THE AUTHORS

KURT BRENT

is a prolific writer, lecturer and broadcaster on a wide range
of subjects. He has a First Class Honours Degree from
Cambridge University. He has been creatively involved in
literally hundreds of BBC programmes on subjects ranging
from animal behaviour and psychology to zombies and
things that go bump in the night. Having undergone
analysis himself with one of Britain's leading psychoanalysts, he became deeply interested in, and has continued
to study, psycho-analysis, social psychology and related
subjects.

KAY BATCHELOR

is a professional radio and television journalist, who has
contributed to many BBC programmes, including Woman's
Hour, Today, news and current affairs, before going out to
California as a production assistant for CBS Films. During
her six years in California, living in what she calls a nest of
Beverley Hills psychologists, she became seriously interested
in what makes people tick (including herself). Eventually,
under the guidance and tuition of a professional clinical
psychologist from Yale she began to work as a pupil-
counsellor herself.

YOU

by
KURT BRENT
AND
KAY BATCHELOR

TOPAZ BOOKS
ENGLAND

First published in Great Britain 1977 by
Topaz Records Ltd, 67 High Street, Great Missenden, Bucks

© Topaz Publications Ltd, 1977

ISBN 0 905553 02 0

PRINTED AND BOUND IN ENGLAND BY
HAZELL WATSON AND VINEY LTD
AYLESBURY, BUCKS

CONTENTS

PREFACE

Who is the most interesting person in the world? YOU! To you yourself, at any rate. After all, everything you think and feel, all that you believe, and all that you are or will be or might be, is contained somewhere within the boundaries of the body and the selfhood that belong to you and you alone. And this book is addressed to you—to each unique and separate and individual you who is reading it, and whose face looks back at you from the cover.

Its main purpose, of course, is to *interest* you. That can mean a number of things, though. It may mean that you're going to read the book for simple entertainment—and you can get a lot of pure fun out of answering the questionnaires; or from seeing, from the guide-lines we've given you, what you can find out about yourself (or your family and friends) from your handwriting; or from trying out ancient traditional techniques which claim to help you know more about your life and destiny; and from all sorts of other tests, exercises and suggestions. You will also find plenty of fascinating new and thought-provoking information—including, incidentally, items that may surprise you about recent scientific interest in some of the apparently "way-out" topics.

But if you want to get more out of the book than fun, you certainly can. If you approach it in the right way and in the right spirit, it really can help you to get to know yourself better, to spot your weaknesses and danger-points (as well as your strengths) and to come to terms with them; to see where you might have come to a dead-end, and where the real growing-points for your future development might be; and perhaps to build up a more complete and accurate picture of yourself than you've ever had before.

In order to aim at this we would advise you to read the book chapter by chapter, rather than just dipping into it. It's important, too, when you come to the questionnaires to answer them as conscientiously as you possibly can. You won't get the best out of any of them unless you're absolutely honest with yourself. Don't be tempted to write down what *seems* to be the right answer, even if it's apparently a very obvious one—but the one that's right for *you*. And don't assume that the obvious questions are necessarily the easiest to answer honestly: they may be the very ones that challenge you to think again about some aspect of your behaviour or your way of life.

We certainly DO NOT claim that our questionnaires are anything like as comprehensive and scientifically worked out as psychological tests ideally should be. That kind of test needs to be very long, and in a book of this scope, which aims at variety, there wouldn't have been room for more than one or two of them. If you want to try out some of them, though, you will find suggestions in the book list. We must explain, too, that it's only on the basis of these long and complex questionnaires that proper statistical assessments can be made—and our scoring in consequence isn't meant to be more than a rough guide. On the other hand, all our questions, answers and comments are derived from or based on the soundest sources, including some of the most recent research. If you approach them honestly, if you think *and* feel about them, you can hardly fail to learn something about yourself. But it's entirely up to YOU!

KAY BATCHELOR   KURT BRENT
OXFORD 1977

CHAPTER ONE

YOU AND YOUR BODY

CHAPTER ONE

YOU AND YOUR BODY

Before you read beyond this first sentence close the book, get a piece of paper, and write down as quickly as possible twenty things you are aware of at this very moment . . .

Now look at your list. The larger the number of items you have written down that relate in some way to your own body—including sensations of sight, touch, sound and smell, and observations involving these senses—the greater the likelihood that you are on good terms with your body, comfortably and creatively in it.

If you try out this test at intervals (as spontaneously as possible) and you consistently score a high proportion of "body points" (never less than ten, say) then it's also likely that you have a more than average interest in aesthetic and artistic matters, or even that you yourself have artistic talents. The artist cannot help being, in some way or another, in profound touch with nature—and where can understanding of nature more naturally begin than with one's own body?

Your body, in fact, seems the obvious starting-point for knowing yourself. After all, you've been landed with it, for better or worse. For one reason or another you may lose friends, lovers, relations—but your body is always with you. Now ask yourself these two basic questions:

> Do I look on my body as a friend and ally, with whom I gladly co-operate, and to whose messages I listen?

or: Do I regard it as an enemy, or at best as a mysterious and rather disreputable stranger I'd rather not know to much about?

It seems a pretty obvious conclusion that if you can unhesitatingly say YES to the first of these questions, then you are likely to be a happier, better integrated person—*more in command of your self.*

It's a commonplace that bodily symptoms can affect behaviour. To take an obvious example: a headache can make your irritable—"like a bear with a sore head", as the old saying wisely puts it. But there are thousands of other ways in which your body and your attitudes towards it affect the way you live. It's astonishing, though, how many people are *not* fully aware of their own bodies and of the rich and varied messages they have to offer. For a variety of reasons, among them the hangovers of Victorian prudery, an over-strict or over-anxious upbringing, or the pressures of a machine-orientated, depersonalising society, these messages get blunted, distorted or suppressed. Getting them unscrambled again, sorting them out, and clearing the channels is one of the ways of increasing your happiness and effectiveness. Knowing yourself better could begin with knowing your body better.

The preliminary questions that follow don't of course pretend to be comprehensive or scientifically detailed—but your answers will tell you something about your relationship to your own body, and perhaps help you to live in greater harmony with it. Needless to say, if you are suffering from severe pain of body or mind, it's not to this—or any other—book you should turn, but to your doctor.

A. PRELIMINARY QUESTIONS

(Answer YES *or* NO*)*

This group consists of very simple questions, merely designed to confront you, in very obvious ways, with your receptivity towards your body and some of its signals.

1. Do you know at once when there is a marked change in the weather?
2. Do you duck instinctively if you are passing under a very low doorway?
3. If a ball is suddenly thrown in your direction, do you make an immediate attempt to catch it?
4. When you are sun-bathing, do you know when your

skin has had enough?

5. Do you jump out of the way quickly if a car is bearing down on you?

6. At your regular meal times, do you always eat more or less the same amount, whether or not you are really hungry?

7. Do you usually stop eating as soon as you are full?

8. Do you adopt the timetable of your bowels, or insist upon imposing one of your own?

9. Do you insist upon giving yourself a certain number of hours in bed, whether you are feeling sleepy or not?

10. Do you stay up long after you have begun to yawn?

11. Do you make love
    (a) at set times, or
    (b) when you really want to?

12. Do you feel worried if you're doing an unusually long stint of physical work, even if you're not feeling tired?

13. If you are working in the garden (or at any other stooping job) do you stop as soon as—or shortly after—your back begins to ache?

14. When you have a sudden yen for salt, vinegar, fruit, vegetables, meat etc., do you usually pay attention to it?

15. When you get a sudden impulse to jump, dance, sing, run, shout, do you usually try to obey it?

16. When everybody else is hurrying (e.g. during the rush-hour) do you nevertheless go at the pace your body wants to?

17. Do you usually "bite back" your laughter or tears?

18. Do you resist the impulse to go for a walk before going to bed, or on getting up?

19. Do your ears perk up at an unfamiliar sound?

20. Do you enjoy the rhythmic movement of your own body?

❖❖❖❖❖❖❖❖❖❖❖❖❖

SECTION A: ANSWERS & COMMENTS

1-5.   YES   This probably means that you are in reasonably good tune with the more immediate of your body-signals.

6.   NO ⎫   The body usually tells us if it is hungry or full
7.   YES ⎬ —but how often do you listen to it?

8.   YES   Because the body knows best—whatever we may "think".

9-10. NO   Your body tells you when it needs sleep, and how much. Its judgement is better than that imposed by your will or by an outside authority. Yawning, incidentally, can mean you're short of fresh air, not necessarily of sleep.

11.   (b)   The more often you can follow the body's genuine desires rather than decisions imposed by the will, routine or fashion, the happier you are likely to be.

12.   NO ⎫ If you do accept these signals from your body
13.   YES ⎬ you will be in harmony with it, and (in all
14.   YES ⎭ likelihood) fitter into the bargain.

15-20.   If you can honestly say YES to questions 15, 16, 19 and 20—and NO to 17 and 18, then you are probably more than usually receptive to your body and what it has to tell you.

B. ACCEPTANCE OR REJECTION

(Answer YES *or* NO*)*

Here are some rather less obvious questions which should indicate whether or not you are really in tune with, and at peace with, your own body.

1. Are you
   (a) uncomfortable at the sight of your naked body?
   (b) able to look at it with pleasure, or at any rate with good-humoured, acceptance?
2. (a) Are you inquisitive about the less accessible and easily seen parts of your body?
   (b) Do you deliberately ignore or avoid them?
3. Do you have strong taboos on certain parts of your body?
4. Do you take a pride in caring for and grooming your body?
5. Do you enjoy stroking your skin, flexing your muscles, brushing your hair etc.?
6. Are you particularly embarrassed about your natural functions?
7. Are you only fully aware of your body when it is sick or in pain?
8. Do you find you have to bath or wash more frequently than most people you know?
9. Have you the reputation of being particularly fussy about your house-keeping—following people around with a dust-pan and brush, not allowing them to go into certain rooms? Or similarly nit-picking at your office or other work place?
10. Are you seriously upset if you run out of deodorants?
11. If you do sedentary work of some kind, do you have sudden urges for strenuous exercise—and do you try to follow them?
12. If you take a special interest in some form of exercise or outdoor activity, are you intolerant of those who don't?
13. Do you find that prolonged bouts of watching television make you long for fresh air and exercise?

14. Do you look upon a tool or gadget as
    (a) in some way an extension of your own body?
    (b) as something separate with a hostile will of its own?
15. Do you have dreams or fantasies of your body melting away, and do they upset you?
16. Do you enjoy rhythmic exercises like dancing, running, swimming etc.?
17. Can you wake up at a certain hour even without the use of an alarm-clock?
18. Does the thought of merging with someone else in the act of love-making disturb or exhilarate you?

✦✦✦✦✦✦✦✦✦✦✦✦

SECTION B: ANSWERS & COMMENTS

1. (a) NO Obviously if you can accept your body as it is,
    (b) YES without exaggeration and self-glorification on the one hand; or guilt, disgust, or depreciation on the other, you are likely to be a reasonably balanced and well-integrated person.

2. (a) YES A reasonable degree of inquisitiveness about
    (b) NO your own body is natural and healthy. A lack of it might indicate an uneasiness about the worth or "niceness" of your body.

3. NO If you can't easily think about or mention the more private parts of the body—when it's natural or necessary to do so—you may be having difficulty in accepting your own body. On the other hand, using all the words (four-letter and otherwise) at times when it's not really necessary—or going out of your way to be naked, for instance, in front of your children—may equally mean a secret fear and denial of your body. (In fact, most psychologists are now agreed that it is not a good thing for adults deliberately to show

their nakedness—which must seem gigantic and terrifying—to their children).

There is such a thing as trying too hard to be natural!

4-5. YES Up to a point, caring for your body and delighting in its smooth, efficient working suggests that you respect and value it—so long as you don't get too self-absorbed, vain, or over-anxious about it.

6. NO There's not much point in being embarrassed, because you can't avoid them anyway. However, if you think or talk about them too much, the odds are you haven't entirely accepted your physical being, or that you look down on the body as something rather disreputable and dirty.

7. NO You can't avoid having some body sickness and pain—but there are some people whose only means of reassuring themselves that they really do have a body is to exaggerate every ache and pain, or even invent them. If you are fully alive in the body of course, you will respect and co-operate with it when it is sick, and rejoice with it when it is healthy. Respect is the key word. That is something we must have whatever kind of body we have got.

8-9. NO Worrying too much about the cleanliness and neatness of your body or of the house you live in (which seems like an extension of the body) would usually suggest that you still feel, at some level of your being, that there is something dirty and perhaps threatening about bodies, which can only be overcome by continuous and frantic cleaning. On the other hand, of course, extreme untidiness or squalor or dirt would suggest a lack of proper respect for the body—and therefore for the self.

10. NO You shouldn't be. Naturally you want to be clean—but to respect your body is also to accept—and, indeed, to take pleasure in—your natural body odours (so long as they're not stale).

11. YES The old saying "a healthy mind in a healthy
12. NO body" has a great deal of truth in it. Over-emphasis on the body, however, can be just as suspect as neglect. You need always to remember that your brain is part of your body. At the same time, those students and scholars who despise physical exercise of any kind have in a way cut off their heads from their bodies—and so are inevitably out of touch with the world of nature and often with reality itself. If you do have a sedentary or brain job but are ready to listen to your body when it tells you it wants fresh air and exercise, you are much more likely to be a balanced person—and to be more efficient at your job!

13. YES We hope so. We all live in a world where machines are increasingly doing the jobs which once needed human sweat and muscle; and this means quite often that your body isn't really being used and valued as it's meant to be. The tv set can be one of the most menacing of these machines. You hardly need to do anything except switch on and focus your eyes, and then your body can become almost entirely passive. If you are an extreme tv addict you are in danger of spending a large proportion of your waking hours in a state that resembles babyhood, with the tv set standing in as a teat or dummy (why else is it called The Boob Tube?). Needless to say, if used with intelligence and discrimination, tv can provide genuine stimulus and entertain-

ment (as other machines can save us labour) —but if your body periodically revolts and demands to be let out, to be given movement or absorption in other tasks and interests and if you follow its promptings then it's likely that you are still in close communion with your body, and therefore a truly independent being.

14. (a) YES The more you enjoy using a gadget or tool,
       (b) NO treating it as an extension of your body and concentrating your mind, nerves, and muscles on its operation and control, the more likely you are to be in harmony with your body.

15. YES This sort of dream or imagining is quite common, but NO it won't worry you if you have learned to be confident in the possession of your own body.

16. YES Such sports and exercises (including relaxation exercises of the yoga type) can be a means of securing body-awareness and harmony.

17. YES This may be another indication that your mind and body are in harmony and that you have trust in them.

18. Hopefully, it exhilarates you, because that would mean that you are joyously confident of your whole body and therefore have no fears in temporarily giving it to someone you love.

C. BODY CONFIDENCE AND BODY DOUBT

(Answer YES *or* NO*)*

The set of questions you have just answered are mostly about the way in which pride in the body is seriously challenged by the materialistic, mechanised kind of society we live in. It is natural, therefore, that doubts about the secure possession of the body are likely to be quite frequent. Here are some further questions which may help you to decide whether or not you suffer from this kind of body-insecurity; and perhaps make you determined to take steps to help yourself get over it.

1. Do you have frequent fears that burglars are going to break into your house?

2. Do you worry a lot about how strong your country is; and about the possibilities of an enemy invading it?

3. Do you tend to get exceptionally hot and bothered if what you regard as your special territory is encroached upon—for example, if someone parks his car very close to your own car-space; if someone passing by breaks a twig off your hedge; if someone appropriates your favourite chair or couch, or in cramped conditions (such as camping) sits on your bed rather than his or her own?

4. Do you have strong feelings of dislike and impatience towards people of other race or colour or religion than your own?

5. Do you find watching acts of violence on the tv screen or in the cinema almost more than you can bear?

6. Are you excessively cautious about taking body-risks— e.g. jumping over stiles, diving into water etc.?

7. Do you feel uncomfortable in an open-plan kind of house or work-place, with a lot of glass walls and big windows?

8. Do you prefer small rooms, well-filled with furniture, to bigger rooms with fewer bits and pieces?

9. In a strange city do you tend to feel safer in the narrow

crowded roads than in wide streets with tall buildings?

10. Do you feel rather uncomfortable living in the country?

11. If you do live in the country, do you prefer valleys and small villages to hill tops and the wide open spaces in general?

12. Do you tend to stand away from other people at parties?

13. Do you tend to discourage body contacts at parties— e.g. hand-shaking, hands on shoulder, squeezing of arms etc.?

14. Do you dislike sitting with your back to the other people in a room—e.g. in a restaurant?

15. Do you feel uncomfortable if the doors of a room are left open?

16. Do you make a habit of touching certain parts of your body—e.g. bite your nails, pick your nose, gnaw your lips, rub your hands together, chew the ends of your moustache etc?

17. Are you mad about body-building, organized nudism, or any course of exercise designed to develop one particular part of the body?

18. Do you rather frequently hunch up your body, square your shoulders, straighten your back, rise on tip-toe, expand your chest, flex your muscles?

19. Do you feel unduly uncomfortable without your favourite ring, close-fitting bracelet or belt etc?

20. Do you like to carry a walking stick with a heavy knob, an umbrella with an outsize handle etc.?

21. Do you like to camouflage areas of your body—e.g. wear dark glasses, false eyelashes, heavy cosmetics, wigs, tattooing?

22. Do you find yourself taking various tablets and medicines, even though you don't really need them?

23. Are you uncomfortable unless you have your radio or record-player on full blast?

24. Do you always have to have a transistor radio with you?

25. Are you particularly dependent on nicotine, alcohol, spicy foods?

26. Do you feel unpleasantly surprised or uncomfortable the first time you see a new photograph of yourself, or hear a recording of your own voice?

27. Do you tend to think of yourself as smaller than you really are?

28. Do you tend to exaggerate your height?

29. Do you frequently have Alice-in-Wonderland feelings —i.e. sensations of unaccountable shrinkage or expansion of your body or parts of it?

30. Do you try to identify and explain small aches and pains instead of immediately imagining there is something terrible the matter with you?

31. Do you over-protect your children by trying to stop them playing energetic games or taking reasonable risks?

32. Do you discourage your children from making new friends?

33. Do you discourage your older children from exploring further than their own garden?

34. Have you ever experienced "eye or ear hunger"? That is, have you ever suddenly felt that you would burst if you didn't see new faces or scenes, if you didn't look at some unfamiliar buildings or pictures, or buy a new book or record, or hear the sounds of the country or the sea?

35. Do you encourage your children to have new experiences—e.g. painting, climbing, reading, swimming, playing music etc?

36. Do you set your children an example by being ready yourself to adventure out into new physical, emotional, intellectual and artistic experiences?

❖❖❖❖❖❖❖❖❖❖❖❖

SECTION C: ANSWERS & COMMENTS

1-3.   NO   At least, *ideally* we should all be able to say NO to these questions. But if you have to say YES, such fears and worries might indicate that you have doubts and uncertainties about your body boundaries—that you are not comfortably and confidently in your body.

4. Hopefully   People who in some way dislike or feel
     NO   ashamed of their own bodies—*and don't know it*—are more likely to dislike and reject other people and *their* bodies especially when they seem in any way strange and different. This is particularly the case where colour is concerned. Psychologists have found that there is in some people's minds a definite connection between skin colour and dirt. The person who hates anyone else because of differences of colour or race or religion is most likely feeling his own shaky grasp of his own body boundaries threatened by having anything to do with such a person. It is partly because of these unreasonable and morbid feelings—unfortunately very widespread—that the negroes of the USA have coined their slogan "Black is Beautiful". (Incidentally, the negro himself, of course, can have the same sort of morbid or negative feelings about white skins.) The more secure we all are within our body boundaries, the less likely we are to hate and fear anyone in this way.

5.   YES   If you are sensitive you will naturally be upset. But if you find yourself feeling over-anxious, afraid to go upstairs alone afterwards etc., it may be another indication that you are insecure in your possession of your body and afraid that its boundaries may be destroyed.

6-11. NO   If you answer YES to most of these questions, it could mean that you are not altogether comfortable or secure in your body.

12-13. NO   If you have to say YES to these questions, the probability is that you feel your body-boundaries threatened in the presence of "dangerous strangers", i.e. other people. If the questions seem to you ridiculous, the odds are that you are in confident possession of your body and of your Self.

14-15. NO   If you answer YES to these questions (which are about the space round your body) then you are still probably insecure not only in your body, but in the "buffer-zone" space immediately surrounding it—because rooms, possessions, etc. are like an extension of the body, and it seems as if you are afraid of an attack on it and them.

16. Ideally NO   But we all have our little habits, and these can mean a need for reassurance that the body is really there, sound and whole.

17. NO   Too fanatical an adherence can indicate over-anxiety and uncertainty about your body, and fears that parts of it are useless.

18. NO   At least, strictly speaking it's NO—though it is very common to use these techniques as a means of bolstering confidence in your body —and your Self. If carried to excess, however, it can again mean that you are over-anxious and uncertain about your body.

19-25. Ideally NO   These are other bolstering techniques often used by those who are not in confident possession of their bodies. If you have answered YES to as many as six of these questions, it would suggest that you need to take stock of yourself in this respect. If you gave as many as six NO answers, this would be pretty satisfactory.

26. Ideally NO   If the answer is YES for you, it would indicate some uncertainty—but a large number of people do feel uncomfortable in these circumstances partly because, for instance, you normally hear your own voice from inside your own head and it is bound to sound very different when heard from outside on a tape—

and this can understandably make you feel that you don't know the sound of your own voice any more.

27.   NO   If you answer YES, the odds are that you are in a depressed state, or that you lack confidence generally—or that you still want to play at being a child!

28.   NO   If you persistently exaggerate your height, it would suggest that you feel a need to assert yourself. In the case of a man it could indicate, in addition to a strong wish to prove himself a go-getter, some inner wish to dominate his women.

29.   NO   Hopefully. If the experience really is frequent, then it is likely that you have not yet learned to accept your body, and still experience feelings of guilt and shame about it.

30.   YES   It's pretty obvious that this is to be hoped for; the more familiar you are with your body, and the more at home you feel in it, the more likely you are to know instinctively whether or not there is anything seriously wrong with it.

31-33.   NO   It is certainly to be hoped that you can say NO here. Some people, however, tend to feel their children to be extensions of themselves —and to express their fears about the security of their own bodies in the form of overanxiety about their children's.

34.   YES   This would be an encouraging sign both as to your possession of your body and your ability to respond to its creative promptings. The need for these experiences is often felt as a physical want. People often find, for example, that after looking at pictures in a gallery, at country scenes, or at the sea, their eyes feel as if they have been "washed" and strengthened.

35-36.   YES   If you can say YES to these, then both you

and your children are lucky people. A readiness to open yourself up to aesthetic and other experiences (which always involves venturing into unknown territory) and to encourage those nearest you to follow suit, means that you have few fears or uncertainties about the truth and independence of your body—or of the Self to which the body is a guide and indicator.

BODY LANGUAGE

There are, of course, all kinds of other little everyday actions and movements which, unknown to ourselves, reveal what we are feeling. Close observers of human nature have always been aware of these, and creative writers throughout the ages have made great use of them, often to most telling and subtle effect. Needless to say Shakespeare was one of them. In his play *Troilus and Cressida*, for example, he lists quite a range of unconscious "body signals" (as a modern psychologist would call them) in order to convey the essential flightiness and sensuality that underlie Cressida's professions of life-long fidelity to her lover Troilus:

There's language in her eye, her cheek, her lip,
Nay, her foot speaks, her wanton spirits look out
At every joint and motive (i.e. motion) of her body.

Shakespeare understood intuitively and imaginatively what the social psychologists have recently been proving scientifically. To quote one of them: "there is a 'language' of movement comparable to spoken language, both in its structure and in its contribution to a systematic ordered communicative system". Often, indeed, these non-verbal communications are more reliable than spoken language, because they are, for the most part, involuntary, spontaneous, and therefore directly related to our true emotions. And what the psychologists have been doing in recent years is to codify and systematise them into a coherent scientific structure -and quite a number of their findings were incorporated in the questionnaires you have already answered.

To begin with the "language" of the eyes—a great deal is now known scientifically about its workings. For hundreds, perhaps thousands, of years it has been suspected, for example, that the pupils of the eyes dilate when the person concerned is sexually aroused or attracted to someone of the opposite sex. It was this suspicion, in fact, that lay behind the cosmetic use, in centuries past, of belladonna. The scientific name for belladonna (or deadly nightshade—it was also used as a poison is *Atropa belladonna*—and it contains atropine, which oculists use now (in a synthetic form) in order to enlarge the pupils of the eyes, and so make their examinations easier. It's significant that belladonna is Italian for "beautiful lady", and Italian beauties (especially courtesans) used the drug in order to make their eyes appear big and sexy. Now it's been scientifically proved that this dilation of the pupils is an involuntary, and inevitable, accompaniment of sexual attraction.

The social psychologists have also established that what they call "eye gaze"—how we look into other people's faces and eyes when we're talking to them—plays an important part in communication, and follows regular patterns. It serves both as a kind of "feed-back"—so that we are kept informed as to how we're getting on in the conversation— and as a signal that we're still interested in continuing it, that the channel is, so to speak, still open—and it's very closely synchronized with our speech. In speaking to someone, after all, it's polite to keep looking at them from time to time in order to reassure them of our concern and interest. The amount of eye-contact, though, varies quite a lot according to circumstances, personality, status, and even sex. If, for instance, a man is being interviewed for a job he's likely to look at his potential employer more frequently than a woman does in the same situation. Both men and women look more if the person concerned is a high-up of some sort— naturally enough, because in such cases they're indicating respect, perhaps even awe. It's been found, too, that extroverts tend to use slightly more eye-contact than introverts, and that their glances are nearly twice as long. A very shy or anxious person, as we all know, doesn't find it easy to keep up eye-contact—and neither, incidentally, does the person who's trying to pull a fast one (hence the popular expression "shifty eyed"). A word of warning here, though—the really foxy person can fake a long, candid gaze in order to con you into believing in his honesty and sincerity. So the eyes like the face aren't always a reliable guide. People also tend to break off eye-contact if an intimate topic is touched on in the conversation (except sometimes when the two people concerned know each other very well). For most people, in fact, eye-gaze that goes on too long arouses anxiety or discomfort—but it won't surprise you to learn that there's an important exception: the more you find yourself liking the person you're talking to, the longer you're able to look at them—and vice versa of course. Long glances between members of the opposite sexes, indicate (as we all know from experience) the beginning of sexual attraction—and, as we've seen, the attraction will have gone even farther if the pupils of the eyes dilate.

When that happens you probably don't mind how close you get to the other person, but generally speaking this matter of eye-contact is closely linked to distance, and in normal social situations it's been shown that you nearly always have to break eye-contact if you're too much on top of your partner in a conversation.

As a matter of fact people of different races and nationalities vary quite a lot in this respect. Investigators have demonstrated that, in ordinary social situations, North Americans feel uncomfortable if they're standing or sitting less than eighteen to twenty inches away from the person they're talking to, and the same is probably true of Englishmen and most Anglo-Saxons. On the other hand Latins and inhabitants of Middle Eastern countries prefer to get much closer. Some primitive tribes in Africa and Indonesia maintain actual bodily contact of some kind throughout a conversation. Human beings aren't unique, of course, in this matter: each animal species also has its characteristic individual distance, as well as a maximum social distance between the members of a group.

The distance at which people stand or sit when they're talking to you can in fact tell you a good deal about them. For example, introverts tend to place themselves slightly farther away than extroverts (the latter, by the way, are also more likely to enjoy dancing cheek to cheek!). It's been noticed, too, that people tend to stand closer to members of their own racial group -or to those of the racial groups they most approve of. Members of the same "peer group" also tend to get closer to each other—you will have noticed, for example, how at a party teen-agers (if they've got over their initial shyness) tend to gang up. Another interesting little finding is that when women friends talk to each other they get much closer than men friends in a similar situation. Generally speaking if the person you're talking to doesn't show that he minds being fairly close to you, it's a more positive and friendly sign than if he deliberately "keeps his distance"—and if he begins leaning slightly backwards it's a sign that he's feeling distinctly uncomfortable (though it may only be because you've been eating garlic). Generally speaking, too, people who know each other well, and/or who are of a similar social or professional standing, tend to get closer than strangers or people in contrasting walks of life. And, again, it won't surprise you to learn that if you're liked the person you're talking to will tend to get closer.

Recent research has also shown that our various postures send out definite "messages". One psychologist has postulated four major ones. The first of them is the "attentive posture" (that is, showing interest, concern, and probably sympathy and liking)—and consists of a forward leaning of the body. The second is the "withdrawing posture" (symptomatic of a lack of interest, and perhaps of dislike or disdain) —expressed in a slight drawing back of the body, often accompanied by a slight turning away—for example of the shoulder (we talk of giving someone the "cold shoulder"). Then there is the posture of the proud, arrogant, conceited person—a very erect or even backward leaning trunk, erect head and raised shoulders, and a puffed out chest. And lastly there's the "depressed, downcast or dejected posture" —a forward-leaning trunk, bowed head, drooping shoulders, and sunken chest.

Posture is of considerable importance in signalising a person's status—or at any rate the idea he has of it. It has been found, for example, that at board meetings and similar gatherings the more high-up a person is (or conceives himself to be) the more relaxed or even slumped his posture will be (with the feet on the desk in extreme cases!), while the juniors or those with less self-confidence adopt a more upright and formal posture. In addition, of course, postures reflect emotional states—a relaxed one obviously indicates relaxation, while an awkward, contorted one indicates uncertainty and stress.

The trunk and the head, the researchers say, play a particularly important part in all this. A consistently raised head, for example, points to a sense of superiority and a lowered one to a feeling of inferiority. Someone who keeps nodding the head is someone who needs to win the approval of the person he or she is talking to (especially if it's accompanied by anxious or ingratiating smiles). But other parts of the body also play their parts. If, for instance, the arms are held akimbo (perhaps with the hands on the hips) a decidedly unfriendly and often superior or even aggressive attitude is to be deduced. In popular fiction a virago is often depicted as standing and yelling insults "with arms akimbo", but in fact it's been shown that women adopt this stance much less than men. If, though, the arms hang down in front of the body, and especially if the hands are also clasped and the head and one shoulder turned away, the person concerned is the shy, shrinking violet type. If the arms are held close to the sides, and especially if accompanied by a stiff, upright stance (like a soldier standing at attention) then an over-respectful, perhaps servile, attitude is to be inferred. If, on the other hand, the arms fall into a naturally easy, open position, warmth of nature is indicated.

This is particularly so in the case of a woman who likes the man she is talking to—though investigators have also found that the "open arm" position is often one of the signs of the kind of relaxation that goes with the assurance of success and high status.

But the movements of hands, legs and feet are, in the view of recent researchers, of particular value, because they are the least subject to conscious control, and therefore "a good source" (to quote from one of the researchers) "for leakage and deception clues". In other words, these movements can be real give-aways. Some of the more obvious hand indications for example are: the clenched fist, with its message of anger and aggression; the holding out of the palms of the hands as a token of peace or submission; the gripping of the hands together (usually accompanied by a twisting of the fingers) as a sign of anxiety; and the clasping of the raised hands in prayer or supplication.

But perhaps it's the legs and feet that are the most revealing of the lot. Often they tell the truth when all the other indications—including the words that are being spoken—point in the opposite direction. For example, someone may be talking in honied phrases—while the tapping of a foot shows boredom and impatience, or a rapid scuffling or little kicking movements reveal hidden anger and aggression—a desire, in fact, to boot you out of the way. Or again, a woman may be outwardly behaving in a very proper manner—while unconsciously revealing a provocative amount of leg. Frequent crossing and uncrossing of the legs, too, indicate uncertainty and inner tensions, while a comfortable leg position—say with one ankle across the other—is an indication of relaxation and confidence.

These, then, are some of the many "non-verbal signals" which have been established by recent research. They should help you to spot further tell-tale signs in yourself and your friends.

CHAPTER TWO

FACES AND FEATURES

CHAPTER TWO

FACES AND FEATURES

If the body can tell us a good deal about ourselves, it seems logical to suppose that the face will too—perhaps even more so. It is, after all, the only part of the body that's never covered up—unless you wear a yashmak, and even then your eyes and forehead will be showing. Your face, too, is the window through which you look out on to the world. It's probably because the face *is* so exposed, though, that, as modern research has shown, it's not always to be trusted. As it's the most obvious screen on which your inmost thoughts and feelings can be projected, it naturally tends to be the most carefully guarded. Whereas, for example, the involuntary movements of the hand and foot are nearly always instant giveaways, the features of the face can often compose themselves in a deliberate or calculated way. And there are all kinds of social and cultural conditionings and pressures that affect and add to this process.

All the same, people can't be on their guard all the time. Whether we like it or not our feelings often slide into our faces without our conscious control. This is particularly the case with strong, spontaneous feelings. Lovers know from experience that you can read each others' faces. So do loving parents and children. At one time it used to be thought that the size and arrangement of the various features of the face were themselves certain guides to the characters of the people concerned. It was an over-simplification, of course. Life just isn't as cut and dried as that. We know now that facial like other bodily characteristics are inherited—and it really would be unfair to jump to the conclusion (without any real evidence) that a man was necessarily weak-willed, for example, because he had a small chin—when he's merely inherited it from his father or grandfather.

Nevertheless these ancient ideas about the human face didn't grow up by accident. Although they were much too rough-and-ready and had no scientific backing, they were the results of observation and experience. They should be taken with more than a grain of salt, but there was something to them. In addition, some of the most distinguished minds of the past were interested in them. The great Ancient Greek philosopher and pioneer scientist, Aristotle, for instance, had some intriguing theories about noses. He argued that they pointed (so to speak!) to broad types of character, which could be compared to certain animals or birds.

There's no harm in joining in a game with Aristotle: so— without jumping to rash conclusions about your own or anybody else's nose—see if you can enter opposite each of these descriptions by Aristotle, the appropriate character-type, together with the corresponding animal or bird:

QUESTIONNAIRE A

1. A nose with a thick, bulbous end.
2. A sharp-tipped nose.
3. A large, rounded nose with a blunt end.
4. A slender, hooked nose.
5. A round-tipped, upturned nose.
6. A nose with a slight notch at the root.
7. A snub nose.
8. A nose with large, wide-open nostrils.

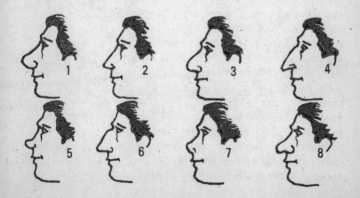

ANSWERS
& ARISTOTLE'S COMMENTS (in brackets)

1. Insensitive (swinish)

 2. Short-tempered, easily provoked (like dogs).

3. Magnanimous (compared to the lion).

 4. Noble, but grasping (eagle-like).

5. Luxury-loving (like barn-door fowls).

 6. Impudent (crow-like).

7. Luxury-loving and lustful (like deer).

 8. Passionate (no comment from Aristotle here!).

SCORE: Counting a score is really irrelevant in this one, because Aristotle's categories are too broad to be very reliable—even though there may be something in them. But if you got five character-types and five animal analogies right, then you are perhaps above the average in perceptiveness. If you got them all right, then you must be on the same wavelength as Aristotle! On the other hand, if you were suspicious of such a sweeping approach and either got them all wrong or refused to answer the questions at all—no one is going to penalize you!

❖❖❖❖❖❖❖❖❖❖❖❖

Our ancestors came to many conclusions about the features of the human face, nearly all of which were taken seriously by investigators at one time or another—including the one about weak chins we've already mentioned. Here are some of them—beginning with two further observations about noses. Again without taking things too seriously, write opposite these brief descriptions which qualities, moods or emotions are, according to folk-lore, usually associated with them.

QUESTIONNAIRE B

NOSES

1. A long nose, with a thin, pointed end.
2. Quivering nostrils.

CHEEKS

3. Cheeks that blush easily and frequently.

EARS

4. Big, protruding ears.

CHINS

5. Jutting chin.

MOUTHS, LIPS, TEETH

6. Narrow mouth.
7. Sucked-in mouth.
8. Pursed, narrow mouth.

9. Wide mouth, lips neither too thin nor too thick.
10. Mouth with corners turned down.
11. Thin lips.
12. Thick, moist lips.
13. Gritting, grinding teeth.
14. Large front teeth with gap between them.

HEADS

15. Low forehead, sloping back.
16. High forehead, bulging temples.
17. Red hair.

EYES

18. Eyes set very close together.
19. Large, well-shaped eyes, set well apart.
20. Eyes upturned, with faraway expression.

QUESTIONNAIRE B—ANSWERS & COMMENTS

These facial characteristics are popularly supposed to indicate:

1. Inquisitiveness (the Paul Pry nose).
2. Rage or sometimes passion (a romance-writer's cliché).
3. Shame or modesty.
4. Clumsiness.
5. Determination or obstinacy.
6. Self-righteousness.
7. Caution or miserliness.
8. Enviousness.
9. Generous nature.
10. Unhappiness, depression.
11. Meanness.
12. Sensuality.
13. Determination.
14. Sensuality, love of pleasure (Chaucer describes his Wife of Bath, in *The Canterbury Tales*, as "gat-toothed").
15. Stupidity ("foreheads villainous low" Shakespeare says in *The Tempest*).

16. Intellectuality.
17. Passionate nature ("hot stuff").
18. Cunning, untrustworthiness.
19. Sincerity, candour, honesty.
20. Religious devotion.

SCORING: Bearing in mind that these represent popular folk ideas about certain features and their corresponding characteristics (not scientifically tested ones), it might nevertheless be justifiable to conclude that if you got 15 or more answers correct, then you are both observant and a good judge of character. 15-12 would suggest that you are fairly observant and a reasonably good judge of character. If you scored under 12, then perhaps you need to look about you more and be cautious in your dealings with other people.

Incidentally, there's another bit of folk-lore which might be added here—that is, the size of a man's nose corresponds to that of his sex organ, though there seems to have been no scientific research on the subject, so perhaps it's a case of wishful thinking. You will probably be able to think of some other—more respectable—examples. Write down those that occur to you in the blank space and see if you agree with the characteristics they are popularly supposed to denote.

In the eighteenth and nineteenth centuries, physiognomy (which the Concise Oxford Dictionary says is the "art of judging character from features of face or form of body") was eagerly pursued by a number of scientists. Their findings and theories were in turn carefully studied by Charles Darwin, author of the famous pioneer work on evolution, *ORIGIN OF SPECIES*, published as long ago as 1859. Darwin was particularly interested in the correspondences between the facial expressions, and the muscles that control them, in human beings and in animals. His book *THE EXPRESSION OF EMOTION IN MAN AND ANIMALS* (1872) is still considered by modern scientists as a classic on the subject.

ARE YOU A GOOD JUDGE OF CHARACTER

The Questionnaire that follows is derived from Darwin's findings, supplemented by more recent investigations along similar lines. It is designed to test how observant you are about human facial expressions and if you are good at drawing the appropriate conclusions.

QUESTIONNAIRE C

What emotions, attitudes or moods would you suppose from the following facial expressions? (If you can't "see" these expressions from the descriptions, try them out in front of a mirror. As you twist the facial muscles, you will almost certainly feel something of the appropriate emotions —and it'll be very good practice if you are an actor or actress!).

1. Eyes and mouth wide open, eyebrows raised.
2. Eyes sparkling, skin a little wrinkled round them, corners of mouth slightly drawn back.
3. Glaring or contracted eyes, probably bloodshot; red face, veins of forehead and neck standing out.
4. Eyes staring, hair of nape of neck bristling, cheeks and lips trembling.

5. Hissing through clenched teeth.
6. Whistling through pursed lips, and perhaps with hand over mouth.
7. Eyes wide open, pupils enlarged, skin beneath eyes appearing slightly swollen, forehead wrinkled in many folds.
8. Wide open eyes and mouth, eyebrows highly arched; arched, curved lines on forehead.
9. Frequent blinking of the eyes.
10. Frequent smiling, with smiles coming and going in snatches.
11. Face tense and flushed.
12. Difficulty in meeting other people's gaze.
13. Marked dislike of being watched.
14. Head continually lowered, often accompanied by fixed smile.
15. Raised head, unsmiling mouth, eyes fixed on other person.
16. Readiness to accept prolonged eye-contact.
17. Fondness for dancing cheek to cheek.
18. Hooded eyes – i.e. upper lids drooping and half-concealing the eyes.
19. Features slightly swollen, coarse-skinned, and apparently misshapen.
20. Hollow cheeks, line of nose sharpened, eyes glittering; thin, slightly smiling lips.
21. Glowing face, features either smiling or looking as if they have just been smiling, or might soon do so again.
22. Bright eyes, curved smile, rounded cheeks.
23. Appearance of thinning face, shadows in cheeks, round eyes; pallid, slightly yellowish or greenish complexion.
24. Crooked smile, with one corner of lip raised over eyetooth.
25. Frowning face, with wrinkles across forehead; skin beneath lower eyelids wrinkled.
26. Mouth firmly closed, slight frown, lowering eyebrows.
27. Compressed nostrils, slight protrusion of lips, as if to make a small blowing out of breath.

28. Wrinkled nose, lower lip turned down, upper lip slightly raised, together with a sudden blowing out of breath.

29. Partial closing of eyelids, reducing the eyes to slits, together with a slight turning away of the eyes, or even of the whole head.

30. Wandering eyes, accompanied by sudden, darting glances.

❖❖❖❖❖❖❖❖❖❖❖❖❖

QUESTIONNAIRE C—ANSWERS & SCORES

1. Surprise.
2. Cheerfulness, good spirits.
3. Rage.
4. Fear.
5. Intense hatred.
6. Astonishment.
7. Grief, or extreme anxiety.
8. Terror.
9. Inattentiveness.
10. Excessive desire to please.
11. Anxiety.
12. Nervousness, shyness.
13. Extreme self-consciousness.
14. Submissiveness, feelings of inferiority.
15. Dominant or even domineering nature.
16.
17. } Both symptoms of an extrovert, self-confident nature
18. Suspiciousness, lack of trust.
19. Habitual brutality.
20. Cruelty.
21. Happiness in the knowledge of being loved.
22. Tenderness.
23. The classic symptoms of love-sickness.
24. The mechanics of sneering—if frequent, they denote a sneering, contemptuous nature.

25. The most obvious manifestations of deep thought.
26. Doggedness, sometimes obstinacy.
27. Contempt.
28. Disgust.
29. Disdain.
30. Guilt, cunning.

SCORING: 20 and over more or less correct answers would suggest that you are exceptionally observant and understanding about the messages conveyed by the facial expressions of your fellow men and women. 15 to 20 would be a fair score. 10 to 15 would be poor; and below 10 would suggest that you should pay more attention to other people, and that you should try to react more sympathetically to them.

❖❖❖❖❖❖❖❖❖❖❖❖

Now here is a similar test of your observation and judgment of character, but this time it is pictorial:

QUESTIONNAIRE D

Study these drawings carefully; and then indicate (by ticking A or B or C) which characteristic you would normally associate with each:

A. meekness.
B. contempt.
C. insecurity.

A. anxiety.
B. distrust.
C. profundity of thought.

3.

A. generosity.
B. superiority.
C. harshness.

4.

A. gentleness.
B. cruelty.
C. imperiousness.

5.

A. rapture.
B. fear.
C. surprise.

6.

A. resignation.
B. submissiveness.
C. self-pity.

7.

A. reliability.
B. humour.
C. cunning.

8.

A. disdain.
B. generosity.
C. modesty.

A. grief.
B. compassion.
C. anger.

A. irritation.
B. concentration.
C. anxiety.

A. self-command.
B. boldness.
C. sentimentality.

A. tartiness.
B. coldness.
C. natural sensuality.

QUESTIONNAIRE D—ANSWERS

1. B	5. C	9. C
2. C	6. A	10. C
3. B	7. C	11. C
4. C	8. A	12. C

Now to alter the approach slightly. Examine these pairs of faces, and according to the questions, tick A or B.

QUESTIONNAIRE E

1.

Question: If you are a man, which of these two women would you choose for your wife? (Women also to answer).

2.

Question: If you are a woman, which of these men would in your opinion make the better husband? (Men also to answer).

3.

Question: Which of these two men would you rather have as your boss?

4.

Question: Which of these two generals would you have most confidence in?

5.

Question: Which of these two men would you consider the tougher in a crisis, possessing the greater stamina?

6.

Question: Which of these two women would make the better mother?

QUESTIONNAIRE E—ANSWERS

1.	B	4.	B
2.	B	5.	A
3.	A	6.	A

✧✦✧✦✧✦✧✦✧✦✧✦✧

SCORING & COMMENTS
QUESTIONNAIRES D AND E

Check how good a judge of character you are according to the number of correct answers you gave:

16 to 18   VERY SOUND   Your responsiveness and judgment of character are excellent. You nearly always succeed in drawing the correct conclusions from facial expression, and you are not easily deceived.

13 to 15   SOUND   You are a reliable judge of character. You are observant of the signals given off by other people's faces, and nearly always interpret them correctly.

11 to 12	AVERAGE TO SOUND	You are average in your ability to respond to facial expression and in coming to the right conclusions about it—and you have the potentiality quickly to improve in these respects.
9 to 10	AVERAGE TO POOR	You could not be called unobservant or a bad judge of character, but you do not always pay sufficient attention to the facial expressions of others, or spontaneously understand what they convey. You should set out to improve your capacities in these directions.
8 & under	POOR	You have at present little skill in evaluating other people from their facial expressions. This makes you susceptible to misunderstandings which might be dangerous, to deception by other people, and perhaps even to exploitation by them. You would be well advised to try and improve your powers of observation and your sensitivity towards other people.

CHAPTER THREE
YOU AND YOUR CLOTHES

CHAPTER THREE

YOU AND YOUR CLOTHES

Your body and your face, then, are obviously enough, important parts of the total you. But the great nineteenth century psychologist William James (brother of novelist Henry) pointed out that clothing is as much part of the Self as the body—part of the "material me" as he put it. So the things you put on (or leave off) can convey a good deal of information about you. Perhaps more—because you can choose your clothes!

Research has shown that dress (and under that heading, ornaments, hair-styles, make-up and various kinds of body decoration should be included), does undoubtedly have a powerful effect, both upon other people and upon the wearer. But we have to be very cautious in drawing conclusions about character, personality or mood because so many factors are involved.

To understand these factors we ought to consider briefly some of the possible reasons why clothes came into existence at all. The first men and women presumably went naked—as indeed the Old Testament story of Adam and Eve in the Garden of Eden before the arrival of the serpent, symbolizes.

The formula, clothes = human being, isn't, after all, absolute. We must remember that there are parts of the world—for example corners of the South American jungle—where men and women are still living partially or completely naked. What is more, modern anthropologists are agreed that the naked Indians of the South American forests are probably the most perfectly adapted to their environment of any human beings—far more than western industrial man.

ORIGINS OF CLOTHING

One of the most obvious reasons why our distant ancestors took to clothes was, of course, to keep warm, in the colder regions of the world, or when drastic climatic changes like the ice-ages took place. They saw that animals adapted by growing thicker fur coats, and as they couldn't do that themselves (though they probably did become more hairy) they copied the animals by confiscating their fur coats for

themselves. Another reason for adopting clothes was, perhaps, that in some circumstances they were—like fire and primitive tools—an extension of man's control over his environment and his own capacity to survive in it. By wearing clothes man could in effect carry a shelter on his back and thus extend the length of his working day; or by putting a string round his waist he could carry weapons or other necessary implements, and so leave his hands free; while his woman, by using a sling, could carry her babies on her back.

In many so-called primitive tribes, the sling is still used in this way—and in many cases that's the only "garment" the women do wear.

Often, though, bunches of leaves, feathers, or pieces of bark-cloth are suspended from the waist string. It is doubtful whether the original purpose of these additions was to conceal the sexual organs, or whether they were used to protect the wearers from insects, brambles and so on. Many primitive jungle-living tribes do quite well without any such protection, however. Eventually, though concealment in many cases did come into it, although concealment alone is only

VISITORS TO THIS
GALLERY MUST
WEAR A FIG LEAF

ADAM & EVE

half of the story. Hiding anything also inevitably draws attention to it, and so we have the element of "attraction by mystery"—as one anthropologist called it. In other words, clothes also began to serve the purposes of sexual decoration and enticement. Some psychologists, indeed, believe that this was related to the increase in unconscious fears about sex in the human species. To counterbalance these fears and to recapture some of the pleasure lost because of them, artificial stimulants had to be found—and clothing was one of them. Dr. Edmund Bergler, an American psychologist has in fact suggested that "clothes are, perhaps, the last refuge of diminishing sex." And even more provocatively, he adds: "women's clothes are aphrodisiacs for man's vanishing potency."

NAKEDNESS AND MODESTY

It is a big mistake to assume that the wearing of clothes necessarily implies a greater degree of modesty. Shocked Victorian missionaries hurriedly bundled their naked converts into constricting and unsuitable garments—and usually, by destroying the natives' natural relationship with their environment, gave them their first taste of dirt and disease. In fact, the Victorians' sense of shock was quite misplaced. Anthropologists have shown that those peoples who go naked are conspicuously modest in their behaviour, and often far more moral than we are in matters such as promiscuity and adultery. In some cases, indeed, they are subjected to a positively Puritanical code of conduct, with all kinds of prohibitions and taboos.

Moreover, we must remember that ideas of modesty vary from age to age, and from region to region. Leaving the breasts uncovered, for example, was at one time considered not in the least immodest, while in many Muslim cities today even the exposure of a woman's face is considered indecent.

One explorer, too, has related how, when he surprised a group of women bathing naked in a remote part of the Sudan, they rushed out of the water –in order to cover their faces, not the rest of their bodies. Naga women are most careful to cover their breasts, but feel no concern about whether or not their genitals are exposed.

There are no hard and fast rules, therefore, about modesty in dress. The important point is that clothes are meaningful only in a particular cultural setting. And that, of course, applies to us—so that any conclusions we may come to about the psychology of dress, are applicable only within our own western type of society.

The missionaries who were so shocked by the natives'

nakedness would have been even more outraged if it had
been pointed out to them that the tight-laced corsets of
their Victorian young ladies were in the main designed to
push the breasts up, and, by making breathing difficult, to
cause sexually interesting flutterings and movements of the
bosom; or if they had been told that the bustle was meant to
accentuate their pretty little bottoms. To be fair, these aims
operated, of course, almost entirely at the subconscious
level, as do similar features in modern dress. The fact that a
woman wears clothes that have these sexual connotations
does not necessarily mean she is showing her availability. On
the contrary, it may mean that she sets a high value on her
sexuality. At the same time, the underlying sexual motives
in dressing are inescapable. Mate-seeking is, after all, a
perfectly natural occupation, and we can all think of hundreds of examples among animals and birds of special
behaviour, including the display of plumage and so on, which
come into play when they are enticing their mates.

In human societies, though, there is another factor in
dress almost as powerful as the subconscious sexual mate-
seeking motives: namely, Keeping up with the Joneses.
Dress is one of the oldest and most obvious ways in which
men and women establish their status or group membership
in society. At one time this was a much more cut and dried
business than it is now. Special kinds of clothes belonged to
special kinds of individuals or social groups. In imperial
Rome, for example, no one who wanted to stay alive would
dream of wearing the purple toga of an emperor. Laws
were often passed forbidding people of one class to wear
the clothes of another. In Henry VIII's England, for
instance, a woman whose husband was unable to afford to
keep a horse exclusively for the King's use, would not be
allowed to wear a velvet bonnet or a gold chain. At one
time in New England, a woman whose husband was worth
less than $1000 was not allowed to wear a silk scarf, and there
are dozens of similar instances. Right up to the 1914-18
War and even beyond it, it was possible to pin-point a
person's class by the clothes he or she wore. Really, it was

the coming of mass-produced clothes and the possibility of imitating different "classes" of clothing which altered the whole situation. Everyone, for example, could pretend, by wearing hacking jackets or polo-necked sweaters or yachting caps, that they had the money and time to hunt or play polo or go sailing. But as the old status symbols in dress lost a lot of their meaning, new ones were invented. At present there is a whole range of specific clothes and personal decorations to show that you are "with it".

Even the amount one's skin was tanned used to have important social significance. At one time the possession of a white skin was jealously guarded and lovingly worked on, since this implied enough money not to have to go out to work in all weathers. Much later, the Mediterranean sun-tan became so fashionable (because this time it meant enough money to be able to travel south in the winters) that cosmetic firms marketed bottles of stuff guaranteed to give

an artificial tan. But now that every sort of package holiday is available to every sort of person, this kind of distinction is fading. At the same time, the deep psychological need to make such distinctions, to show that one belongs to a particular group, doesn't go away so easily. Here is an exercise to see how aware you are of the signs and signals of some of these groups. And think, while you are doing it, to which of them you feel you belong:

EXERCISE A

See if you can list the dress habits, use of words, life-styles, type of food, housing, social relationships, etc., of the following different groups of people:

1. Under thirty-five "young executives".
2. Alternative Society followers (vegetarians, wholefooders, environmentalists, etc.).
3. Teenagers (town and country versions).
4. The Jet Set.
5. The arty-crafty.
6. Smart pub, fast car crowd.
7. Middle-aged, *Guardian* newspaper reading liberals.
8. Well-heeled industrial workers.
9. The Establishment (i.e. managing directors, high-up Civil Servants, top Service brass, etc.).
10. The unchanged and unchanging true countryman.

Of course, within all these social groups, there is, naturally, some distinction to be made between men and women, and the different ways in which they express these things. In the animal kingdom, of course, it is usually the male who has to make the display in the mating process—and at certain periods of history the human male, too, has been more splendid in appearance than the female—as in the days of long curly hair, lace ruffles, and gorgeous cloaks for men.

At one time, too, men as well as women drew deliberate attention to the sexual areas of their bodies. The tight breeches of the eighteenth century, for example, left no one in doubt as to the wearer's sex; neither did the even tighter hose of an earlier epoch—which were not unlike those of the male ballet dancer of today. Indeed, hose was so tight that separate accommodation had to be thought up for the male genitals—hence the quaintly-named cod-piece. This provocative article of men's clothing lasted roughly from 1400 to 1575. At first it wasn't much more than a cloth pouch hanging from the front of the hose. But soon it became a truly gorgeous affair, made of silk or velvet, and often decorated with ribbons, gold and jewels. By a bit of obvious wishful thinking, it also became larger and longer. François Rabelais, in his book about "the Great Gargantua", was really making fun of the fashion when he described the huge cod-piece worn by his hero:

"For the codpiece 16 yds. of material was required. The shape was that of a triumphal arch, most elegant and secured by 2 gold rings fastened to enamel buttons, each the size of an orange and set with heavy emeralds. The codpiece protruded forward as much as 3 feet."

Notice the rings and buttons—they were for the purpose of keeping the codpiece permanently erect. Perhaps Rabelais was also making fun of man's everlasting (and hopeless) ambitions in this matter. Even suits of armour at that time would often have a huge helmet-like codpiece, sometimes with a spike at the end, or in the shape of a cockerel. The joyous, unashamed assertion of virility could hardly go further!

Such open flaunting of the male sex organ was eventually swamped in the dull decency of trousers—though the sporran of the Scotsman's kilt is, according to some specialists, a continuation of the same old idea. Interestingly enough, there has recently been something of a revival of all this in the deliberately tight crotches of present-day jeans for young men. The widespread appearance of long hair on men is another example of the revival of an earlier symbol

of virility—which could partly explain the extreme hostility to it from the short-back-and-sides brigade. It is, though, difficult to come to firm conclusions about the clothes habits of this group, because so many of the fashions (including the carefully cultivated dirt and shabbiness) are also symptoms of the usual revolt of the young against their elders and against society as a whole. They use clothes not so much to express personality as to assert their loyalty to their own peer-group. In a sense their way-out clothing styles are as conformist, as much a uniform, as the bowler-hat, pin-striped pants and rolled umbrella of the city executive.

Many older men today are also more relaxed and colourful in their dress than they used to be, and psychologically this is probably a very welcome sign. On the whole, though, men in the past couple of centuries have been less concerned about their clothes than women. One of the reasons for this, perhaps, is that they are less in touch with the body than women, less sure of what to do with it or how it fits into the total situation. It is also probably true that a man does not believe that the way he looks mirrors his true self as much as a woman does. That is, he doesn't equate his bodily appearance with the Self as much as a woman does. It has been said, in fact, that *whereas women regard clothes as a means of winning approval, men look upon them rather as a means of avoiding disapproval.*

The greater naturalness and spontaneity of women in relation to their bodies naturally makes them enjoy displaying them to the best advantage through their dress and general appearance, and more ready to experiment with different styles and colours. To some degree this is simply another form, at a deep subconscious level, of the mating game, the search for ways of attracting a mate, often in fierce competition with other women. In our present society (it doesn't by any means apply to all societies) the different devices of attraction must not be allowed to grow stale. New methods must be found: hence what fashion experts call the "Law of Shifting Erogenous Zones"—legs one day, bottoms or breasts the next. And the search for so-called new methods of display are artificially speeded up, sometimes to the point of frenzy, by the huge fashion and cosmetic industries, and their incessant advertising campaigns, by the images or ideals put over in films, television, and so on.

Mini-exercise

Just for fun see if you can list—honestly, mind—the number of times you have changed your style of dressing, e.g. lowered or raised your hemlines; tried out new and weird eye-shadows, and beauty aids; tried for a Taylor-type cleavage; or draped yourself from the ears to the toes—all because you'd seen it on someone else or in a magazine or on the screen.

It is of course true that the relationship of women to clothes and fashion is to some extent at least a symptom of their position in a still male-dominated society. Hence— as an extreme reaction against that position—the burning of bras, and—in a less far-out way—the increasing number of younger women wearing little or no make-up, having simple and natural hair-styles and trying, in spite of fashion-conscious shops, to dress to please themselves.

All the same, there are still large numbers of women (and, after answering that Mini-exercise, you may realise that you are among them) who are very much affected by the dictates of fashion. Apart from the obvious uses during the mating-game, it could also be that as women are still restricted in their activities to some extent, they find adventure and colour and excitement in the constantly changing kaleidoscope of fashion. Another theory is that women's submission to fashion is part of a general masochistic tendency (though that, too, could have been socially conditioned). Perhaps Oscar Wilde had something of this sort in mind when he quipped:

"Fashion is a form of ugliness so intolerable that women have to alter it every six months."

All the factors mentioned above must be kept in mind when trying to draw conclusions about the relationship between your dress and your personality. Nevertheless some fairly positive deductions have been made by various researchers into the subject, and the questionnaires that follow are based on them. Most of them apply to women. But in spite of this, and even though most men's attitudes towards clothes tend, at present, to be rather less clear-cut, we are starting with a **MEN ONLY QUESTIONNAIRE** (though that needn't stop women from answering it too).

QUESTIONNAIRE A (MEN ONLY)
(Answer YES *or* NO*)*

1. If you have to wear a suit to work, do you keep it on when you get home or change into something more relaxed, or at least take off your tie?
2. Do you very often wear an old school or club tie?
3. Do you like wearing a blazer with brass buttons and perhaps a crest on the pocket?
4. Do you go in for tattooing?
5. If you wear conventional clothes for special evening occasions, do you like experimenting with different colours, type of shirt, or neck tie?
6. Do you tend to grasp the lapels of your coat, hitch your thumbs in your waistcoat upper pockets or in your belt?
7. Are you addicted to leather jackets with studs on, or to heavily studded belts, or thick chunky rings?

8. Do you tend to dress as inconspicuously as you possibly can?

9. Do you favour clothes with a semi-military cut or appearance (e.g. uniform-type jackets)?

10. Do you frequently finger your tie or cuff-links or ring, or shoot out your shirt-cuffs?

11. Do you cling to old garments long after they are really wearable?

12. Do you particularly enjoy having your shoes cleaned by a shoe-shine man?

13. Do you usually wear dark glasses and bulky enfolding clothes?

QUESTIONNAIRE A—ANSWERS & COMMENTS

1. Ideally
   YES

If you stay formally dressed when you get home, a reasonable conclusion is that home is less important to you than your business. If you take off your jacket and loosen your tie, you are at least capable of relating to the home atmosphere. If you change into a casual outfit the odds are that you have other sides of your personality to cultivate, and that you are a more interesting companion for your wife and children (or whoever). If you change in a rushed, rather frantic way, it may mean, however, that you are in the wrong job.

2.   NO

Over-addiction to the old school-tie (or other similar "badges") usually suggests extreme conservatism, a clinging to the past, anxiety about your status and a desire therefore to advertise it.

3.   NO   Like the old school-tie addiction, this may point to anxiety about status, whether or not you are entitled to the crest or buttons—and especially if the crest is a made-up one. There are, of course, also perfectly natural occasions for such decorations—when taking part in sports, at school or college reunions, in hot weather, at the beach, etc.

4. On the whole   Tattooing is not in itself bad, but if
   NO   carried to excess is often indicative of a desire for camouflage (similar to an excessive use of make-up in women), and therefore is often a sign of anxiety about hidden inner feelings. It is noticeable, for example, that male teenagers, who are still searching for their full masculine identities, are fond of tattooing: it is regarded as an unmistakable sign of masculine toughness. In adult men, too, of course, tattooing could suggest an over-anxiety to assert masculinity. Women and girls who tattoo their bodies obviously haven't much confidence in the feminine appeal of their skins, and therefore of their bodies.

5.   YES   The willingness to experiment within a restricted form of dress probably indicates flexibility and originality. On the other hand some men can't be bothered and regard the occasion which calls for evening dress a bore which doesn't deserve any extra effort. Some men, too, are sufficiently confident of their appearances to feel that the very conventionality of evening dress makes them look more not less distinguished.

6.   NO   These are well-known and well-attested symptoms of a desire to dominate, and sometimes of downright aggressiveness.

7.   NO   These, too, are symptomatic of a desire (sometimes an anxiety) to stress masculinity, and also of aggressiveness.

8.   NO   Studied inconspicuousness of dress is usually a sign of a strong desire to be inconspicuous in general—which mostly means extreme lack of self-confidence; or sometimes irrational feelings of inner guilt—and trying to be inconspicuous then would mean an attempt to avoid probing eyes by being as nearly as possible invisible. (This would apply, too, to women who cancel out their natural attractiveness by drab clothes and a generally mousy appearance.)

9. Generally NO   Although these may just be the clothes that suit you best, a fondness for military styles often indicates status anxiety and a desire to emphasize male attributes (this could also apply to women who like this type of clothing for themselves).

10.   NO   These are often symptoms of strain, and need for reassurance.

11. On the whole NO   The fondness for an old jacket may be no more than male conservatism, but if carried to excess it may indicate a need

for reassurance and continuity—as with the child who clings to a much-battered but much-loved teddy bear.

12. NO Investigations suggest that this indicates an enjoyment of servility from other men (the shoe-shiner is literally "at your feet"). It has been observed that whereas young shoe-shine boys (in those countries where they are common—because any job is better than no job) kneel at their customers' feet, when they get older they try to assert their selfhood and independence by sitting on stools or inverted boxes.

13. Preferably If these are featured together, it would
     NO indicate a strong desire for camouflage, for a mask that would ward off the world's prying into inner feelings of guilt and shame (whether or not they were real).

If 10 or more of your answers agree with those given above, it would probably suggest that you are an exceptionally stable, mature and adult male. A score of 8-10 would be more likely, and very satisfactory. 6-8 would probably be average. 6 and under would seem to suggest a considerable degree of masculine inconfidence and possibly immaturity.

Now for some **WOMEN ONLY QUESTIONNAIRES** —beginning with one designed to test how secure and contented you are in your femininity:

QUESTIONNAIRE B
(Answer YES *or* NO)

1. Do you go in for very tall hair styles or hats?
2. Do you use padding (in bras, shoulders, hips)?
3. Are you drawn to military tunic type clothes, or large cloaks?
4. Do you like very full and voluminous clothes?

5. Do you like wearing heavy, dangling pendants, long flowing hair, and skirts down on the ground around you?

6. Do you go in for bright scarlet lipsticks, which you lay on with a trowel?

7. Do you pluck your eyebrows almost completely off?

8. Do you force your feet into shoes that are obviously too small?

9. Do you frequently worry about whether or not your skirt has ridden up or got caught up?

10. If you are wearing a necklace, pendant or bracelet, do you keep handling it?

11. Do you find yourself stopping whenever you pass a mirror anywhere, and checking out your face and hair quickly?

12. If you are feeling depressed, do you put on your drabbest clothes and hardly bother about grooming your face or hair?

13. Do you take great pains to see that your children are immaculately turned out, while you yourself dress rather drably?

14. Do you habitually wear dark glasses, wigs, false eye-lashes or nails, change your hair colour completely, etc.?

QUESTIONNAIRE B—ANSWERS & COMMENTS

1. Preferably NO — It has been shown that these attempts to exaggerate height are often a sign of feelings of insecurity or vulnerability about feminine selfhood, and a desire to compete with men. Sometimes, too, the towering hair-style or dramatic hat is an attempt to draw attention to the head (i.e. to the intellectuality of the wearer) and to divert attention from other, more specifically feminine, parts of the body.

2. NO — Obviously the adoption of these devices shows a dissatisfaction with your body as it is, and probably a lack of confidence in your own femininity and personality.

3. Preferably
   NO

Although these may happen to be the styles that suit you very well, they can also be signs of trying to feel bigger and stronger or even more aggressive (i.e. more like men) than you really are. They may also point to a failure to come satisfactorily to terms with the masculine side of your nature. The well-known theory that women have a masculine element in their make-up and men a feminine one is basically correct. The balance and integration of these elements is a true sign of full maturity.

4. On the whole
& 5.   NO

These somewhat dramatic methods of self-enhancement often signal a strong need for security and probably an inner timidity.

6. Qualified
   NO

Inasmuch as it's part of the mating-game, you needn't bother, because in fact a great many men don't like heavy make-up. Usually the message contained in over-red, heavily painted lips is addressed to the wearer herself—a reassurance of a kind of super-femininity, and therefore a sign of some anxiety on this score.

7. Hopefully
   NO

This, too, is usually a sign of a somewhat anxious wish to stress femininity. The subconscious logic suggested in a recent investigation, goes something like this: "Men very often have hairy, bushy eyebrows—therefore I am going to show how very unmasculine I am by showing I have hardly any eyebrows."

8.   NO

This tendency (a very common one, of course, especially when pressured by fashion trends) is of a similar kind. Small feet are considered typically feminine, so some women struggle to prove, no matter how painful it may be, that they too possess this attribute.

9. NO The frequent fussing about how your skirt arranges itself is usually an example (a very common and human one too, and often quite endearing to the man) of an ambivalence of attitude. Your feelings of modesty may dictate that the upper thigh shouldn't be showing—yet a frequent tugging and rearranging of your skirt inevitably draws attention to that very area!

10. NO This is a sign of shyness, nervousness or anxiety (similar to the frequent handling of the tie, cuff-links, ring, etc., in men).

11. Preferably Excessive "mirror-peeking" pretty ob-
    NO viously indicates anxiety about your female image. If it is a fairly constant habit (and not only in moments of stress) you are probably in need of reassurance either from a man or from yourself.

(Incidentally, on the general question of feminine attractiveness, you might be surprised by the results of a recent experiment in which, putting it simply, a cross-section of young men were shown a selection of photographs of unknown young women, ranging in looks from the ravishingly beautiful to the positively plain. Asked to choose those which most attracted them, the young men were far from being unanimous in voting for the prettiest girls; and indeed every young woman, even the plainest, received some votes. Attractiveness among human beings is a mysterious business —and there is always someone who will find each of us attractive, thank goodness!

And if and when you long to be incredibly beautiful yourself, you might do well to remember that the very beautiful woman has special problems of her own. Often she feels bored with the constant attention she receives; she suffers from the feeling that she is valued only for her looks and not for her true and inner self; and she often has feelings of guilt, because she knows that the inner self cannot possibly measure up to the perfection and beauty of her appearance. It is quite common for a very beautiful woman to try, at some time or other in her life, to dowse her beauty in unbecoming clothes, by refusing to make up or by neglecting her hair, nails, etc.) Anyway, back to the answers:

12.	NO	Some women do, of course, But obviously it's better to make yourself up with special care—i.e. *put a brave face* on the world—and, by putting on some of your brightest clothes, things you feel really good in, you may very well end up feeling more cheerful!
13.	NO	This sort of thing is frequently seen in women suffering from feelings of unworthiness, usually of course quite irrational (or rather, rational only in the long vanished setting of childhood fears and anxieties). By making her children look just too sweet and clean and nice, the mother is often (in effect) pushing them forward into the limelight and hiding herself behind them—from what she unconsciously imagines are probing and accusing eyes.
14.	Hopefully NO	If you do, it seems obvious enough that you feel considerable uncertainty, dissatisfaction and perhaps anxiety, about your whole body image. You are probably still searching for your true identity —and it may be that you want to disguise certain things about yourself which you feel aren't so good (without any real reason, of course). These feelings are probably very similar to those of the man who hides behind bushy beard, low-brimmed hat, bulky clothes, etc., as well as the inevitable dark glasses.

QUESTIONNAIRE C — (MOSTLY FOR WOMEN)
(Answer YES *or* NO*)*

Now here is a list of more general questions which deal with some of the indications of character and personality conveyed by your relationship to clothes and some of the signals you are subconsciously giving out through them. Although the questions apply mostly to women, men can try answering for their girl friends and wives (and see where it gets them!).

1. Do you cling to fashions that have gone out of date?
2. Do you (if you can afford to) immediately change your wardrobe as soon as fashion changes?
3. Do you worry if your clothes are not in the latest fashion?
4. Have you strong ideas as to the kind of clothes that suit you best, and do you try to adapt new fashions to these ideas?
5. Do you go in for the most daring, avant-garde fashions?
6. Are you unconcerned about whether or not your clothes are socially acceptable, or currently regarded as modest?
7. Do you wear false eye-lashes and/or a good deal of mascara, eye shadow, etc.?
8. Do you go in for large checked patterns?
9. Or do you like small designs?

10. Do you, either habitually or at certain times, like to cover up your arms?
11. Do you particularly like very smooth, silky garments?
12. Do you tend to add some garish, unnecessary item to your get-up, even though you don't particularly like it?
13. Do you like deep shades and saturated colours in your dresses, etc.?
14. Do you like broad, flowing skirts?
15. Do you spend an exceptionally long time grooming yourself (brushing hair, massaging skin, etc.)?
16. Do you sometimes feel you want to wrap yourself up in your clothes more than usual?
17. Do you feel uncomfortable or unhappy when taking your clothes off during love-making?

QUESTIONNAIRE C—ANSWERS & COMMENTS

1. To cling to outdated fashions (especially if they never particularly suited you anyway) obviously suggests a clinging to the past and a fear of experimentation that may be morbid. .
2. On the other hand, the woman who is a frantic slave to fashion is usually uncertain and anxious about her body-image and her identity. It can also be a means of self-effacement—following too closely other people's ideas of what she should wear turns a woman, in extreme cases, into a kind of puppet or dummy.
3. The mature and well-balanced woman enjoys new fashions and uses them as a means of self-expression, without worrying too much one way or the other.
4. Strong ideas about your body image and the styles that best suit it, together with a readiness to be independent of the dictates of fashion, usually indicate a strong, independent and well-formed personality.
5. This may indicate daring and flexibility—or it may mean you have a strong exhibitionist streak.
6. A somewhat ambivalent indication. It may mean a high degree of independence in your character—or it may mean that you have rather exaggerated self-esteem.

7. Calling attention to the eyes, and accentuating the fluttering movement of the eyelashes, are pretty obvious signals (whether conscious or not) of invitation to further intimacy (though there's no reason of course why you shouldn't use them).

8. Research has shown that loud colours and large check patterns are attempts at reassurance about body boundaries and therefore indicative of uneasiness about them. It is a commonplace that very fat women, who are unhappy about their size, often seem to choose loud clothes (though it's obvious these are least likely to suit them).

9. Here also research has shown that women who prefer smaller designs are likely to be especially feminine and interested in making a good impression.

10. Covering the arms is frequently indicative of a reluctance to reach out to other people, and especially to men. It is noticeable that women who usually have no particular objection to half-sleeves or sleeveless dresses, tend to go into long-sleeved garments when they are feeling hurt, offended and hostile towards their men.

11. A marked fondness for these kinds of material has been noted in women who in childhood did not have sufficient caressing or other forms of body-contact with their mothers.

12. If the rest of your get-up is in good taste, the garish addition is often symptomatic of a subconscious wish to guy a mother who was insufficiently loving and was also competitive in her attitude towards her daughter.

13. Women who go in for deep saturated colours are usually more extrovert and sociable and less submissive than others.

14. There is no reason why you shouldn't—but obviously this kind of skirt is designed (not consciously, of course) to accentuate the pelvic region, and thus to draw attention to maternal capabilities.

15. All women, of course, spend a good deal of time grooming themselves. There is probably something in

the old observation that women tend to be more narcissitic than men (though this may be a part of social and economic conditioning). But although a certain amount of self-grooming is natural and desirable, when it is carried to excess it often becomes a form of self-babying (craving for maternal care)—and those women most addicted to it, it has been observed, are those most in search of love and affection.

16. It has been found that many women wrap themselves up when they feel depressed, rejected or hurt in their feelings (i.e. being treated coldly). An investigation among college girls in America showed that they tended to do the same thing when they were feeling especially homesick.

17. Fear of taking off your clothes often indicates anxiety about your body-boundaries, and a feeling that they are vulnerable and easily threatened. Some women can't achieve orgasm unless they are partly or even almost fully clothed. The retention of a token article of clothing during lovemaking (stockings, perhaps, or a scarf) is quite common.

There are no scores for this section, but, hopefully, plenty of food for thought.

We should like to conclude this chapter by saying that it is difficult to compile questionnaires of this kind without feeling a sense of respect and tenderness for all human beings—together with the age-old conviction that love and tenderness are the only relevant answers to most human problems, difficulties and doubts. Did you feel like that as you answered the questionnaires? If you did—you haven't a lot to worry about!

CHAPTER FOUR

YOUR EVERYDAY SELF—
AND THE INNER YOU

CHAPTER FOUR

YOUR EVERYDAY SELF— AND THE INNER YOU

Close observers of human nature have always been aware that our everyday words and actions can provide clues to our secret motives and desires, and dramatists and novelists often make very effective use of these in depicting their characters. In fact, anybody who wants to understand himself or herself better should be on the look-out for these clues. They crop up in the most unexpected places and circumstances.

One of the most fascinating examples is the song or tune which suddenly pops into your head when you least expect it—and often sticks there, like a toffee-paper you can't shake off your fingers. It may simply be because it's a catchy tune that you've got on the brain—but if you examine the words that may go with the tune, in a surprisingly large number of cases you will find that some part of them—it may be one of the verses, or a phrase, or even a single word— holds a special significance for you and your life at the time.

Here are two examples:

(a) A woman we know had had a particularly happy night with her husband when she felt she'd been at her best. Next morning, while busy with the housework, she suddenly found herself humming an old-fashioned music hall song which she hadn't heard for ages, and which she was surprised in fact to realize that she knew at all. When she tried to recall the words, the only ones she could remember were the last two lines: "Whoa mare! whoa mare! you've earned your little bit of gin!"

She couldn't help laughing as she realized how comically apt these words were to her feelings of emotional and physical satisfaction with the previous night's performance.

(You should be warned that the subconscious is often a bawdy and uninhibited joker!)

(b) Another woman we know who was unhappily married had a particularly angry row with her husband one morning and they parted in mutual fury. As she drove to work later, still feeling furious, she was amazed to find herself singing a bright West Indian calypso. She couldn't understand how she could actually be singing at such a time—until she suddenly realized that these were the words of the song:

"Stone cold dead in de market
Stone cold dead in de market
Stone cold dead in de market,
I killed nobody but my husban'"

Both these examples are, of course, fairly obvious ones. Many songs and tunes are not as straightforward in their meanings. Often you have to think quite hard about the melodies and words. Often, in order to see how they fit in, you have to examine the whole context surrounding the song—the other things you were thinking about at the time, what physical and emotional states you associate with the day and time, the decisions that are facing you, your joys and worries, the general course your life is taking, and so on. Quite often, too, they link up with the dream or dreams that you had the previous night—that's why these disguised singing messages frequently arrive in the morning—while you're in the bath or shower, for instance.

What is certain is that if you do work at these tuneful clues from the subconscious, they will tell you a good deal about yourself. They may very well be pulling your leg, or brutally pointing out to you things you'd rather not face, or making caustic, irreverent and bawdy comments on your high-falutin' pretensions—but you can be sure it's all for your own good. They are real allies, and they can shine a sudden dazzling light into all sorts of dark inner corners.

EXERCISE

It's a good idea, therefore (and first-class entertainment into the bargain) to keep a note-book of these uninvited tunes.

Write down the titles of the songs or pieces of music, and then as many of the words (if there are any) as you can remember. Sometimes it's only a few that come to mind— but these may be the key ones. At other times it's the words which elude you most strenuously that are the truly significant ones.

At the end of every month look back through your notebook. You may have compiled quite a personality programme of tunes. By looking at them in a batch you may learn a good deal about the whole *tenor* of your life (it's impossible to write about this kind of material without the unconscious taking a hand with word-play and puns like that!). You may find warnings and sign-posts. It may even be a way of conducting a kind of mini psychotherapy, or auto-analysis.

Making notes like this is something you can do with other people too. You may take note of the songs your husband

sings in the bath or while he's shaving, for example. You can swap songs, and analyse each other's. You can get your friends to tell you their recent tell-tale experiences of the same kind. Not a bad party game, in fact, but beware: the more conscious you are about it all, the less the subconscious will co-operate. It may even take its revenge on you by feeding you with false clues! It's only the tunes that really do occur to you unexpectedly and spontaneously that are any good to you.

Our everyday words and actions can be just as meaningful. We've all had the experience of meaning one thing and saying another or, if it comes to that, the other way round as well, saying one thing and meaning another. We've all had the experience, too, of forgetting names we normally know perfectly well, or of leaving out key words or phrases in letters, or of misspelling or mispronouncing familiar words for no apparent reason. Sigmund Freud, the father of psychoanalysis, applied to all the various slips of tongue, pen, eye, memory, etc., the term *parapraxes*. He also closely associated with them the more physical kinds of "slipping up.", to which we are all subject at one time or another.

Fatigue, illness, extreme distraction can, of course, account (at least in part) for some of these slips and mishaps. Freud himself admitted that when he had an attack of migraine coming on he tended to forget people's names. But it was he who first systematically studied these fascinating phenomena, and showed (in some of his *INTRODUCTORY LECTURES*, and in his most popular book, *THE PSYCHO-PATHOLOGY OF EVERYDAY LIFE*) that the vast majority of them

"can be traced back to incompletely suppressed psychical material, which, although pushed away by the consciousness, has neverthe-less not been robbed of all capacity for expressing itself."

Freud of course gives dozens of examples, each of them most carefully documented and analysed. Many of them are, obviously, beyond the scope of the amateur. But here are three of them, dealing with verbal slips, that can easily be understood by all of us:

1. An energetic and decidedly bossy lady reporting on a visit which her husband had made to his doctor, said: "the doctor told him he had no need to diet; he could eat and drink what *I* want." She meant, of course, that he had been told he could eat and drink what *he* wanted. Her slip made it pretty clear who wore the trousers in the relationship, and whose tastes really mattered.

2. A professor of anatomy, at the end of a lecture on the nasal cavities, asked his students whether they had understood. When they all said that they had, he told them: "I can hardly believe that, since even in a city with millions of inhabitants, those who understand the nasal cavities can be counted on one finger. . . . I beg your pardon, on the fingers of one hand."

   But his "accidentally" abbreviated phrase had an unmistakable meaning too—that is, he was the only one who really understood the subject.

3. A notorious murderer who posed as a bacteriologist in order to obtain from scientific institutes the cultures of highly dangerous pathogenic organisms—which he then used to kill off various near-relatives—sent a letter to the director of one of these institutes complaining that the cultures supplied to him were not very effective. Instead of writing in his letter "in my experiments on mice or guinea-pigs" he wrote "in my experiments on men". The doctors at the institute were intrigued by the strange slip of his pen—but they didn't realise that it was really a murderer's subconscious mind giving him away.

EXERCISES

1. KEEP A RECORD of the slips of the tongue which you make, including mispronunciations, jumbling of words and phrases, accidental puns, etc. At the end of a week look

through them and see if they tend to be of the same kind or to point in one direction. You may find that the majority of them concern one particular person, or one particular set of circumstances. This could help you to a better understanding of the relationships and situations in your life that are bothering you. To take two very obvious examples:

(a) If you persistently addressed your lover or husband as Tom when his name was actually Tim, you'd probably be well-advised to reassess the strength of your feelings towards him . . . especially if you knew somebody else whose name *was* Tim!

(b) If you said "I abhor my job" when you had intended to say "I adore my job", you would be right to wonder whether or not you really were happy in your work.

2. RE-READ YOUR LETTERS BEFORE YOU POST THEM, and note the words you have missed out or the words you have "accidentally" muddled. Consider these omissions and mistakes carefully: they may contain clues as to your hidden motives and wishes. This is most likely to happen if you are writing to someone you know well, and with whom you often correspond. Here are some obvious but real-life examples:

(a) A young man who was secretly flirting with another girl began a letter to his fiancée like this:

"Darling, I was so glad to deceive your letter . . ."

He had, of course, meant to write *receive*, but the slip of the pen revealed his guilty conscience about the other girl.

(b) A man writing to a friend who had lent him £50 some time ago, added this postscript to his letter:

"P.S. I have forgotten the £50 I owe you."

The omission of the "not" before the word "forgotten" pretty obviously indicated a reluctance to repay the debt.

(c) A woman writing to a lover of whom she was tiring, ended her letter as usual with the words "My

fondest love"— but omitted to sign her name,
thereby demonstrating her desire to be "out of it".
(N.B. Of course you can also study the letters you receive
for give-away clues; though not many of them are likely
to be as straightforward as these examples).

3. ARE YOU THE ABSENT-MINDED PROFESSOR-TYPE?

If you are, it's a good idea to take note of the things,
people, or situations you're absent-minded *about*. As
often as not you really want to forget them, because your
real wishes belong somewhere else. The professor in the
old joke who absent-mindedly got on the 'bus taking
him back home instead of the one going to the lecture-
hall was probably expressing his real preference!

But it's what Freud called *bungled actions* that lend themselves most readily to question-and-answer. Here are two
questionnaires, derived from the findings of Freud and
others. The first of them concerns the relationship between
the sexes.

Consider carefully the actions or situations described in
the questions and see if similar ones might apply to you.

❖❖❖❖❖❖❖❖❖❖❖❖❖❖

QUESTIONNAIRE A

1. Have you ever, intending to telephone your boy/girl friend, or your husband/wife, dialled the number of another man/woman instead?

2. Have you ever, in setting out to keep a date, found yourself heading in the direction of the place you used to meet a former partner?

3. Have you ever, after visiting the home of a married friend, found that you have inadvertently brought some small object—e.g. a box of matches—away with you?

4. Do you habitually, after visiting your boy/girl friend, find you have left something behind?

5. Have you ever, when called upon to pay a forfeit at a party game, offered, or been tempted to offer, your wedding or engagement ring?

6. Do you habitually finger your wedding-ring, or keep pulling it on and off?

7. Do you rather frequently find yourself forgetting the name of your companion of the opposite sex?

8. *(For men)* Have you ever, when travelling on a 'bus with your girl-friend or wife, found yourself asking the conductor for only one ticket?

9. *(For men).* Have you ever, when taking out a new girl to whom you are strongly attracted, left your wallet behind?

10. Have you ever forgotten to post a love-letter?

11. Have you ever found yourself, when on a crowded pavement, dodging backwards and forwards in order to pass someone?

12. *(For men)* Are you in the habit of leaving behind your pen, pencil or penknife when you visit your girl-friend?

13. *(For women)* Have you ever left your handbag or purse in the room of a man you have recently met?

14. *(For married women)* When you first married, did you find yourself still signing your maiden-name on cheques, documents, etc.?

❖❖❖❖❖❖❖❖❖❖❖❖❖❖

QUESTIONNAIRE A—ANSWERS & COMMENTS

1. If you dial the wrong number it's quite likely that for some reason you don't really want to ring the right one. If in addition the number you do dial is that of someone of the opposite sex whom you know, it's a reasonable assumption that he/she is the person you'd rather be talking to. It's quite a common experience, too, for someone "accidentally" to ring the number of a former partner when the relationship hasn't really been brought to a proper conclusion, or when strong feelings of guilt are still there about it.

2. This course of action, too, shows that the new love has not yet really displaced the old.

3. Usually this would indicate a measure of jealousy or envy, or a desire to have a share in the relationship.

4. This suggests a considerable reluctance to leave. It may point to a wish to share or merge possessions— i.e. to set up house together. This would be especially so if the object left behind had an obvious symbolic significance—a latch-key, for example.

5. If so, it's a signal that your marriage or engagement is in danger. You wouldn't be tempted to offer something so deeply symbolic of a close tie or commitment, unless you had really had doubts about the latter's value and durability.

6. This action, though not as serious as the one above, is nevertheless indicative of some doubt and anxiety about the relationship. If you catch yourself doing it, it's probably a sign that you should take thought—and action.

7. It's pretty obvious that if you can easily forget the name of the person you're with, you wouldn't find it difficult to forget him/her altogether.

8. If so, the odds are that you really wanted to be alone or perhaps in somebody else's company.

9. There are various possible interpretations. You may be just plain mean and not want to pay the bill! Or you may not, at any rate on this particular occasion, value

sufficiently the person you are taking out. Or you may have a poor valuation of yourself. Or again, you may be experiencing anxiety as to whether or not you are up to the situation.

10. If so, the chances are that the impulse behind the writing of the letter wasn't very strong, or that you are doubtful as to the sincerity of its contents.

11. This usually indicates a spontaneous attraction towards the other person and a desire for physical contact, especially if the person you are dodging about in front of is of the opposite sex.

12. In this case, you are indirectly expressing your physical desires. The subconscious isn't at all delicate in its behaviour; pens, pencils and penknives are phallic symbols (they even sound like PENIS).

13. This, too, is a hint on the part of your subconscious that you find the man concerned attractive. It may make you blush to contemplate the fact, but handbags and purses are among the most common vaginal symbols.

14. If so, you hadn't yet completely surrendered yourself to your new relationship to your husband. You were still clinging to your old single status—and possibly to the father whose surname you bore before your marriage.

❖❖❖❖❖❖❖❖❖❖❖

QUESTIONNAIRE B

And here is another set of questions derived from similar sources, but of a more general nature. Think about the actions or situations contained in them and see if you can work out their implications:

1. Have you ever found yourself trying to insert your own key into the lock of a house you are visiting, instead of ringing the door-bell?

2. Have you ever found yourself trying to open the door of your office (or other place of employment) with the key of your home—or vice-versa?

3. Have you ever, on your arrival at your home, locked the door after you, even though you knew callers were expected?

4. Have you ever found yourself stumbling or slipping more than usual, and for no apparent reason?

5. Have you ever had a spell of accident-proneness banging into things, cutting yourself, etc., more frequently than usual?

6. Have you ever found yourself, over a period of time, suddenly losing things you value?

7. Have you ever arrived at the theatre, cinema, etc., and found you've left the tickets behind?

8. Have you ever found yourself unexpectedly finding things—e.g. coins in the road?

9. Have you ever, after paying a bill, left your purse or wallet behind?

10. Are you in the habit of flinging doors open and going into rooms without knocking?

11. Do you sometimes make mistakes about the date or the day of the week?

12. When a new year starts, do you tend to go on, for quite a long time, dating letters, cheques, etc., with the previous year?

13. Do you sometimes count the chimes of a clock incorrectly?

14. Do you sometimes forget to wind up the alarm-clock, even though as a rule, you do it automatically?

15. Do you, when you are in someone else's company, sometimes "accidentally" scatter your small change?

16. Do you sometimes "accidentally" give a beggar a bigger coin than you had intended?

17. Do you sometimes, although normally not a clumsy person, have a spell in which you keep breaking things?

❖❖❖❖❖❖❖❖❖❖❖❖❖

QUESTIONNAIRE B — ANSWERS & COMMENTS

1. It's a pretty clear indication that you'd like to belong to the house concerned, and perhaps that you prefer it to your own.

2. An equally clear indication that you'd much rather be at home. If it's the other way round, then either you are deeply absorbed in your work at the time, or you're not particularly happy at home.

3. Obviously enough, you want a quiet evening at home, and the callers are going to be unwelcome ones!

4. Usually this means that you are in considerable doubt about some particular course of action, or about your way of life in general. You need to think about them very carefully indeed. Stumbling is often followed by falling—but if you stop yourself in time (if, that is, you work out the reasons for your doubts) perhaps you won't fall into something you don't really want.

5. Very often this indicates that you are feeling guilty and conscience-stricken about something, and that subconsciously you are inflicting punishment on yourself. You need to work out whether or not the punishment is justified, or if the guilt belongs to some far-distant and vanished state of affairs, and therefore has no substance in reality. Sometimes, though, the "accidents", especially the more serious ones, are subconscious means of preventing you from undertaking something you just don't want to tackle.

6. This, too, is a symptom of inner guilt. By losing something valuable you are making a kind of sacrifice—trying to propitiate the gods rather as primitive peoples still do.

7. Simple enough—you really wanted to stay at home!

8. It's a very good sign. It shows an unconscious eagerness to look for something new in life. As professional scavengers and beggars know, quite a number of coins and other objects get dropped, especially near ticket offices, etc., but one has to be in a mood of readiness for new experiences to find them.

9. If so, it's likely that the bill shocked you. In effect you were saying "You may as well take the lot, you robbers!"

10. This habit is common with people who in childhood suffered a good deal of anxiety (still unresolved in adult life) about what was happening in their parents' bedroom.

11. Usually this indicates that you didn't really want to keep the appointments scheduled for the date in question; or that there was something else you would much rather have been doing.

12. If so, you probably regard the new year with some apprehension. In some cases it indicates a tendency to cling to the past.

13. There is some hidden reason why you don't want to know the right time—a meeting you don't want to go to, for instance; or the sudden memory of something unpleasant that happened at the relevant time in the past.

14. Pretty obviously you are reluctant to face the next day.

15. Quite frequently this is a contemptuous gesture on the part of your subconscious—you are showing the person concerned that you don't value him very highly.

16. This is another common sacrificial or propitiatory action, designed to appease fate—and indicative therefore of some degree of guilt or anxiety.

17. Of course you do. We all do. Sometimes it may merely be because we are exceptionally tired. But often there are reasons, buried in our unconscious minds. It's worth-while thinking carefully about the broken object —who gave it to us and when; what associations, past and present surround it; what exactly was happening in your life when you broke it; who else was present at the time, or had recently been with you—and so on. Here is a true example which will show the kind of unconscious motivations that can lie behind such acts of temporary clumsiness:

> A woman who had devoted herself for years to her rather exacting and finicky invalid widowed

mother, one day swept a valuable china figure off a shelf while dusting, though she had been dusting the same shelf for the past twenty years without mishap. The figure was a dainty, simpering shepherdess, who looked as if she had never done a day's work in her life. It was one of a pair of figures originally given to her parents as a wedding present—the other figure being of a shepherd.

On the previous day the woman had run into a man whom she had known and been fond of years before. The "message" of the breakage is pretty clear. In her unconscious mind the woman wished her mother dead so that the bond could be broken and she could lead her own life. It was, moreover, the shepherdess that had been broken, not the shepherd—so that the woman was also expressing the wish that it had been her much-loved and independent-minded father who had survived rather than her mother.

CHAPTER FIVE

YOUR DREAMS

CHAPTER FIVE

YOUR DREAMS

Dreams are something which our modern industrialized society, with its emphasis on materialistic values, tends to treat as being of little value, except for impractical, "dreamy" people. So let's begin with a few practical, scientifically established facts about dreaming.

We all dream every night. We spend about 20%—say, about one and a half hours—of our total sleeping time in a dream state. And that means, on average, we spend four years of our lives at it!

Are those four years wasted ones? To start finding out, here's a questionnaire which will test your knowledge and understanding of dreams, get rid of some of the popular fallacies about them, and bring up quite a lot of fascinating and important points.

❖❖❖❖❖❖❖❖❖❖❖❖❖

QUESTIONNAIRE A
(Answer TRUE or FALSE)

1. There are some people who never dream.
2. It is possible to tell whether or not a person is dreaming.
3. We only remember a fraction of our dreams on waking up.
4. Although dreams may seem to last a long time, in fact they only last a few minutes.
5. The ancient theories about dreams are all valueless.
6. There are considerable differences between those who remember their dreams and those who don't.
7. People who remember their dreams easily are more dreamy and unrealistic in their daily lives than those who don't.
8. We always dream in black-and-white.
9. Women recall dreams more often and more completely than men.

10. Dreams can be caused by indigestion and other bodily disturbances.

11. Drugs and alcohol increase and enrich our dreaming.

12. Sex dreams are the direct result of the sexual sensations we had just before we went to sleep.

13. Dreams are merely the result of the irritation of certain cells in the brain.

14. Dreams are purely the result of things happening around us.

15. Dreams are sometimes a means of drawing our attention to likely illnesses in our bodies, not yet recognized by our consciousness.

16. Dreams are merely reproductions of past events.

17. Some dreams are racial rather than personal in origin.

18. Dreams always go by opposites.

19. It is the most dramatic and emotionally highly-charged part of a dream that is the most significant.

20. Dreams sometimes take place in parts or sequences.

21. Dreams can be interpreted in a number of different, but equally valid, ways.

22. Dreams are much too weird and far-fetched to have any real relationship to the truth.

23. Dreams relieve our tensions and so encourage sleep.

24. Most dreams are chiefly personal, and refer only to our own experiences and problems.

25. The characters in our dreams are mostly representations of our selves.

26. Every dream is concerned with a problem.

27. Some dreams cheat us with false "solutions".

28. Some dreams never solve the problem they are dealing with.

29. Important practical problems can be solved in dreams.

30. Dreams which don't suggest a solution are valueless.

31. Dreams only reveal the negative sides of our natures.

32. Dreams are valueless unless they are interpreted.

33. It is sexual problems which are most commonly dealt with in dreams.

34. There are differences between an ordinary dream and

a nightmare.

35. Most "night terrors" in children are associated with guilt.
36. Dreams can be telepathic.
37. Dreams can foretell the future.
38. Dreams can provide artistic inspiration.
39. It is dangerous to make special efforts to reject our unique dream images.
40. We can choose and control our own dreams.

❖❖❖❖❖❖❖❖❖❖❖❖

QUESTIONNAIRE A — ANSWERS & COMMENTS

1. **FALSE** We all dream—and we dream every night (as do all mammals and many birds). People who insist they never dream really mean that they don't remember their dreams.

2. **TRUE** There are many scientific techniques for detecting when a person is dreaming. Research has established, for instance, that rapid eye movements (REMs for short) almost always accompany dreaming—almost as if the dreamer were following the action of his dream on a screen—and the REMs stop when the dream is over.

3. **TRUE** The average adult during an average night's sleep, has four or five REM periods. As a rule these periods occur every ninety minutes during sleep. Every person tested, in the numerous dream-laboratories in many parts of the world, has been found to show these periodic REMs. Most of us, however, only remember a small proportion of our dreams on waking—and sometimes none at all.

   (Incidentally, it has been found that newborn babies spend as much as 45-65% of their sleep time in dreaming; between 18 and 30 years old people spend 20-25% of sleep time in dreaming; after that it drops to between 13% and 18%.)

4. FALSE   This used to be a common belief, but modern scientific research has shown that our shortest dreams last ten minutes, and the longest can be anything between 30 and 45 minutes. We usually start with a short dream, and have the longer ones towards morning.

5. FALSE   —or partly false. A lot of them were based on magic and superstition, although some shrewd and accurate observations were made by some ancient commentators on dreams. The Ancient Greek philosopher, Aristotle, originated the theory which Jung (and others) later took up— namely that there are some dreams which "call attention to incipient morbid conditions of the body which have escaped the notice of our waking state".

6. TRUE   It probably depends whether or not we are interested. If we are impatient about our dreams, and think they are nonsense, then we're not likely to remember them very well. Tests have shown that cool, analytical people who have a very logical and unimaginative approach to their feelings tend to remember fewer dreams than those who are more imaginative and more open and flexible in their attitudes to life. It has been shown, too, that introverts—not surprisingly—remember their dreams more readily than extroverts. Other researches have found that those who don't recall their dreams are, in general, confident and self-controlled, but also conformist, defensive, not very self-aware, and tend to repress or deny their feelings; whereas those who readily remember their dreams are less self-confident and more anxious, but have much

greater self-understanding.

7. FALSE　The ability (or willingness) to recall dreams is one of the ways of making contact with the inner life—and those who have that contact are more lik ly to be balanced and mature (more truly realistic) than those who don't. The kind of material contained in our dreams is frequently what we need for the fulfilment of our lives. If these potentialities are consistently ignored or repressed, considerable damage may be done to the personality.

8. FALSE　This used to be believed, but when researchers wake up their subjects from an REM period to question them about colour, the immediate answer is almost always that they have seen colours in their dreams. Most researchers agree that we *do* dream in colour, probably most of the time.

9. TRUE　It may have something to do with physiology and biology—or it may simply be because in our kind of society it's still considered a waste of time for go-getting males to bother about dreams—whereas it's quite all right for women!

10. TRUE　—or at any rate, very likely. A heavy meal late at night means that the digestive system has to draw on increased supplies of blood, so that the circulation to the brain may be affected, and this in turn may be one of the causes of dreaming. But although this may partly explain why we dream, it doesn't of course account for *what* we dream—apart from a few obvious and exceptional cases (for example, if you were actually dying of thirst in the desert and dreamt about lakes of water, then it's likely that both the fact and the content of your dream would be caused by your raging thirst!).

11. FALSE　—or largely false. Most drugs almost certainly tend to suppress REMs during sleep, so there

are fewer dreams to recall. Scientific research
suggests that among these drugs are the bar-
biturates, the phenothiazines, the ampheta-
mines—and alcohol. The fact that they stop
dreaming may be one of the reasons why
depression so often follows taking these drugs.
The benzodiazephines, caffein and aspirin, on
the other hand, don't seem to have much effect
on the amount of dreaming experienced. As for
the quality of the dreams, it does not follow that
drugs necessarily enhance it, although they may
increase the intensity of dreaming. Quite often
drug-takers are deceived by this additional
intensity and believe that the dreams themselves are richer and more significant. And this
false belief carries over into waking life too.
Experiments with writers who had been given
the drug LSD showed that they produced
work far below their normal standards—though
they may have felt, while they were "high",
that they were surpassing themselves. And
with opium-takers (like the poet Coleridge)
the dreams become more and more terrifying
as their addiction increases—and in Coleridge's
case, eventually prevented his writing effec-
tively. All this does not mean of course that
normal dreaming isn't good for the creative life.

12. TRUE   —within limits. A state of physiological arousal
and tension can often make us have sexual
dreams—but of course other reasons have to
be found for the *kind of* sexual dream it is
(whether, for instance, it is heterosexual or
homosexual).

13. FALSE   —on the whole; because if it were true, dreams
would be purely accidental (depending en-
tirely on what particular bit of the brain was
being affected) and would therefore have no
psychological significance. But there is ample

scientific evidence to show that dreams certainly do matter psychologically.

14. FALSE that they are purely the result of outside occurrences (noises etc.) but TRUE that these can trigger off a dream that may be closely related to them. For instance, the alarm clock ringing quite often results in a dream about the ringing of a church or front door bell. But this sort of instance doesn't prove that dreams originate in the sounds and different sensations that surround us, sleeping and waking. Why should the ringing of an alarm-clock produce a dream, while, say, a fly crawling over our nose doesn't? The answer is that the one thing (alarm bell) acted on something that was already being thought about in some part of the mind—like not wanting to get up in the morning; so the dream takes the sound and turns it into another sort of bell which didn't mean having to get up, so allowing the dreamer to go on sleeping.

15. TRUE —quite probably. It does seem that the sensations caused by parts of the body in the early stages of illness can be subconsciously recognized in dreams before they begin to register themselves on the consciousness (see Answer No. 5).

16. FALSE —or rather, it's a theory that has to be modified, because when we dream about a past event, even one that happened a few hours before we went to sleep, it's hardly ever exactly the same in detail or emotional tone. When we do dream about one particular event out of a thousand others, it's most likely to be something that has some special meaning to us at the time of the dream; often it has some connection with a current problem or one that we've had for some time and haven't yet properly understood or dealt with.

17. TRUE OR FALSE Perhaps there can never be a definite answer. The common dream of falling is often quoted as a typical example of a dream belonging to the whole human race—coming from the experience our distant ancestors must often have had of falling out of trees when they were still living in them. And it was Jung who pointed out that, though many dreams come from personal experiences, we also dream of things which we can never have experienced personally—and claimed that these things belonged to the collective race memory still tucked away in all of us. But the falling dream can also have a purely physical explanation, because just before we *drop off* to sleep there may be a sudden dropping of the blood pressure. And of course, this dream could also be caused by an actual fall in childhood which left an unconscious fear of falling. Or it could even mean a subconscious fear of falling into disgrace, or debt and so on.

18. FALSE Many of the old dream books made this claim, but although some dreams do turn everything upside down (in order to conceal the real truth), by no means all of them do. And it has to be said that there's little scientific evidence to support the value of such popular dream books.

19. FALSE It is, on the contrary, the part of the dream which seems the most unimportant and trifling that is often the most significant. This is the result of a process which Freud called *displacement*—that is, the switching of the feeling and emphasis in a dream, in order to escape the disapproval of the censor who lives inside all of us. It was Freud, of course, who first established the study of dreams on a proper scientific basis, in his famous book *THE INTERPRETATION*

OF DREAMS, published early this century.

20.   TRUE   Sometimes a whole sequence of dreams may keep nagging away at the same problem. Sometimes one dream may put the problem and a sequel give the answer—though of course in both cases it's all wrapped up in dream language and images.

21.   TRUE   The first three great psychoanalysts—Freud, Jung and Adler—did, of course, interpret dreams in different ways. Freud's theory was that dreams nearly always "treat of sexual material and give expression to erotic wishes", which come from the unconscious and have been repressed during the waking hours. Alfred Adler also believed that dreams were a form of wish-fulfilment, but that the suppressed wish was for power and superiority over others to make up for feeling inferior as a small child; it was Adler who originated that much-used phrase "the inferiority complex". And Jung advanced his theory of the collective unconscious containing "not only every beautiful and great thought and feeling of humanity, but also every deed of shame and devilry of which human beings have ever been capable", and supplying material for our dreams.

All these theories and the many variations of them—as well as the physiological and biological approaches—can show us aspects of the truth about ourselves.

22.   FALSE   No matter how strange dreams may be, they are dealing with the truth. Often, indeed, it is the very oddity of their images and symbols that forces us to face the unpleasant facts we may be trying to dodge!

23.   FALSE   —in all probability. Some dreams are just as likely to disturb our sleep as to encourage it, for the simple reason that they are concerned

with disturbing problems—and there have been some specialists (like J. A. Hadfield) who insist that this is primarily what they are for. Such dreams won't let us sleep properly because it's much more important to solve the problems they are presenting.

There are exceptions, though, as with dreams of sexual pleasure, when tension is obviously relieved (and in some cases, wishes fulfilled).

24. TRUE —on the whole. It's true that Jung argued for a collective unconscious—but he also believed in the existence of a personal unconscious. Some dreams are of a common type, and some of them may have a universal application, but usually they also have meanings unique to the individual dreamer as well. In fact it can't be stressed too strongly that theoretical interpretations of dreams are of very limited value. Most dreams are personal, and refer to the dreamer's individual experiences and problems. Therefore, *their meaningful interpretation depends as much on the dreamer's personal material and associations as on the dreams themselves.*

25. TRUE But usually only the imaginary persons in our dreams, which are nearly always parts (actual or potential) of ourselves.

26. TRUE —in all probability. Most specialists would be likely to agree that there is always some sort of movement in a dream towards resolving some hang-up in the dreamer—whichever of the many theories they may base their interpretations on.

27. TRUE Some dreams, when they fail to find a way out of a particular difficulty they have been tackling, get out of a tight corner by *pretending* that the problem's solved. A common example is that of the child who needs to get up in the night to go to the lavatory, but who is too lazy

or comfortable to do so, and instead *dreams* that he has got up, been to the lavatory, and returned to bed   only to find when he wakes up in the morning that in reality he has wet the bed.

28. TRUE   Some dreams don't get any further than presenting the problem over and over again. Hence the repetitive dreams and nightmares that we had as children—and perhaps still have.

29. TRUE   There are several dramatic examples of scientists dreaming the answers to scientific problems. The German professor, Kekulé, for instance, was puzzling over various problems in organic chemistry. He fell asleep by the fire and a dream presented him with an entirely new idea which subsequently revolutionized the whole subject. There are examples, too, of crossword addicts hitting on the correct answer to a clue in the course of a dream.

30. FALSE   In some cases the fact that a particular dream doesn't offer a solution may be a sign that the time has come for the dreamer to tackle the problem in his waking life.

31. FALSE   Dreams often do reveal the dark sides of our natures, of course, but they can also show the potentialities which, for some reason or other, we have been repressing. Dreams can and often do help us to enrich our lives.

32. FALSE   Interpretation (if properly carried out) adds to the value of a dream because it encourages us to think about the whole subject logically. But sometimes we respond to the meaning of a dream intuitively, without putting it into words. Often, too, a dream can have a profound and healing effect on us without any conscious effort at understanding. You've probably had the experience yourself of feeling good or bad during the day, because of a dream the night

before—even though you can't remember what it was about at all.

33. TRUE —in all probability. Most of us suffer, one way or another, from sexual hang-ups dating back to our early years. As sex is still probably the most inhibited area in us, it is the one most likely to present problems—and therefore to appear in our dreams. This does not, of course, necessarily mean that there aren't all the other urges and influences at work in us—as described by Jung, Adler and other psychologists.

34. TRUE —but only in the sense that we define nightmares as dreams which are dominated by monsters of one sort or another—hence the name. Ernest Jones (one of Freud's most distinguished followers) thought that terrifying animals in nightmares represented the dreamer's parents—and are connected with all sorts of childhood unconscious fears and desires. Some nightmares are pretty obviously sexual—those with witches riding broomsticks, or those in which a girl finds something huge and hideous lying over her and half-suffocating her—though suffocation experiences in dreams can also derive from unconscious memories of the difficult birth of the dreamer.

35. TRUE It has been noted that they often start when a child is about three years old—when a conscience is developing, and also a strong sense of guilt which is often connected with sexual curiosity and the feeling that this has to be suppressed. Parents who are too severe and disapproving, and who punish children for comparatively innocent behaviour (such as "playing doctors" and examining each other's sexual parts) are very often responsible for those children suffering from continuing nightmares.

36. TRUE —in all probability. There are a large number

of authenticated dreams in which the dreamer has learned of events or had experiences which have later proved to have been taking place at the same time as the dream, even though at a considerable distance away. These cases cannot at present be accounted for by any other explanation than some form of telepathy.

37. NOT PROVED   —is possibly the best answer. It's true that many dreams which seem to foretell the future can be explained by being just chance. It's also true that in the dream-state literally thousands of possible events pass through our minds, but we only remember any of them when one particular happening actually does occur later, in waking life—and put it down to dream premonition. Having said that, we must admit that there are still quite a number of well authenticated dreams about events—and the details connected with them—which occur in exactly that way, perhaps several years later. The famous theory of relativity has after all taught us that time isn't anything like as straightforward as we used to think, and perhaps the dream-state is in some way outside the kind of time we measure by clocks and calendars.

38. TRUE   This we can say most emphatically, since one of the present writers not only dreamed practically the whole of a play which he subsequently wrote and had produced on radio, but also the plots of several successful short stories. There are many other instances of dreams providing musicians with themes for pieces of music, painters with ways of painting a picture, and so on. Such works of art can be very successful and often have a special dream-like quality and intensity—so long as the necessary talent is there and the equally necessary and hard technical work has been done!

39. TRUE   These unique dream images are very much a part of your total self. To ignore them is to run the risk of psychologically hurting yourself.

40. TRUE   —to a considerable extent, and after a good deal of effort. It is, for example, one of the practices of the yogi of Tibet; and we can learn a lot from such techniques—which include deliberately making ourselves confront and overcome the hostile and terrifying figures in our nightmares. Some western experimenters have succeeded in training themselves to have certain dreams of a healing and enriching kind, and even claim to be able to "enter into" their dreams and stay in them, watching, as conscious observers.

SCORING: This is a difficult questionnaire, so if you have come to the right conclusions in over 30 of the questions, you have a very sound and mature knowledge and understanding of dreams and what they imply. A score of over 20 would still be pretty sound; 15 to 20 would be fair; 10 to 15 rather weak—and anything under 10 would probably suggest that your attitude towards life in general and your self in particular tends to be rather narrow and unimaginative.

✦✦✦✦✦✦✦✦✦✦✦✦

As we have already emphasized, dreams cannot be successfully interpreted by outsiders, and they can only give their full meanings when they are looked at in connection with the personal associations of the dreamer.

All the same, we can learn a good deal more about dreams in general by considering some of the most common types. It is, in any case, a comfort to know that a certain sort of dream (which may worry us because it's so odd and we think *we* are odd because we're the only people to have it) is shared by thousands of other people, all over the world.

HERE IS A SELECTION OF THESE COMMON DREAMS

AGGRESSION AND RESCUE

Dreams of beating up and chasing thugs and so on are sometimes trying to make up for the frustrations and inferiority feelings experienced by rather timid people. This type of dream can also indicate a determination to overcome the wild desires charging about in our unconscious minds. Dreams of being heroic, rescuing someone from a fire and like disasters, are of a similar kind. We often *day*-dream this sort of story with ourselves as heroes, too.

ATTACK AND ASSAULT

In some cases, the sexual meaning is obvious in dreams of this sort—as with the adolescent girl who dreams of a burglar breaking in. Sometimes, when the attacker is particularly terrifying, there are deeper and more complicated unconscious sexual fears which would need a specialist's explanation. It might also be that the attacker represents the dark side of our natures (like the really shocking thoughts which occasionally flash into our waking minds) which Jung called the Shadow, and which may be asking to be let in and acknowledged by us. Generally speaking, it is probably better for our wholeness and effectiveness if we can admit this side of ourselves and even make friends with it instead of treating it as an enemy.

BURDENS AND WEIGHTS

Dreams in which we are struggling under the weight of heavy loads or trying to shift heavy pieces of furniture, machinery and so on, may refer to the burdens which we may actually be carrying in our daily lives and which are beginning to get too much for us. They may also indicate personal problems of a deeper kind which are "getting us down". If you dream that you are carrying the weight more easily than you expected, or that you are beginning to shift the heavy object, then you are making real progress in solving the problem, whatever it is.

CHASING AND RUNNING AWAY

These are a bit like attacking dreams, except that the emphasis is on the running away. And with these too, there is sometimes an obvious sexual interpretation—there is a wish in all inexperienced people to be pursued or wooed, though the idea is partly pleasurable and partly terrifying. It's been pointed out that the word *chased* is a pun on the word *chaste*—you can watch out for puns in your dreams, it's a frequent way of getting across a lot of meaning in a single word or two (Freud called it "condensation"). In running dreams, too, we often find we can't get a move on, our feet are clogged in mud, we're caught back by brambles etc.—or even that we're completely paralysed. This can be associated with sexual orgasm (especially when it's a new experience) and so can feelings of breathlessness, heart-thumping and other sensations connected with running hard. Sometimes the particular feeling of paralysis is connected with babyhood experiences—the baby, for example, who may have longed to run away from something or someone terrifying, but of course lacked the ability to get on its feet and run. These dreams of running away often indicate a general insecurity.

CLIMBING

These dreams are often associated with the falling dreams we've already mentioned. In some cases this may be connected with the rise and fall of sexual experience, trying to reach satisfaction. But the climbing may also mean social climbing, or the struggle to reach the top in some career or course of study or simply the determination to "get on top" of some problem or difficulty. If you do reach the top in any of these dreams, it is usually a promising indication that you have achieved success, or that you are now in a position to do so.

CRIME AND PUNISHMENT

There are few of us who haven't had this dream in one form or another, since all of us are potentially wicked somewhere in the bottom of our hearts and souls, and even awake we've all had thoughts and wishes that have shocked us (or our super-ego, to use Freud's word for the severe, disapproving part of ourselves). Whether or not we are aware of them, we have all had murderous feelings when we were babies and small children about not getting enough milk from our mothers, perhaps, or feeling jealous and threatened by the arrival of a baby brother or sister (often throwing leaves or earth into the cot or pram in an attempt to do away with or "bury" them). The emotions roused in these situations are very powerful—and so is the

fear of the parents' anger and disapproval. A sense of guilt persists long after, and expresses itself in dreams of severe punishment, including torture and execution. Even more powerful (and deeply buried) are the emotions connected with secret incestuous wishes. Sometimes after an upsetting dream of this sort we experience a feeling of well-being and relief—partly perhaps sheer thankfulness that it was "only a dream", but perhaps partly because the so-called crime has been punished in the dream, and we are free to go on without that particular guilt at least to make us unhappy.

DEATH AND DYING

In fact it's impossible to dream of not existing at all; if we dream about our own deaths, we are always still there as spectators. Sometimes these dreams may signify a wish never to have been born rather than a longing to die—a desire, that is, to return to the supposed bliss and security of the womb. When we dream of someone else's death, it is often a secret, though probably momentary, wish for it to happen. Shocking, no doubt—but then we have to get used to being shocked by some of our dreams and the sooner we do so the less anxious and guilty we shall be. Death in dreams—and particularly if it is the death of a stranger—is often a very hopeful sign, because it can mean the death of some part of yourself that you no longer need—such as the "little girl" or "little boy" in you that made you go on running to someone for advice and help even though you were now grown up.

TESTS AND EXAMINATIONS

The commonest form of this dream is sitting down to take an examination and finding you can't answer a single question out of the whole lot. There may be a straight-forward explanation if you really are working for an examination at the time—you'd better work a lot harder! But as a rule the dream represents some trial or test facing you in your life in which you're not feeling very confident. Sometimes you are being "put to the test" over some emotional problem or family situation, and sometimes it's to do with your career—it's the sort of dream very common in our strongly competitive, go-getting societies. It may even be advising you indirectly to get out of the rat-race!

FLYING AND FLOATING

This is often a very pleasurable sort of dream, and the sensation of moving freely and lightly through air or on water can be delightful. It may in fact be drawing on buried memories of pleasure—as far back as floating freely in the waters of the womb, or lying without effort in the mother's arms while feeding—or perhaps more recent sexual pleasures. It is easy to see why we enjoy dreams like this. But their meanings may not always be pleasurable; they can, for instance, indicate a severe inferiority complex, which the dreamer is trying to feel better about by trying to rise above everyone else. They may, on the other hand, simply indicate the desire to rise above difficulties. Or they may express feelings of bounding optimism—getting "high". It's also been suggested that such dreams have lingering racial memories from the days when our remote ancestors still lived in the water or in the trees.

In this type of dream—as indeed in all others—it's very important when you think about it afterwards to assess the emotional tone or atmosphere. If, in relation to flying dreams for instance, it is one of high hopes, then the more optimistic and happy interpretations can be made; if, on the other hand, the atmosphere of the dream is anxious or doubtful, a different meaning must be taken.

LOOKING FOR A ROOM

This kind of dream is more common among women than men. If the woman is single, it usually relates to her wish to get married, set up house and have babies—that is, in dream-punning language, to have her womb "occupied". If the dreamer is looking over several rooms, it may mean that she is searching round for the most suitable mate—and the most suitable place and circumstances in which to have a baby (a bit like a cat prowling round to find the safest corner to have kittens!). If the woman is married, it may be that she is looking round for a new "lodger"—another baby perhaps. Applied generally to both men and women, this type of dream can mean that the dreamer is looking for the *right room*—that is, his or her true self. If in the dream you are exploring a large, rambling house and excitedly come across new and unknown rooms, you may be entering into a particularly exciting and unexpected phase of your life. Again the tone of the dream is important, because if you feel anxious or worried in your search—it may be a bad dream in the sense that you are trying to find somewhere to be safe—even trying to go back to the remembered safety of your mother's arms.

LOSING MONEY AND VALUABLES

Sometimes these dreams may simply mean that you have actually lost something but haven't yet consciously realized or accepted the loss, or that you are in danger of losing something because you are being too careless in looking after it. But they may also be a warning that you are in danger of losing some less tangible value or belief in your life which, with part of your nature at any rate, you cherish.

MISSING TRAINS

Any dream of travelling is basically about the journey through life which we all have to make. When you miss a train (or any other form of transport) it may be a reassurance that you are not going to die yet. It may, on the other hand, be telling you that you are neglecting some opportunity in your life, that you have "missed the bus"; or that you're in danger of being left behind in the race of life; or that you are bothered by your failure to "get on"; and it can mean that you are suffering from arrested development—you've stopped growing up, "moving on".

NAKEDNESS

There may be a sexual significance to these very uncomfortable embarrassment dreams in which we suddenly find ourselves naked or only wearing one very short garment in public. They may, however, recall painful experiences in childhood when some innocent piece of exhibitionism, showing yourself off in some way, was frowned on by adults —and a sense of guilt about the naked body was started. Or again, they can mean a desire to show yourself as you really are (more dream puns here, about "baring our souls" and knowing "the naked truth"), and in this case the embarrassment in the dream may mean you're afraid that others will not accept you as you are.

REBELLION

This kind of dream takes distressing forms sometimes— you are, for example, shouting defiance at, or hitting, or even trying to kill parents or other figures of authority. This doesn't, of course, necessarily mean any real hatred or wish to kill—the people you are furiously trying to conquer may in waking life be ones you are very fond of. In fact, this may be the trouble—especially if it's parents who are involved: the dreamer is finding it difficult to break away from the bonds of affection. Sometimes, too, the parental figure is really the inner disapproving part of the dreamer's own self. In any case, don't worry; basically the dream is healthy, a sign of the inevitable struggle to achieve individuality, and of having the necessary courage and determination to go through with it. In some dreams of this type, the authority which is trying to hold you back may be represented by a crowd of people at a conventional social gathering of some sort—and you disgrace yourself by shouting and acting in a decidedly unconventional way

TEETH FALLING OUT

Although, according to Freud and others, this dream can represent some sort of sexual loss connected with your own body, there are plenty of other interpretations which may be equally valid. If may refer to memories of losing your first milk teeth—and may thus be a hopeful "growing up" dream. Or it may indicate that something you've done has made you "lose face" or "spoil your image"; or that in some way you've been "lying in your teeth" and are being punished (and to dream of false teeth does often point to deceit or self-deception). Or again, teeth can stand for aggression—in dream-pun terms "baring your teeth"— in which case the loss of them would suggest a failure to be firm or decisive.

TELEPHONES

These dreams usually take the form of forgetting to 'phone someone, of forgetting the number or failing to find it in the directory, of failing to find the money for the coin-box, or of failing in some way to get through. Usually they point, rather obviously, to some breakdown in communication in your personal or inner life (as do dreams about letters or telegrams you've somehow failed to send). In other words, you aren't connecting either in your personal relationships or to some part of yourself which is waiting impatiently for a call.

TUNNELS

Dreams of exploring or struggling to explore tunnels and narrow passages are quite often recalling the actual experience of your own birth.

UNPREPAREDNESS AND ARRIVING LATE

These dreams are usually about performing in some way— you're either acting in a play and suddenly realize you don't even know what the play is about, let alone which part you're playing, and you're due to go on any minute; or you're appearing on television without the least idea of what you're supposed to be doing; or you're arriving late to give a lecture and you don't know what you're supposed to be talking about; or you're making a speech and you've left your notes behind and you don't know what the function is. Such dreams may refer to some actual laziness or lack of preparation on your part; or they may mean that you are feeling worried about some part you are supposed to be playing in your life and you're not sure what to do about it; or they may come from the nagging and impossibly demanding inner voice we all have which is trying to tell you (quite unreasonably) that you are no good and can't possibly succeed in anything you set out to do.

VANISHING OBJECTS

This includes dreams in which you are trying to get somewhere but the familiar road, stairway, door, building, etc. has unaccountably disappeared. Such dreams usually indicate that you are in two minds about some situation or project, either in your outer or inner world, or that there are strong forces (sometimes hostile but sometimes friendly—only you and your associations will tell you which) that don't want you to arrive or succeed, and don't perhaps think your journey is really necessary.

WATER

This is rather a big category of dreams. A large expanse of water—a lake or ocean—often represents the unconscious itself, suggesting all the growth and change taking place in the bottomless depths of your being. The dream in this case may be urging you to pluck up courage to dive into the depths, to explore the unknown parts of yourself. Dreams of being in water may also point to a desire to "wash away" bad deeds, to "come clean" and start again. When the dream is about a spring, that also often means the beginning of fresh life. A river may indicate the flowing of life from its beginning to its end—and people who have grown old peacefully and happily often dream of walking beside a boundless ocean when they are close to death and eternity.

To be swept away in a dream by waves, floods or tides is often a way of showing you that you need to let your emotions go, flood over you. And though they may sometimes contain warnings, generally speaking dreams about water have some positive things to tell you.

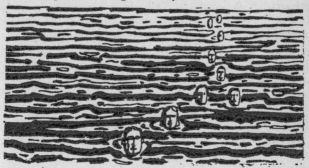

DREAM SYMBOLS

As we've just explained, dreams frequently make use of symbols (that is, an object or a person or an animal or an event representing a vhole section of your life or experience) as a quick way of getting a lot into a short space of time. And although the full interpretation of these symbols depends very much on what they may mean to you personally, there are some general meanings which may be of use to you. Here is a short ABC of the most common symbols, many of which you may have come across more than once in your dreams:

ANIMALS: usually stand for the animal part of our nature, sometimes tamed (when, for example, we dream of our pets), sometimes wild and dangerous. In any case we usually need to meet them and let them out, remembering that all animals have to be understood and treated carefully.

BASEMENTS: like cellars and other underground places in dreams, usually signify our lower natures; or sometimes the unconscious itself.

BAYONETS: like swords, spears, long knives and so on, these often figure in sexual dreams. They can also mean that some important thought or wish is trying to pierce our defences.

BLACK MAN: usually represents a forbidden object of sexual desire, which strikes our conscience as "dirty" (i.e. black). But it can stand, too, for the dark side of our natures.

CAVES: again this can have a sexual meaning (the obvious feminine counterpart to the bayonets), though Jung saw the cave as a place of mystery and magic (as it often is in fairy stories) where healing can take place.

CLOTHES: a common symbol of your *persona*—the appearance you present to the world. If you dream of changing your clothes, your personality is usually about to undergo some sort of change.

CROWDS OF STRANGERS: according to Freud this means a secret—which is, of course, hidden from the dreamer's conscious mind.

DIRT: this can mean that you are unconsciously "doing the dirty on" some perfectly natural desire which—perhaps from childhood experiences of being scolded too severely for having fun with all sorts of mud and filth—your conscience has labelled as dirty.

EYES: naturally stand for seeing—or not seeing, if the dreamer's eyes are blinded, blindfolded, or if (as often happens in dreams) the eyelids are stuck together.

EXPLOSIONS: usually mean what you'd expect—that eruptions are taking plac in your unconscious, or that you wish they would.

FIELDS AND GARDENS: these suggest that your personality is ready for fresh growth, particularly if the ground is ploughed or dug over. Sometimes women dream about them when they are pregnant or wish to be.

FIRE: usually signifies sexual passion, but could also mean the "flare up" of rage.

FOREIGNERS: often refer to parts of your self you don't understand, or don't want to—because you feel they are "foreign" to your more conventional self.

GESTAPO: together with other frightening kinds of guards, policemen, etc., usually refer to the stern parental figures of childhood.

GIANTS: often refer to childhood memories of yourself as a pygmy surrounded by gigantic adults. Or they can signify the people round you in your adult life who make you "feel small"

GOVERNESS OR SCHOOLMISTRESS: often stands for an over-strict mother.

HAIR: often symbolizes growth, but when it is falling out or being cut off, it can express sexual anxieties.

HOLES AND TIGHT CORNERS: usually mean what they say that you are hemmed in by some problem.

MASKS, MIRRORS, PHOTOGRAPHS: all these often indicate that you are dodging looking at your true self.

POLICEMEN: nearly always stand for the disapproving part of your personality.

PRINCES AND PRINCESSES: Over-fond parents often turn their sons and daughters into princes and princesses, both in their waking lives and in dreams. These dreams frequently feature actual members of the Royal Family, and when this happens they can be a way of dignifying or glamourizing desires which you're secretly ashamed of or think little of; or it can simply mean a habit of self-glorification.

PRISONS: often suggest either that you are locking up a part of your personality that wants to be free, or that you are punishing yourself for some imagined crime.

SNAKES: can be a straightforward sexual symbol, or (as Jung pointed out) can stand for wisdom and healing.

STORMS: a sign of disruption and disorder.

TRAMPS: a common symbol for the more unrespectable parts of our personalities.

VEILS: sometimes stand for marriage, and sometimes for those aspects of ourselves we are in fact hiding behind a veil.

WALLS: usually represent the barriers we are trying to erect round parts of ourselves which are really depicting growth and freedom.

These are only a few of the many thousands of dream symbols, and you will probably be able to think of many more typical examples from your own dreams and those of your friends.

DAY DREAMS

A lot of what can be said about sleeping dreams also applies to day-dreams—those fantasies which we probably all indulge in during our waking hours. In a society like ours, with so much emphasis on *getting on*, hustling and bustling about—*achieving* as the Americans put it—it's often implied that day-dreaming is only indulged in by dopey, impractical people. This is not by any means true. Recent research has shown, for instance, that children with rich fantasy lives (and who play a lot at "make believe") are *not* less in touch with life than the more unimaginative children. In fact, it has been found that they are more likely to learn and understand, and more likely to be original and independent in their thinking, as well as being psychologically more balanced and tranquil. Children without an inner fantasy life are often more restless and frustrated, more easily bored and distracted, and much more dependent on their surroundings for satisfaction and excitement. Studies of delinquent adolescents, indeed, have shown that their aggressive actions—taking it out on their surroundings by smashing things up and so on—are often caused by a lack of anything interesting *inside* themselves (which might also lead to something interesting to do). It's no mere chance that these young people find it particularly difficult to remember their sleeping dreams.

Much the same is true of aggressive, anti-social adults too. It has also been found that excessive over-eating is often an expression of a *hunger* for the kind of pleasures and satisfactions that can't be got out of outside surroundings alone, but must be made out of the inner life. Anyone who has ever made anything—cut a rug, put up a shelf, planted garden seeds and seen them growing, painted a picture, gone carol-singing (the list goes on, thank goodness, for as long as human imagination lasts)—anyone who has ever done anything like this will know this to be true.

There seems little doubt, in fact, that our day-dreams, like our sleeping ones, are tremendously important in helping to keep us mentally healthy and creatively happy. So don't despise *any* of your dreams!

❖❖❖❖❖❖❖❖❖❖❖❖❖

WHAT YOU CAN DO WITH YOUR DREAMS

1. FIRST AND FOREMOST, if you have scoffed up to now at your dreams and daydreams—change your attitude now!

2. BEGIN TO TAKE MORE NOTICE of them all. They can help you to understand yourself better and perhaps to resolve some of your hang-ups—and they can make your personality and your life more interesting.

3. IN ORDER TO DO THIS, begin keeping a dream diary. If possible, write down your dreams as soon as you wake up, together with the date and any other relevant information (where you are, what the weather's like and so on).

4. THEN WRITE DOWN ALL YOUR ASSOCIATIONS TO THE DREAM —that is, what you personally connect with the various objects and people and happenings; you'll be surprised how this will help you to understand the dream more

clearly. Don't go only for the spectacular part of the dream; often it's the apparently unimportant bits that give the real clues—a few words, a stray gesture, a detail that didn't seem to matter—and don't forget the dream puns!

5. LOOK BACK OVER YOUR DREAM DIARY FROM TIME TO TIME, and note the themes and symbols that keep cropping up —these are most important in giving you a kind of outline of your basic problems and of the various neglected parts of your personality.

6. LEARN TO RECOGNIZE THE KIND OF DREAM THAT MAKES YOU FEEL GOOD—and try willing yourself to have that particular dream again—and again. You will find you can control your dreams in this way, so that they become health-giving and enriching.

7. FACE THE TERRORS of your nightmares and, if you can, fight the monsters, try to subdue them, calm them down; and then try to find the positive good things they represent.

N.B. Needless to say, if you are suffering from a mental illness of some kind you should take professional advice.

Finally, remember that your dreams belong to you alone. In every case you must make your own personal associations before the meanings and helpful influences of each dream can be found.

CHAPTER SIX

YOUR HANDWRITING

CHAPTER SIX

YOUR HANDWRITING

The possibilities of telling character from handwriting have fascinated people for hundreds of years. But the earliest attempts were all made by amateurs, who—though often achieving remarkable results—were practising an art and not a science. As a science graphology (to use its proper name) didn't really establish itself until the 1920s, when Dr. Robert Saudek published *THE PSYCHOLOGY OF HAND-WRITING* and *EXPERIMENTS WITH HANDWRITING*, based on a systematic examination of the handwriting of tens of thousands of men, women, and children, of many nationalities, classes and standards of education; and including the left-handed as well as the right-handed, the short-sighted and the long-sighted, those who were healthy and those suffering from various diseases and muscular

troubles—and even those who had lost their hands and had learned to hold the pen with their feet or their mouths.

To-day there are many employers—mostly in Europe—who engage graphologists to report on the character traits revealed by the letters of people applying for jobs (handwritten letters are obviously insisted on). Sometimes, too, graphologists are called as expert witnesses in court cases involving the dating or genuineness of letters or documents. The methods they use are generally based on Dr. Saudek's thorough and pretty complex findings—which you would need to study too, if you wanted to be a really competent judge of character from handwriting. All the same, it is possible here to indicate some of the broad principles of the science of graphology, and some of the more straightforward interpretations.

For the sake of simplicity these interpretations must be based on three facts:

1. That *you are British, or have had a British type of early education.* Correct interpretation of character from handwriting largely depends on the kind of writing you were taught at school. Some foreign methods of teaching children to write (including some American approaches) are quite different from ours. You would have to be very expert to take these into account. To take an extreme example, if you were Chinese you wouldn't even write from left to right across the page!

2. That *your style of handwriting is reasonably mature.* Telling character from handwriting depends on a more or less easy flow of the pen across the page. Children are too busy trying to form the letters to be able to manage this, and so it's practically impossible to analyse their handwriting.

3. That *you are in reasonably good health.* Your natural characteristics only show themselves when the pen is moving rhythmically, and making alternate thin and thick, up and down, strokes (even biros and pencils allow you to do this)—and this is impossible if illness is badly affecting your muscle control.

Here is a specimen of the writing of the novelist, Charles Dickens, in good health:

And here is part of a letter which he wrote the day before his death:

In the first example, you will see that the alternation of thick and thin strokes is strong and rhythmical. The lines, too, have an energetic, slightly upward tilt. In the second example, on the other hand, poor Dickens's muscles weren't functioning properly, and his hand could hardly move across the page, producing only feeble, pasty strokes. Note, too, that the lines dip downwards, usually a sure sign, in this kind of writing, of poor health and low spirits. If you study these two specimens carefully, in fact, you will probably be able in future to spot the handwriting of someone in poor health or physical condition.

❖❖❖❖❖❖❖❖❖❖❖❖

SIGNATURES

Now to get on to some of the more obvious points. It's often claimed that you can tell a lot about a person's character by his or her signature alone. In fact, by itself it is only of limited value because hardly anybody is entirely himself in signing his name. There's always something a little artificial about it. At some point in our lives we have all deliberately chosen a certain style of doing it (and no two signatures are exactly alike), and although we may vary this—in fact never do it identically—the signs of deliberate choice are always there. Usually, too, we are concerned in our signatures with the kind of person we want the world to think we are—we're thinking of our *public image*, in fact.

For people in high places, of course, this public image is of tremendous importance, and a great deal may depend on it. Here, for example, is a signature that clearly shows its writer's high sense of authority and of the dignity of the individual destiny:

From Hasberige scribled this 27ᵗ of October.

Your lovinge systar Elizabeth

It is, as you will have guessed, the signature of Queen Elizabeth I. She usually wrote, incidentally, in an upright hand. Sloping handwriting only began about the middle of the sixteenth century; Queen Elizabeth would still have been unfamiliar with it when she wrote the piece above, and that helps to explain some of the formality of the writing.

A few other points might perhaps be made in connection with this particular signature. Although it is elaborate, it doesn't somehow seem coarse or self-important (which is what we do feel about some very flowery signatures when we see them). At the same time it isn't the signature of a shrinking violet (which a tiny, obviously self-effacing signature would probably suggest to us). Queen Elizabeth's signature is a decidedly regal affair.

Although we have looked at this by itself, as a rule *signatures are most valuable when taken in conjunction with a fairly lengthy piece of handwriting*. Say, for instance, that somebody writes you a letter in a hurried slapdash and careless manner—but signs his or her name with a tremendous flourish, taking great care with each letter and underlining the whole—then you can be fairly sure that the writer of the letter regards himself or herself as far more important than what he or she has written about—or than you, the recipient.

On the other hand, a carefully written letter with a modest unpretentious signature in the same style of writing, would generally indicate that the writer is more interested in the subject of the letter—and in you—than in cultivating his or her personality. A lot of people, of course, have unreadable or nearly unreadable signatures (busy doctors are famous for it). But here's a warning. If you come across an almost illegible signature which nevertheless shows signs of having been written slowly and with care (individual letters touched up, for example), you would be well advised to be cautious in your dealings with the writer.

I . . . AND YOU

You can probably learn more from the capital letter "I" than you can from signatures. It is the only letter (apart from *a*—as in a cat—and perhaps *O!* as an exclamation) that makes a word all by itself; and English is the only language in which the first person singular is written with a capital letter. So it is uniquely the symbol of the self. Every time you write "I" you are in effect showing yourself to the world—or at any rate your estimate of yourself and the way you want to be estimated.

The vain, self-important, self-assertive person, therefore, will tend to write the letter *I* with great pressure of the pen, to exaggerate its size and in some cases, to add all kinds of twiddly bits to it. In the following example, you will see that the *I* is a good nine times larger than the *a* of the next word, and twelve times larger than the *m*:

If you had a piece of writing in front of you in which all the *I*'s were written like that, or in some other equally self-assertive way (for example, as a carefully made block letter in the middle of ordinary writing) you could be even more certain in your conclusions. But don't pay too much attention to the *first I* in a letter. Most people give that a bit more emphasis; it's the later ones that really matter.

Completely opposite to the "great I am" sort of *I*, is that of the self-effacing person who hates to thrust himself forward, and therefore cuts down the size of the capital *I* so that it's often smaller than the ordinary letters surrounding it—or writes it in an unemphatic, rather wavering form. Here are two obvious examples:

> *... will obtain receipt*
> *which I will send*
> *direct to you.*
> *I trust this will be*
> *satisfactory*

In between the two extremes is the *I* of the person with a firm grasp of his or her own personality, who doesn't need to keep thinking self-centredly when writing *I*, either by lingering lovingly over it, or hurriedly to try to smother it. The specimen (at the beginning of this chapter) of Charles Dickens's writing when he was in good health illustrates this. You'll notice that each of the two *I*'s is full of individual character in the way they're shaped, but written rapidly and set in with the rest of the writing without any over-emphasis. The more careful formation of the second *I* is pretty obviously due to the fact that Dickens was coming to the end of his letter, where a touch of formality and politeness naturally came into it.

SINCERITY AND PRETENCE

There are of course other clues to help us decide whether or not a writer is being sincere, or is putting on an act. Here are some of the most important of them:

Starting—and tailing off

The ways in which a writer begins a letter and carries it on can be most revealing. Take a good look at this example:

The very first word speaks volumes, you might say. The capital *D* is written with a tremendous flourish; the next letter is still quite bold and assertive, but the *a* is badly formed, and the *r* practically non-existent. In other words, the letter was written by someone trying to put on a show of forcefulness, but almost entirely lacking in it. You'll see that the *Sir* is much smaller than the *Dear*. The *I* which begins the next line is again quite strong, but the second *I* has shrunk to half the size of the first. There's another effort by the writer in the word *phones* (at the end of the second line) to pull himself up and concentrate on what is in fact the subject of the note. But the *the* before it is tiny and poorly formed. Then, in the second line, in the word *spoke* the *p* has next to no downward stroke, and although there's a flattering flourish on the *you*, the *d*s in *did* look more like *a*s. The words in the third and fourth lines become progressively smaller and more feeble, until the writer makes one final effort with the *Yours Faithfully*, and there's an appearance of energy in the long, rightwards projecting bar of the *t*—though many of the letters even in these two words are flaccid and wavering.

This short note of seven lines, then, has revealed a sham aggressiveness and energy, and the conclusions reached in connection with the very first word are fully confirmed.

And here is an extreme example of the attempt to put on a show.

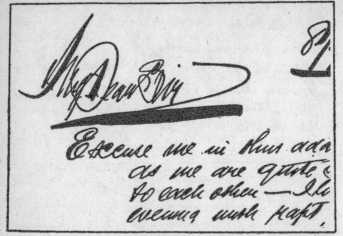

You will see that the writer has started off on his *M* with
a bit that looks almost like a separate letter (the technical
term for the way we begin a word is *initial adjustment*). Then
he dashes upwards with a long, thin stroke, and then down
again with a stroke so thick and heavy that he practically
tears the paper. He tries to demonstrate a powerful personality in the *D* of *Dear* too—but he has already almost
exhausted himself, and the other strokes in the *Dear Sir* are
thin and spidery—though he has another go with his savage
and self-important underlining. Although there is a fresh
display of showing off with the *E* of *Excuse*, the rest of the
passage has no particular pressure. This is the writing of
a man (probably a bully) who huffs and puffs but has little
stuffing in him, and who is quickly exhausted. Note also
that extreme exaggeration like that shown at the beginning
of this letter often points to a state of mind verging on the
pathological.

THESE POINTS SHOULD ALSO BE NOTED:
1. It's necessary to examine a piece of writing for its con-
   sistency. The person who is writing naturally, eagerly
   going on to say what he or she wants to say, will not

show any marked differences in the style of writing, and it will look much the same all the way through. It's only the person who is striving to make an effect or who has bad hang-ups, who keeps chopping and changing in style—because the pretence can't be kept up, and the real natural style in writing keeps breaking through.

2. This sort of pretence often shows itself, too, in noticeable differences between the beginnings and ends of words.

3. Affectation of some sort or another can also be indicated if the style of writing (especially such features as size, slant, roundness, pointedness or pressure) changes very obviously towards the end of a longish piece of writing— when the writer is getting tired and is therefore off-guard.

4. Always go first for the more conspicuous letters, especially the capitals, when trying to read character from handwriting. It's there that the deliberate tinkering and showing-off can be seen, and not in the small, unassuming *i*, *m*, *n* or *u*. At the same time, if these are shoddily formed and very different indeed from the more showy letters, that is a give-away, too.

TOUCHING UP

Going back over a piece of writing and touching up some of the letters (for example, adding loops to the *l*s, *e*s, *g*s, etc., which were filled with ink at the first writing) might strike one as an obvious sign of insincerity. But in fact such corrections, when found in rapid writing, usually show conscientiousness on the part of the writer and consideration for his reader. On the other hand, if the writing, though mature and educated, is a predominantly slow one, it's one of the signs of over-bookishness. If, however, the touching-up is rather elaborate, with loops and flourishes, it's either the writing of someone in a very lofty position (the specimen of Queen Elizabeth I's handwriting is a case in point) or of someone preparing an official document—or in the absence of these circumstances, it's a symptom of vanity.

INITIAL AND FINAL ADJUSTMENTS

Something more has to be said about the way we begin and end the separate letters of the alphabet. Some people dash straight into them and finish them off quickly, others make a little pause either before they begin writing a character or at the end of it—and sometimes both. This sort of adjustment or pause can, of course, happen in the middle of a word as well.

Opposite are two tables to illustrate this.

The *initial adjustments* are in the table on the left, and the *final adjustments* in the table on the right. The first line in each case shows the quickest and most straightforward adjustments. Then as you go down the columns you will see that the adjustments become progressively slower and more elaborate.

What you can learn from these tables

INITIAL ADJUSTMENTS

1. Generally speaking the writer with a quick and spontaneous mind will make very slight initial adjustments—provided he is healthy. If there are a lot of them, though, in a handwriting which is predominantly quick it shows that the writer, though mentally alert, is in the habit of carefully weighing up his or her plans before setting to work on them.

   If there is a complete absence of these "starting points" in writing of this kind, then the writer is unusually fluent and sure of his judgments, and possibly lacking in forethought.

   On the other hand, if the writing is predominantly slow, the frequency of initial adjustments denotes that the writer is thorough and conscientious in planning and carrying out any project, but perhaps a bit pedantic.

2. Normally the *very* elaborate initial adjustments point to a writer who is either clumsy and slow-witted, or scatter-brained, or rather fussy—or in some cases, has some kind of physical handicap.

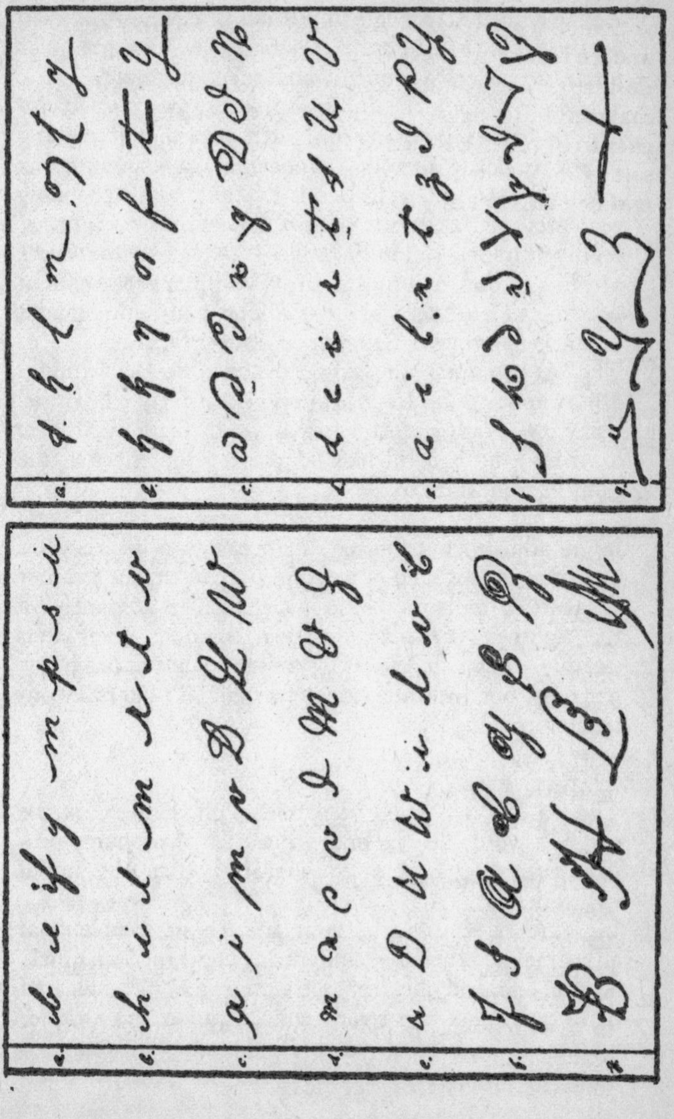

Now look carefully at the two tables.

3. The way the letters begin in the first three lines—marked on the table (a), (b) and (c)—merely mean a muscular habit or perhaps a moment's pause for throught.

4. The fourth line—(d) in the table—shows curved approach-strokes, inclining to the left, and therefore going in the opposite direction from the way spontaneous writing goes (that is, from left to right). This probably indicates mental resistance on the part of the writer.

5. In the fifth line—(e) in the table—you will see that there are lots of dots or upward strokes with sharp angles at the tops. These denote either a long pause for thought before beginning to write, or an indecisiveness.

6. The last two lines—(f) and (g) in the table—show initial adjustments that are obviously excessively elaborate. They could only occur in very slow writing and indicate a writer who is artificial and playing for effect to the point of abnormality.

7. Note that slow writing nearly always contains these initial adjustments. On the rare occasions when they are absent from this kind of writing, we can expect a rather slow-witted individual who is nevertheless convinced of the rightness of his or her own opinions, and plods steadily along, concentrating on the details under his or her nose, but with little idea of a general plan or a convincing conclusion.

FINAL ADJUSTMENTS

1. The ways in which a writer finishes off the letter at the end of a word (i.e. the final adjustments) probably provide even better clues to character than the initial adjustments.

2. In some cases, though, there are no noticeable final adjustments. When the handwriting concerned is a quick, natural one, and obviously the work of a highly educated person, this indicates strong concentration and a rather matter-of-fact turn of mind. If, though, the writing is naturally slow (in speed, that is, not necessarily in intel-

ligence) it points to a person who is conciliatory by nature and perhaps prone to give in to other people a little too easily.

3. The first line in the final adjustment table (the right-hand one) shows a prolonging of the final stroke downwards or to the right, without great pressure, but pretty strongly marked. These features are perfectly normal. In a quick. natural handwriting they often indicate that the writer is careful and responsible in the wording of the text, and possesses a sense of intellectual and even spiritual values, though at the same time tending to have a pretty high opinion of his or her self; a person with an independent mind, and one who likes to have the last word in an argument is suggested. But if, in quick writing of a high standard, the marked final adjustments are accompanied, in the rest of the writing, by considerable differences in size, width, and slant of the letters, and also in the pressure of the pen, then the qualities mentioned above tend to be spoiled by irritability and a kind of nervy stubbornness. You often find these features in the handwriting of very clever young men whose intellectual gifts haven't found their proper outlet. In slow natural writing of a good educational standard, however, marked final adjustments point to a person who, while thorough and conscientious, is pernickety over details, and quite certain that he is always morally right. If the writing is both slow and obviously unnatural, the marked final adjustments indicate boastfulness, conceit, complacency and a bossy tendency.

4. The second line—(b) in the table—shows the final strokes being stretched out and emphasized in a way that suggests considerable affectation.

5. The final strokes in line (c) bend very noticeably to the left, which usually means that the writer doesn't like the effort of writing quickly—and is probably prone to mental laziness.

6. The final stroke in line (d) also turns to the left, but with a short, sharp angle. These are called "harpoon strokes"

and are a sure sign of great powers of perseverance, and inflexibility of will.

7. In line (e) the movement comes to a halt on a distinct blob; this means that the writer has to keep resting, and usually denotes laziness.

8. The final adjustments in line (f), with the strokes going up and to the left, and finishing in a point or little hook, could hardly look more awkward. They are only possible in very slow writing, which borders on the pathological.

9. The final adjustments in the last line of the table are even more exaggerated, and the mental condition of such a writer would be even worse than in the previous example.

SPEED

You'll have noticed several references so far to the speed of a handwriting. In fact *it's impossible to make any really accurate assessment of character from writing without first estimating its speed; because there are many features which mean one thing in mainly quick writing and something quite different in mainly slow writing.*

There are a number of indications which will help you to calculate the speed of a piece of writing with reasonable accuracy.

Here are the chief signs of slow writing:

  (i) Wavering, bent and broken strokes.

 (ii) Upstrokes and downstrokes of almost identical thickness. Or variations in thickness which follow no obvious pattern.

(iii) Lines sinking to the right.

 (iv) Very accurate placing of the dots over the *i*'s and the bars on the *t*'s.

  (v) Careful formation of the letters, and especially those towards the end of a word.

 (vi) Frequent signs of pausing—including final adjustments within words, dots where the pen has momentarily come to rest, etc.

(vii) A linking of the individual letters by angles instead of curves.

(viii) Gradually shrinking left-hand margin, plus other signs in the formation of the letters of a marked tendency to the left.

(ix) Starting off words in a heavy and rather elaborate way.

(x) Narrow spaces between the downstrokes of *m, n* and *u*, and generally rather narrow spaces between letters within a word.

Here are the main clues to fast writing:

(i) Lines tending to rise to the right.

(ii) Inaccurate aim in putting dots over *i*'s and the bars to *t*'s, together with a tendency to make full stops or dots look like commas or accents (obviously it takes longer to make a proper dot).

(iii) Letters obviously hurried—many of them incomplete and becoming almost illegible towards the ends of words, especially long ones (which tend to make the fast writer impatient).

(iv) Very slight final adjustments, and no signs of pausing within the words.

(v) *t* bars and *i* dots frequently linked up to the letters that come next.

(vi) Frequent joining up of words, and of figures in a number.

(vii) A clear drift towards the right (to be expected when the pen is being driven at full speed across the paper) which is shown by an increasingly wide left-hand margin, and by the projecting bits of letters pointing to the right.

(viii) An obvious tendency to reduce even the necessary movements towards the left—as with the loops of *g*'s— to a minimum, and to get such letters driving to the right as soon as possible.

(ix) Hardly any or no preliminary strokes with the pen before beginning.

(x) Wide spaces between the downstrokes of *m, n*, and *u*, and increased space between the letters within a word.

Here are two easy examples for you to practise speed detection on :

> *you will be supplied*
>
> *Thank you very much f m nice. letter, if I suit wi my very best. to please*
>
> *Yours Truly,*

You will, of course, have come to the conclusion that the first example is a *quick* writing, and the second a *slow* one. As a matter of fact, the first of them contains not a single indication of slowness, while the second has only one possible suggestion of quickness—some of the *t* bars and some of the dots over the *i*'s aren't very carefully placed, and in some places the dots look more like commas.

Such clear-cut examples are rare. As a rule the difference between quick and slow signs is much narrower. But no matter how narrow, you have to decide whether the writing is predominantly slow or quick.

Now here are some of the features which have different meanings according to whether the writing is predominantly quick or slow:

1. RISING LINES

   In quick writing, they suggest enthusiasm, zeal, ambitious drive and sometimes optimism. If the quick writing isn't particularly mature, they can point to a tendency towards

> impulsiveness and lack of self-control.

In slow writing, they are merely the result of the angle at which the sheet of paper was placed.

2. SINKING LINES

In slow writing, they denote lack of energy and a tendency towards melancholy.

In quick writing, they show either considerable depression or a very poor state of health. (As in the specimen of Charles Dickens's writing the day before his death.)

3. WAVY LINES

(That is, writing in which some of the words, instead of going in the same general direction as the others, rise above the line or fall below it, thus giving an undulating effect to the line as a whole.)

In quick writing, this feature suggests a high degree of skill, adaptability and tact. But if the writing also varies a good deal in size, width, pressure and slant of the letters, these wavy lines indicate moodiness, inconsistency of purpose and a restless desire for change.

In slow writing, they show timidity, indecision, instability and a marked streak of opportunism.

4. STEPPED LINES

(That is, lines in which the beginnings of the words are at one level and ends on another—like this: m_{an}) although the line of writing as a whole takes a straight course.)

In quick writing, this feature indicates strong self-control, disciplined energy, and a strong capacity for self-criticism.

In slow writing, it also carries these implications—except that there is in addition a tendency towards obstinacy.

5. LIGHT PRESSURE

In quick writing, denotes sensitiveness, delicacy of feeling, and a tendency towards excitability.

In slow writing, the sensitiveness is extreme, leading also to extreme shyness and timidity and a lack of energy—in other words, a typical inferiority complex.

6. STRONG RHYTHMIC PRESSURE

In quick writing, this shows great energy, thoroughness and persistency.

In slow writing, the thoroughness is usually accompanied by a stuffy and slow-witted approach to life.

7. STRONG PRESSURE WITHOUT RHYTHM

In quick writing, this points to excitability and lack of balance, and a decidedly nasty temper.

8. UNIFORM PRESSURE ON ALL STROKES

This produces a rather pasty, smeary effect. If it's combined with sinking lines and broken strokes (again as in the example of Dickens's writing the day before his death) it is entirely due to physical deficiencies. Otherwise, in mature and intelligent quick writing it denotes great vitality and enterprise, combined with a marked love of sensual pleasures.

On page 134 are three examples which bear this out:

In slow writing, although the vitality and enterprise are completely lacking, the sensuality is extreme to the point of grossness.

9. BIG WRITING

In quick writing, this is one of the indications of an enthusiastic, passionate and romantic nature which loves action and achievement.

In slow writing, it denotes dignity and a sense of pride in genuine achievements. But if the slow writing is also obviously pretentious and unnatural, it is a sign of arrogance and a longing to dominate others.

LORD BYRON

LADY HAMILTON

CASANOVA

10. SMALL WRITING

In quick writing, it shows strong powers of observation and concentration, rapidity both in thought and action, and a highly developed critical sense.

In slow writing, it still shows strong powers of concentration and thoroughness, but accompanied by a rather plodding mind.

11. EXTREME DIFFERENCES IN SIZE BETWEEN BIG AND SMALL LETTERS

In quick writing, this characteristic is often found in politicians and organisers who have a genuine gift for public speaking. It usually means clarity of mind and conciseness, as well as versatility and the ability not to get flustered. But if the spacing in the writing is notably bad, a considerable degree of fanaticism is indicated.

12. INSUFFICIENT DIFFERENCE IN SIZE BETWEEN BIG AND SMALL LETTERS

In quick writing, this is usually nothing more than one of the indications of speed.

In slow writing, it suggests laziness, evasiveness, self-consciousness and confusion of thought.

13. WIDTH AND NARROWNESS

Wide writing looks like this:

monument

And narrow writing like this: *monument*

(Note: the *m*'s, *n*'s and *u* in this word monument are practically closed up by what are known as "covering strokes".)

In quick writing, width (especially with pronounced slant) often denotes sincerity, sociability, and a person so fond of talking that he or she often finds it difficult to stop!

In slow writing, width usually indicates that the writer has very little "go" and is much attached to creature comforts.

In quick writing, narrowness (combined with pronounced slant) is one of the pointers to the existence of severe psychological repressions.

In slow writing, narrowness tends to indicate a self-controlled and very reserved nature, which can be over-cautious and suspicious.

14. SIMPLIFICATIONS

(These usually take the form of omitting parts of letters, such as loops—as in this *h*

In quick writing, these simplifications (provided they don't make the writing unreadable) indicate an objective, critical and realistic turn of mind. But if they make the writing practically impossible to read, they suggest slovenliness and self-indulgence, and little consideration for others.

In slow writing, they usually indicate a super-cautious and rather slow-witted person, almost entirely lacking in imagination.

15. EMBELLISHMENTS

In quick writing, the addition of a few extra loops and flourishes plus the exaggeration of ovals, provided they are pleasant to look at, indicate a lively imagination and a delight in graceful self-expression (such as dancing).

In slow writing, these nearly always denote ostentation and quite frequently a tendency to untruthfulness.

16. ANGULAR CONNECTIONS

    (That is, linking up the letters both at the bottom and top in a sharp-angled way—like this:) *Monument*

    In quick writing, this means strong willpower, determination and marked powers of resistance.

    In slow writing, it implies much the same qualities, but if the slow writing is of a poor standard, then harshness of temper, excessive pride and obstinacy are indicated.

17. GARLANDS

    (That is, widely looping connections, like a garland of flowers—like this:) *monument*

    In quick writing, these generally mean a sociable, good-natured and sympathetic person.

    In slow writing, they often indicate laziness and lack of moral will.

18. ARCADES

    (As a rule these only occur to any marked degree in upright or backward-sloping writing. They look like this:) *monument*

    In quick writing, they don't usually have any significance.

    In slow writing, they are indications of a very secretive nature.

19. HALF OVALS, LEANING TO THE LEFT

    (These are only found in slow writing, and look like this: *monument*

    In other words, the lower bits of letters like *m* curve backwards and nearly close up to make an oval.)

    In slow writing, this feature indicates insincerity and great secretiveness. If in addition the piece of writing has *o*s open at the bottom (like this *o*) be on your guard: the writer is not to be trusted and is a chronic liar.

20. DOUBLE CURVES
(These look like this:) *monument*

In quick writing, they have no particular significance.
In slow writing, they are sure pointers to a combination of indolence and secretiveness.

21. THREADLIKE CONNECTIONS
In quick writing, if these occur only at the word-endings they are merely additional signs of speed. But
In slow writing, if they affect the whole of the script, then they are one of the most characteristic features of hysteria and mental instability.

Opposite is a very obvious example

❖❖❖❖❖❖❖❖❖❖❖❖

SOME GENERAL INDICATIONS

The more intuitive amateur students of handwriting have observed that certain writing habits have broad character implications. As we have already said, without previously studying a whole piece of writing to decide whether it is quick or slow, such generalisations have no real scientific basis, and must not be taken as absolutely reliable guides. Having said that, here are some of the more likely suppositions:

1. HOOKS at the beginning of a word—like this: *tat* —can imply acquisitiveness.
2. PLUMP, WELL ROUNDED *e*'s—like this: *bear* —can indicate a tolerant nature.
3. FLAT-TOPPED *r*'s AND ROUNDED *m*'s AND *n*'s—as in this word: *form* —can point to a creative mind.
4. DOUBLE LOOPS IN CIRCULAR LETTERS—as in this word: —may indicate a deceitful nature. *noon*
5. SECOND PART OF THE LETTER *k* GREATLY ENLARGED—like this: —may mean defiance. *cake*

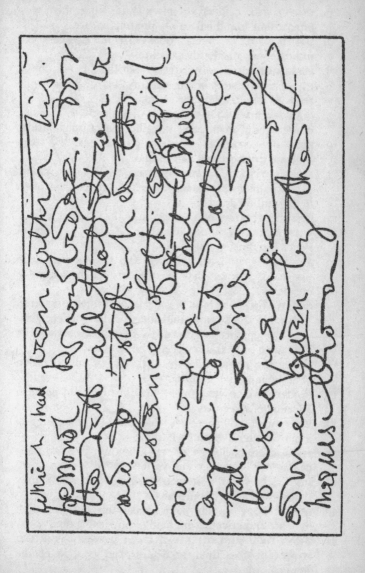

6. BAR OF THE *t* POINTING DOWNWARDS—like this: *t* often seems to indicate a dominating nature.

7. SHORT, SWOLLEN UPPER LOOPS—like this *collar* can indicate someone easily taken in.

8. *t* BAR DETACHED ABOVE STEM—like this: *t* is one of the characteristics of the dreamy sort of person who tends to live in a fantasy world.

9. ROUNDED TOPS TO THE *t* STEM—like this; *tent* is one of the signs of a complacent, rather self-satisfied nature.

10. LONG DOWNSTROKES ON *y* AND *g*—like this: *yg* can indicate firmness and determination.

11. LONG UPTURNED FINAL ADJUSTMENTS—like this: *calls* —can point to a tendency to extravagance, and often to ostentation as well.

12. UPSWEPT FINALS, NOT VERY EXTRAVAGANT AND USUALLY WITH A KINK IN THEM—like this: *sary* is one of the characteristics of generosity.

13. ABSENCE OF FINAL ADJUSTMENTS AND TENDENCY TO CLIP OFF FINAL STROKE—like this: *tape* can be a sign of meanness.

14. CURLY ADJUSTMENTS IN A BACKWARD SLOPING WRITING —like this: *ape* may indicate a tendency to childishness, a reluctance to grow up. (Note: Backward writing itself often indicates reserve.)

15. BIG LOWER LOOPS—like this: *g* can be an indication of an imaginative nature.

16. HORIZONTAL LOWER LOOPS—like this: *y* can point to a feeling of insecurity.

17. VERY SMALL LOWER LOOPS—like this: *y* may suggest a person who likes to go it alone.

18. LONG SLENDER LOWER LOOPS—like this: *y* can indicate a love of change and variety.

19. HOOKS ON FINAL ADJUSTMENTS—like this: *rams* may point to tenacity of purpose.

20. LOWER LOOP ADDED TO *p*'s—like this: *pup* may indicate an active nature fond of physical action.

21. SHORT FINAL ADJUSTMENTS, SHARPLY UPSWEPT, POINTING FORWARD—like this: *first day* can be one of the signs of initiative.

22. HORIZONTAL POINTS OVER *i*'s AND *j*'s—like this: *ī j̄* can suggest irritability.

23. VERTICAL POINTS OVER *i*'s AND *j*'s—like this: *i j* can point to annoyance with oneself.

24. *d* STEMS BENDING BACKWARDS AND *g*'s FORMED LIKE FIGURES-OF-EIGHT—like this: *and give* ·may indicate literary talent.

25. *t* BAR HALF WAY UP STEM—like this: *t* -may mean a practical nature.

26. SHORT WELL-BALANCED *t* BARS—like this: *tent* can be a sign of precision.

27. *t* BARS TO LEFT OF STEM—like this: *lot* may indicate a tendency to putting things off till tomorrow.

28. VERY TALL *d*'s AND *t*'s—like this: *dot* may point to self-pride, vanity.

29. CAREFULLY AND REGULARLY CLOSED CIRCLE FORMS— like this: *look* may mean reticence.

30. OPEN CIRCLE FORMATIONS—like this: *look* can be indicative of a very talkative person.

31. ARCHED *t* BARS—like this: *tent* may mean strong powers of self-control.

32. LOOPED *d*'s AND *t*'s—like this: *dust* can mean touchiness and sensitivity to criticism.

33. VERY LOW *t* BARS—like this: *t* may indicate lack of self-confidence.

34. WEAK *t* BARS—like this: *t* may mean a lack of will-power.

35. HEAVY *t* BARS—like this: *t* can indicate strong will-power.

36. BRACE-LIKE STRUCTURES—like this: *test* can mean stubbornness.

37. ANY TIE STRUCTURE—like this: *for* (i.e. the letter *f* looks as if it's got a knot in it)—may indicate persistency, firmness of purpose.

38. INITIAL WAVE OR FLOURISH TO AN *m* OR *n*—like this: *man* can suggest a sense of humour.

39. WEAK, SPRAWLED OUT *p* AND *s*—like this: *slipper* can point to a pliable, yielding nature.

With the information and hints you now have, you will be able to take the first steps towards treating the subject of character-reading from handwriting as something more than a mere parlour-game, and you will already be able to learn a good deal about the characters of your friends from their writing (you must of course read from a previously written specimen not something specially composed for the occasion) —and you should also learn something about yourself from your own handwriting!

CHAPTER SEVEN

YOU AND YOUR CAR

CHAPTER SEVEN

YOU AND YOUR CAR

In 1960 there were just over 97 million cars in the world Now the figure is over 240 million, and if it went on at that rate, in ten years' time there would be about 373 million. In Britain alone the figure for 1975 was well over $13\frac{3}{4}$ million —and that means no less than 73 cars for every 100 households!

No relationship can exist without some sort of interaction —and this is just as applicable when one of the parties is a machine. The car is no longer looked on simply as a con-

venient method of transport or even as a luxury. It is rapidly becoming a necessity, something most of us can't do without and would find far more difficult to give up than smoking or drinking. It's as important to a lot of us as a home—often in fact it's regarded as a kind of mobile home. Indeed, it's only half a joke to say that many people love their cars more than their nearest and dearest. The man or woman, in

countries like our own, who doesn't have a car, even though one could be afforded, is a rare bird indeed.

RESEARCH EXERCISE

You might find it an interesting piece of research, in fact, to make personality profiles of those people you know (and perhaps you're one of them yourself) who don't own a car, or show any particular wish to do so. First of all, write down their:

name
age
whether married or single
profession
estimated income.

Then list the particular characteristics, as far as you know them, of the people concerned. The following questions might help you. Working out the answers should tell you a good deal not only about them, but probably about yourself too—especially if you happen to be one of them!

QUESTIONNAIRE

1. Would you, generally speaking, regard them as unusually cranky or eccentric in any way?
2. Are they unusually bad at managing their money?
3. Do they strike you as discontented?
4. Do they, as far as you know, lead normal sex lives?
5. If they are married, do they lead an interesting, fruitful family life?
6. Do they have interesting and unusual hobbies?
7. Are they in worse or better health, physical and mental, than the average?
8. Are they fond of exercise, sport and out-of-door activities?
9. Do they take unusual holidays?
10. Do they travel abroad?
11. Are they more, or less, interesting to talk to than other people you know?
12. Do you sometimes think that perhaps their car-free existence is also a care-free one?

COMMENT

It's that last question that's the sixty-four thousand dollar one, because it must have occurred to all of us at some time that we're not just the owners of cars, but also in some degree their victims and slaves. We must have wondered, too,

whether our love affair with the car has made us more like a machine and less like a human being. It's an undoubted fact, for instance, that few of us at any deep level of our being, pay much attention to the grimmer realities of car-ownership. It seldom occurs to us that modern road and traffic conditions put a strain on the driver which is very likely to be too much for him, physically and psychologically. Even more amazing, we seem to have a kind of inbuilt anaesthetic that blots out, or at any rate dulls, any real awareness of the fact that driving a car is almost as dangerous as being in a war. Even if we are ready to admit that a car is a lethal weapon, we seldom apply this to ourselves and our cars. Thus a survey carried out among a cross-section of motorists showed that 70% believed that "it could never happen to me".

It's not that the facts and figures such as the following aren't plain to see:

(a) In 1975 alone, 6,351 people were killed and 318,003 were injured on the roads.

(b) Any person now under the age of thirty-five is more likely to die as the result of a traffic accident than from any other cause (including cancer—and barring another major war).

(c) Nearly 50% of all men who die round the age of twenty, do so in car crashes.

Yet somehow or other, although our eyes scan such facts and figures and our brains register them, they don't really go deep.

❖❖❖❖❖❖❖❖❖❖❖❖

It is sometimes difficult not to conclude that the car brings out the worst in all of us. The psychologist Professor John Cohen puts it like this: "When a motorist sits down at the wheel of his car he becomes partially mechanized . . . He is now a man-in-car . . ." a *bio-robot* as he calls him, adding that there are some people "whose humanity is temporarily obliterated" when they are driving.

Perhaps it's this, combined with the blotting-out mechanism, that lets so many of us make confident assumptions about cars and motoring of a kind we'd look at much more suspiciously if they were made about any other subject. In order to test how realistic and objective *you* are in this respect, examine the following statements.

QUESTIONNAIRE A
(Answer TRUE or FALSE)

1. Extroverts are more inclined to be involved in car accidents than introverts.
2. The more self-sufficient a person is, the safer driver he will be.
3. You are just as likely to be killed in a car as on a motor cycle.
4. Dithering in a motor-car is always dangerous.
5. The person who is tense makes a notably bad driver.
6. The risk of an accident is greater when you are driving alone.
7. Married drivers have fewer accidents than unmarried ones.

8. The driver of the private car is the worst offender on the roads.

9. Young children are better at hearing and seeing approaching vehicles than adults are.

10. The stripes on a zebra-crossing are too slippery for safety.

11. If all drivers had the same high degree of technical skill as professionals have in the handling of a car, accidents would be practically eliminated.

12. The majority of motoring accidents are the result of sheer bad luck.

13. The main reason for bad motoring behaviour is the inadequacy of the roads.

14. When he's driving a vehicle, a person behaves in a manner totally different from his usual one.

15. The serious and persistent motoring offender is unlike the ordinary law-breaker, and is otherwise a perfectly respectable citizen.

16. A driver who is convicted of one of the very serious driving offences very rarely repeats the offence.

17. Most people convicted of a serious driving offence are genuinely sorry about it.

18. The person with a record of previous accidents is a greater danger on the road than the hitherto accident-free driver.

19. The police treat serious motoring offenders as criminals.

20. The police are anxious to catch as many motoring offenders as possible in order to further their careers in the police force.

21. Speed of reaction is absolutely essential to accident-free driving.

22. The driver over 65 years old is much more liable to road accidents than the under-25 driver.

23. Middle-aged drivers are more likely to try and justify their anti-social behaviour on the roads than young ones are.

24. Many people drive better after a drink.

25. Alcohol is nothing like as serious a factor in road

accidents as some people seem to think.

26. Women are more anxious in their driving than men.
27. There are as many women offenders on the roads as men.

QUESTIONNAIRE A — ANSWERS & COMMENTS

1. TRUE The introvert tends to be more thoughtful, and is therefore more likely to think before he acts.

2. FALSE On the whole, a bit of inconfidence makes for greater care and better decisions in the sort of crisis that happens when driving. The bother with the self-sufficient, self-confident person is that he or she can—in certain circumstances—become cock-sure. Unfortunately, the motoring situation seems to bring out our aggressive and reckless tendencies.

3. FALSE Recent statistics showed that for every mile travelled, the chance of getting killed was eighteen times greater for a motor-cyclist than for a car-driver, and that motor-cycles were three times as likely as cars to be involved in both fatal and serious accidents.

4. FALSE — or at any rate partially false. There is evidence that it is not the ditherer but the over-confident, impatient driver who is responsible for most accidents. Dithering may be infuriating to other drivers, but does it really matter all that much—when you remember that the stake may be life or death—so long as the dithering results in the *right* decision?

5. FALSE A degree of tension usually makes for greater concentration and alertness. Any public performer or entertainer would say that a complete lack of tension invariably leads to a below-par performance.

6. FALSE —or rather, false as far as over-25-year-old drivers are concerned. Younger drivers, espe-

cially those in their teens, usually get much more reckless and want to show off if they have passengers of their own age with them in the car even more so if it's a girl-friend with them.

7. TRUE   This, presumably, speaks well for the married state! Needless to say it would be a lot less likely to be true if the marriage was a really unhappy one.   .

8. FALSE   It's the motor-cyclist who is the worst offender. It's worth noting, incidentally, that the record of drivers of goods vehicles is, on the whole, better than that of private drivers; and the record of public transport drivers is by far the best of the lot.

9. FALSE   Although children usually have better sight and hearing than adults, research has shown that they don't interpret what they see or hear as well. It's quite true, too, that they are more careless about traffic   largely because of lack of experience. An investigation in Paris a few years ago showed that 80% of children involved in road accidents stepped off the footpaths without paying sufficient attention to the traffic. (Incidentally, it is significant that children lacking parental affection are more often knocked down than other more fortunate children.)

10. FALSE   In fact special care is taken to see that zebra crossings are non-slippery. But research has shown that in traffic situations we are sometimes prone (whether pedestrians or drivers) to illusions or even hallucinations. The timid driver at night will sometimes mistake a tree or its shadow for a human being, or a piece of paper on the road for an animal   and swerve to avoid the imagined obstacle. It is in fog, of course, that we are particularly prone to such illusions, together with various distortions of vision and hearing.

I TELL YOU IT'S NOT A DOG!

11. FALSE Technical skill by itself is not enough. The higher the degree of skill, the more carefully it has to be used.

12. FALSE The element of luck plays only a minor part in the causing of accidents.

13. FALSE Drivers tend to blame the condition of the roads, but again the scientific evidence convincingly shows that this is not the major factor in causing accidents (though of course every effort should be made to improve roads and make them safer). We may not like it, but we have to face the fact that it is the mistakes of the driver himself/herself that cause the majority of the accidents.

14. FALSE   Sometimes we're surprised because someone we
thought was mild and inoffensive behaves like a
madman when he's behind the wheel, but in
nine cases out of ten (and there are always
exceptions) he's revealing an aspect of his true
nature which he normally keeps out of sight. As
Professor Cohen puts it:

> "By and large a man in a car is anonymous,
> and therefore off his guard. In these circum-
> stances he may throw off his customary mask
> of courtesy and consideration."

There has been a good deal of argument on this
question of a link between a person's driving
personality and everyday self, but most investigators tend to agree with the conclusion reached
by two American researchers, Tillmann and
Hobbs, back in 1949—that by and large people
"drive as they live".

15. FALSE   It may be true, of course, of a number of people
—but on the whole it is false, because research
consistently shows that a large number of the
serious and persistent offenders are not distin-
guishable from ordinary criminals (we're not
talking here of minor mishaps and offences that
are spread over all sections of the motoring
public); in fact, many of this group of offenders
are found to have had previous convictions for
other, non-motoring, offences. As Alan Canty,
an American researcher in this area, says ". . . the
chronic violator is a social problem-child, whose
traffic misbehaviour is but a symptom of his
personality maladjustment."

16. FALSE   After a carefully controlled investigation the
social-psychologist T. C. Willett reported:
". . . the facts do not support this assumption,
whichever group of offenders is considered.
Especially is it untrue of those who drive when
disqualified, or fail to insure against third-party

risks, many of whom fall almost into the category of repeaters or recidivists." Dr. Willett thinks there may well be "a compulsive element" about driving when disqualified which isn't stopped by long terms of disqualification, and in his opinion these may in fact do more harm than good. It's facts like these that make some people say that every motorist should pass some sort of psychological fitness test. But of course psychological disabilities of one sort or another are only too common in our civilisation—and, as one cynic has said, if motorists had to pass a psychological fitness test, the roads would be nearly empty! It's still true, though, that to put a lethal weapon like a car in the hands of seriously disturbed people is obviously dangerous, for themselves and for others.

17. FALSE   Angry self-justification and a holier-than-thou attitude is, unfortunately, the more usual reaction. One scientifically controlled inquiry among such offenders revealed that only 14% felt at all genuinely sorry.

18. TRUE   As a general rule, those who keep on having accidents don't seem to learn by experience.

19. FALSE   Offending motorists who have been arrested often complain that they are treated like criminals, but in fact the police are anxious to regard most serious offenders (such as habitually drunken drivers guilty of manslaughter) as otherwise normal and respectable citizens. Perhaps they feel they've got enough obvious criminals to cope with as it is.

20. FALSE   It's a common accusation, but there's practically no evidence to support it. The paper-work that would be involved in such a policy is in itself enough to make it almost impossible!

21. FALSE   It's a help, of course—but not if it results in the wrong decision and action. Sound judgment is

much more important.

22. FALSE   The driver over 65 may not be a better driver
than he was ten years before, but (so long as he's
healthy and he can still hear and see satisfactorily) if he's always been a good, safe driver,
the odds are he will be quite a good one now—
especially as male aggressiveness (a major factor
in dangerous driving) gets less with age. National
statistics show in fact that the most serious
motoring offenders are those in the age group
21-30.

There are many statistics, from all over the
world, that show that the young, despite their
physical advantages, are the worst drivers in
terms of causing injury and death; and those are
of course the only real terms on which to judge.

23. FALSE   There are, of course, plenty of bumptious middle-
aged drivers who think they know it all. But on
the whole this age-group tend to be more aware
of the need for a civilized code of behaviour on
the roads—and more conscience-stricken when
they do have accidents.

24. FALSE   It's a very common claim, of course, but it's
nothing more than wishful thinking. Some
people are less affected by alcohol than others,
and some take longer to be affected than others.
But there is overwhelming evidence that, for all
types of drinkers, alcohol affects judgment and
discrimination, even when taken in small quantities, and that the sensation of feeling more alert is
one of the more dangerous illusions it produces.

25. FALSE   A Traffic Accident Research Unit in Australia
recently reported that: "Every piece of good
research has indicated that the more alcohol
that is consumed, the greater is the risk of
accident involvement", and that "Alcohol has a
severely detrimental effect on driving skill . . .
research of the highest quality . . . has indicated

that alcohol is an important causal factor in approximately *one-half to three-quarters of all severe and fatal accidents.*"

Incidentally, among the drink and drive motorists, it is the genuine alcoholics who are the most dangerous; for one thing, alcoholism is a psychological illness and the symptoms include a sense of unbearable frustration together with violent impulses towards aggression and self-assertion, often accompanied by strong suicidal tendencies. Anyone like this, of course, is in urgent need of psychiatric help.

26. TRUE   And older women tend to be more anxious than younger ones. But don't jump to conclusions about this until you've read the next, and final, answer!

27. FALSE   Many men are going to hate this, but, on practically every count, women have a far better driving record than men (even after taking into account frequency of driving, mileage covered, etc.). An analysis of statistics in Britain, for example, showed a ratio of twenty-one male motoring offenders to every one woman. And a study of a single police district in England showed that out of the 653 serious motoring offenders investigated, 279 men were convicted of dangerous driving as compared with 6 women; 97 men were convicted of driving under the influence of drink compared with 7 women; 69 men were convicted of driving while disqualified but no women at all—and all the five deaths were caused by men.

In fact, there is only one type of offence which women seem to commit in larger numbers— though the ratio of even this is still 12 men to 1 woman—and that's failing to stop after an accident or to report it. But before we go any further with the obvious (and perhaps to male chauvinist pigs, surprising and unsettling) differences between men and women drivers, let's see how you scored on the Questionnaire above.

SCORING AND COMMENTS

If you got *18 or more* correct answers, then you have a good grasp of the realities of the motoring situation, possess sound judgement in general, and your driving is likely to reflect these qualities. *13 to 18 correct* would be a fair score; *under 13* would suggest that you have poor judgement—and anything *under 6* that you are pretty badly lacking in the qualities and skills needed on to-day's roads.

❖❖❖❖❖❖❖❖❖❖❖❖❖

When you look at the facts and figures, it's almost impossible for any reasonable person to disagree with the conclusion that the case goes against men drivers according to all the available statistics. It's true that women drive differently from men; it may indeed be true that women tend to drive slower, to give confusing signals, and to dither. In some cases these habits (so infuriating to the man driver) lead to accidents, but the scientifically tested evidence shows that these characteristics are only a minor factor in road accidents. Whether they like it or not, men have to face the fact that, in civilized and humane terms, women make better drivers than men.

If the word "better" is more than male egos can take, then let's use "safer". There are a number of pretty obvious reasons why a woman should be more careful and considerate when she is driving. For one thing, she is the one who carries and rears the children—and as we all tend to regard our cars (like our clothes and our homes) as extensions of our bodies, it's possible that a woman has something of the same feelings towards her car and its passengers (especially if they *are* children) as she has towards her body and it's womb. Probably, however, the main reason why women make safer drivers is because largely they lack the competitive and aggressive drives of the men. Women generally speaking don't feel the same need to push ahead, to demonstrate their sexual superiority by forcing the other driver off the road, and so on—as if driving were the kind of locking-horns fight that goes on between stags in the forest.

It seems, then, as if we must all at this point accept the fact that the greatest single reason for road accidents is male aggressiveness. A degree of aggression, competitiveness and adventurousness are, of course, natural and good and biologically necessary to man. Unfortunately the driving situation seems to bring out these qualities in the most primitive and immature (and destructive) forms, together with great anxiety about male-ness and a childish eagerness to demonstrate it. This may be another way of saying that lots of men have never properly grown up. There are of course plenty of anxious and immature women as well, but on the whole they have outlets for their immature impulses other than driving. Interestingly enough, it's those women with an unusual amount of masculinity in their natures, or those who are trying to imitate men, who most frequently get into accidents, and whose driving records on the whole don't compare well with those of more feminine women.

One good sign is that a lot of people have become aware of the dangerous instincts let loose by the driving situation, and that there have been attempts to find outlets for them off the open road. Stock-car racing is obviously one of them; and the Americans have come up with a brilliant idea in creating "drag-strips"—that is, stretches of private road, fitted with safety fenders, along which, for fifty cents, you can race with other cars in conditions of almost total safety. These drag-strips are often quite close to the motorways, so that if a driver has been seething with frustration and mounting rage and aggression and is aware of it, he can let off some dangerous steam along a drag-strip before rejoining the motorway (hopefully in a safer frame of mind).

The more grossly irresponsible and anti-social forms of motoring behaviour are, of course, obvious enough. Here are some of them:

1. Failing to stop and help after knocking someone down.
2. Deliberately charging another car or trying to force it off the road.
3. Driving at reckless speed in a built-up area, or near a school, hospital or old people's home.
4. Refusing to give way at a pedestrian crossing.
5. Persistently driving while disqualified for an offence involving serious injury or loss of life.
6. Deliberately charging over a cross-roads just for the fun of it.
7. Ignoring traffic-lights.
8. Habitually driving while under the influence of alcohol.

If you fall down on any of these, you should seriously consider whether or not you ought to give up driving until you have overcome your defects and/or got psychiatric help. If, however, you find yourself wanting to add other items to the list, you probably possess the basic psychological requirements for a good, safe driver.

✦✦✦✦✦✦✦✦✦✦✦✦

Even though not too many of us can be called potential killers on the roads, there are still a great many dangerous impulses in the best of us. Here is a Questionnaire designed to help you decide which elements in your driving behaviour might make you a menace on the roads—so that you can perhaps take steps to control and even get rid of them entirely:

QUESTIONNAIRE B:

(Answer YES *or* NO*)*

1. Do you only feel really secure and confident inside your car?

2. Do you only feel at ease inside a big, heavy, powerful car?

3. Do you frequently flash your head-lights into the eyes of incoming drivers in order to teach them a lesson about something they may be doing?

4. Do you hate other people overtaking you, and habitually accelerate when they are trying to do so?

5. Do you regard overtaking the driver in front of you as a matter of personal pride?

6. Do you lavish more care on your car than you do on those nearest and dearest to you?

7. If you are married, have you ever put buying a new car before having a baby?

8. Do you experience strong anxiety if your car is older, smaller, slower, etc. than those of your neighbours and friends?

9. Do you get into an uncontrollable fury if someone outwits you on the road?

10. Do you frequently cut across if you are in the wrong lane of traffic?

11. If another driver makes a rude sign at you, do you make one back, or give chase in order to get even with him in some way?

12. Have you ever come to blows with another driver?

13. Do you find yourself becoming exceptionally conscious because another driver is a woman, a foreigner, or someone from a different age-group than your own?

14. Do you tend to show off in your driving if you have a passenger with you (and especially someone of the opposite sex)?

15. When you are driving, do you frequently have fantasies that you are a racing driver, a famous personality, a powerful leader, etc.?

16. When you are choosing a new car, is power your main consideration rather than style or utility?

17. Do you frequently find yourself subject to a craving for high speed, whatever the circumstances?

18. Do you tend to identify high speeds with masculinity, and careful driving with femininity?

19. Do you regard automatic transmission as fit only for women drivers?

20. Do you regard safety-belts as rather cissy?

21. Do you habitually experience a powerful impulse to charge at oncoming vehicles?

22. Do you find yourself becoming extremely irritated by the stickers and/or hanging decorations in other peoples' cars?

23. Do you tend to boast of your sexual prowess to comparative strangers?

24. Would you consider yourself exceptionally impulsive and/or sociable?

25. Do you tend to be on rather bad terms with your father, and to look down on him?

26. Do you have a particularly close relationship with your mother?

27. Do you tend to be over-optimistic?

28. Do you regard your car as your main escape to freedom?

29. Do you frequently use your horn when overtaking on the motorway?

30. Are you convinced that you can estimate speed to the nearest mph?

31. Do you very frequently change your job?

32. Do you suffer from chronic depression?

33. Do you experience feelings of hostility towards a very large proportion of the people you work with and meet in the course of your job etc.?

34. Do you experience feelings of omnipotence and indestructability?

35. Do you have spells of intense self-hatred?

QUESTIONNAIRE B. ANSWERS & COMMENTS

1.   NO   should be the answer, for the obvious reason that if you are really confident and secure it won't only be inside your car. If you have to use your car to bolster your confidence, then clearly you haven't got enough.

2.   NO   If you have some weight and solidity of character, you won't need a car to act as a stand-in for these qualities. You may still choose this type of car for other reasons, however. Research suggests, though, that the possession of this type of big heavy car increases the feeling of psychic size. It is very likely too, that this sort of car appeals particularly to those men who suffer from anxiety and feelings of inadequacy about their sexual potency. Too often the roar of the engine and the thrust of the heavy body are a kind of anxious protestation. The man who is truly potent doesn't need to give off these noisy signals.

3. Hopefully   It's obviously pretty daft to try to teach
   NO   somebody else a lesson by a method that might very well result in death or injury to yourself or your passengers—not to mention those in the other car. It is surely obvious, too, that a man who can get so angry about another human being and do something which might kill or cause him terrible injury, is hardly a mature and balanced human being. If you sometimes feel such irrational and wildly disproportionate feelings welling up in you, then clearly you need to take very careful stock of yourself. The genuinely mature and responsible driver is continually aware, no matter what the provocation, that human life may be at stake.

4. Hopefully   Admittedly it's a common enough impulse,
     NO   but one that must be checked if you are to be a really good and safe driver. The open road isn't a racing track, and it's dangerous to treat it as one. If you think about it, the "no mate, you're not going to pass me" attitude is a pretty childish one.

5.   NO   —for much the same reason as the previous answer. Again, it's pretty childish to feel so touchy about it. Presumably you are driving at the speed that suits you at the time, so why try to increase it just to get one up on the stranger in front of you? If your pride is so closely involved in such a situation, it's difficult not to wonder whether you've got much to be proud about in your life in general.

6.   NO   —we hope! as much for your own sake as for those close to you. There's nothing wrong, of course, in keeping your car spick and span, and a good deal right about keeping the engine in good working order. But an exaggerated concern for your car would probably suggest some sexual anxiety and/or guilt—in Freudian terms, as we all know, a car is a penis symbol, and to be frantically worried about the symbol would suggest a similar attitude towards the thing it symbolizes.

7. Hopefully   To prefer a machine of any sort to a human
     NO   being surely implies a cock-eyed scale of values.

8. Hopefully   We all tend to use our cars as status symbols,
     NO   but if this attitude is carried to excess it probably suggests considerable social uncertainty, and a rather unfriendly relationship with others round you. The really mature attitude towards a car is to treat it simply as a machine bought to serve you for strictly practical purposes—though admit-

tedly there are few of us as mature as all that!

9. NO Is obviously the desired answer—for the same kind of reasons given in other comments—anger of this sort can only make you more of a danger to yourself and others.

10. Hopefully Obviously it's always a dangerous man-
    NO oeuvre.

11. Hopefully The driving situation, because of the strains
    NO it imposes, is one that almost inevitably leads to a lot of irritation and irritability. But blind, uncontrollable anger is one of the surest symptoms of immaturity. The only sane response must be to shrug your shoulders, let the poor fool get on with it, and concentrate your faculties on the job in hand —even if you have to let rip some short sharp and naturally rude words to relieve your feelings!

12. NO Even though an individual punch-up would be immeasurably safer than trying to fight it out with lethal weapons like cars, you're not going to be fit to get back into your car and drive away afterwards.

13. NO —at least we most sincerely hope so. It's a common enough reaction among drivers, but there is no doubt that psychologically it shows a lot of inner anxiety and uncertainty, immaturity, intolerance, and a bad lack of objectivity (especially in view of the statistics discussed earlier in this chapter).

14. Hopefully It's a common enough fault among teenage
    NO drivers (as we've pointed out earlier) but if you're an adult it's time you grew out of it. If you have to show off, make it your biceps or your cleavage!

15. NO We hope, because driving a car needs all your attention.

16. NO Would be the better answer because utility

is the more realistic quality on modern roads with stringent speed limits—although of course there's nothing wrong with looking for a bit of style.

17.   NO   would be the better answer here too. We've come to feel that speed is a normal and essential part of life, although most psychologists are agreed that this is a tendency which should be reversed if possible. Some psychologists see the thrill of speed as a "conative propensity"—that is, something intellectually thought up, deliberately willed, and not *biologically necessary*. They point out that a very marked craving for speed is usually accompanied by *hypomania* (that is, a state of frantic excitement), obsessional desire for hurry, and other signs of a psychopathological nature.

18.   Hopefully   Surely careful driving should be the most
       NO   important consideration, irrespective of sex?

19.   NO   —is probably the better answer. There may be something to be said for the argument that having to handle gears helps to keep you alert when driving. But it is possible, according to some psychologists, that many men like gear-levers for the wrong (and immature) reasons—the shape itself is a pretty obvious penis symbol—which may indicate a need for reassurance over potency, and even castration fears.

It's worth adding that scientific investigations reveal that most women are glad of the convenience of automatic transmission—except those women who have strong masculine characteristics in their natures.

20.   Hopefully   You may have other more rational doubts
       NO   about safety-belts, but you should be convinced by looking again at the statistics—

which show convincingly that wearing safety belts very appreciably reduces death and injury on the roads.

21.   NO   All of us occasionally have this impulse, especially when night-driving. But it is simply not on to give way to it. If you find the impulse so constant and strong that it's worrying you, you'd probably be wise to consult a psychiatrist.

22.   NO   is the desired answer. Many people may be mildly irritated by this sort of thing, but if your irritation is very strong, you are likely to have insufficient control of your temper and be dangerously intolerant into the bargain—and this will make you a hazard on the roads.

23.   NO   It is to be hoped. The tendency usually points to an anxiety about sexual potency, and psychological tests have shown that this tendency makes for dangerous driving—because the driver then tries to use the car as a substitute for sexual performance.

24. Hopefully   Because there seems to be some relation be-
      NO   tween impulsiveness and a very high degree of sociability, and proneness to accidents.

25. Hopefully   The psychologists have shown that a positive
      NO   and affectionate relationship with the father (or father-figure) leads to a greater sense of responsibility and respect for law and order —and would therefore make you more responsible on the roads.

26. Hopefully   Because it would mean you had many diffi-
      NO   culties to cope with in your life—including that part of it you spend driving a car. Delinquent behaviour of all kinds, including that on the roads, is often associated with an exceptionally close relationship with an over-protective mother. It's been found, for

instançe, that youngsters who habitually steal cars or drive them away without permission, frequently come into this category.

27.　NO　Over-optimism may lead to carelessness.

28.　NO　Many people do look on their cars in this way, but if you can honestly answer NO then you are not over-dependent on your car and will have plenty of other interests in your life.

29.　NO　most emphatically. It's a dangerous practice, unnerving to other drivers, and one of the symptoms of gross impatience, aggressiveness and arrogance.

30.　NO　It's known that most people are poor judges of speed, and nearly always underestimate it.

31-35.　NO　is the reassuring answer, because all these characteristics tend to be signs of some psychological disorder, and incidentally are often part of the "alcoholic personality"

SCORING & COMMENTS

As you see, NO would be the best answer to all the above questions; a score of *25 and above* would suggest that you are a mature and adult individual, and therefore likely to be a good, safe driver. *Over 15* would be fair. If you score *under 15*, there really is a serious chance that you are a positive menace on the roads. You should think very seriously about any incorrect answers you made.

Keep this Questionnaire with you. It may help you to spot your main personality defects, as they affect your driving, and perhaps encourage you to try to correct them. Test yourself with the questions from time to time: when you can honestly answer NO to a good proportion of them, you will have taken some important steps towards greater knowledge and understanding of your self and your driving standards will have improved enormously.

CHAPTER EIGHT

HOW INTELLIGENT ARE YOU?

CHAPTER EIGHT

HOW INTELLIGENT ARE YOU?

In this chapter we are going to give you an Intelligence Test, which you can apply to yourself, or to your friends, or members of your family—provided they are over thirteen years old. But whatever you do, don't exaggerate the importance of this or any other intelligence test. They all have their limitations and none of them claims to be perfect. For one thing, all those you are likely to come across will have been devised by people belonging to societies like ours for people belonging to societies like ours, so they will inevitably tend to measure the kind of mental qualities which are most highly valued by such societies.

They won't be much use, for example, for Indians living in the South American jungles, who can't read or write, who probably can't count beyond the total of their fingers and toes, and who haven't the foggiest idea about the laws of gravity or the motions of the world on which they live, or of its place in the cosmos. Yet anthropologists who have lived among them have been impressed by the success with which they have adapted themselves to their particular environment (far more successfully than industrialised man) and by the quickness of their natural intelligence. It's likely that some of their chiefs and medicine men are in the genius class—but obviously if they were asked to take the test you're going to do, they'd register as morons!

Different societies, after all, expect different things from people, and make quite different demands on them. That's why it would be unfair to apply our kind of intelligence tests to immigrants to this country, for example, who haven't had a western type education. They come from an entirely different culture than ours, and it takes them a considerable time to get acclimatized to the kind of demands it makes. A striking illustration of this point comes from the USA, where educational psychologists have given the same Intelligence Tests to groups of white and Red Indian children. It was found that the white children quickly understood the instruction (usual in many of the tests) that if they couldn't immediately answer one of the questions, they should go on to the next one, and perhaps go back later if they had time, to the ones they couldn't answer at once. But the Red Indian children had been trained by their tribes to believe that it was more important to get an answer right than to be quick about it. In consequence when they came up against a difficult question early in the test they tended to stick at it until the time for the whole test had run out. Their scores were, of course, bound to be low—but clearly that had no relation at all to their intelligence.

In fact even within our own kind of western societies, there are variations in background, upbringing and so on, which affect performance in the usual type of Intelligence Test, without necessarily indicating any lack of intelligence. It has been found that this often applies, for instance, to the children of gypsies or bargees, who tend to live in a world of their own, separated from many of the stimuli of their neighbours in the same country—even sometimes cut off from newspapers, radio and television. It has been found, too, that even to-day there are some facts and concepts more available to town dwellers than to country people. And the other way round too—it has been noted that children in towns have a vaguer and narrower understanding of what is implied even by such simple words as cow, crop, harbour, and ship, than those who live in the country or near the sea. Then again, children who were deprived in their early years and did not get enough love and affection (and the over-all stimulus that goes with them) often seem less intelligent than other children for the simple reason that they never received the encouragement to get to know their environment or to go out and meet it.

It has also been argued that there is a class basis to most Intelligence Tests—that they are really devised for middle-class children whose parents know the kind of things that are expected of them in the educational rat-race, and are therefore better able to push them and encourage them than working-class parents who may have missed out on their own educations—and that in any case a middle-class home provides a background of sophisticated talk, books, and activities that give their children an unfair advantage. We have been talking, incidentally, mainly about children; but generally speaking the points we have made apply to adults as well.

The truth of the matter is that no Intelligence Test is universally valid. In every case it is applicable only to the particular section of the particular community for which it was devised. *And even then it has limitations.* The most obvious of them is that most of the Intelligence Tests, in order to get a cut-and dried scoring system, rely mostly on closed questions (that is, questions which have only one correct answer). Now there is evidence that the more creative sort of people are best at open questions (that is, questions to which several more or less correct answers can be given, and which offer a better chance of being truly original) whereas they tend to make careless mistakes with the closed questions on which another, more precise sort of person would answer very well. Some critics of Intelligence Tests argue that if these tests are used as an actual means of selecting people for higher education or for jobs, then those who might (by their particular sort of intelligence and temperament) have become artists or scientists are perhaps being lost to the community.

And yet another disadvantage is that very intelligent people often see the right answer to a question straight away, but think it's too obvious, and so spend a lot of time puzzling out what the questioners were really getting at—and trying to outwit them!

A common criticism of these Tests is that people can be coached for them, so that those who come to a Test unprepared are at a considerable disadvantage. There is a good deal to be said for this criticism. It has been shown in America, for example, that a course of study using teaching machines can greatly improve speed of performance in Intelligence Tests. Most educational psychologists, too, agree that coaching in the kinds of questions and answers to be expected can indeed put up the score. This doesn't much affect the results from the very bright people, but in the medium range the difference in the results between those who have been coached and those who have come fresh to the test can mean the difference between getting a place in an educational establishment or even a job.

It is generally acknowledged that this is something that must be changed—though in practice most of those concerned with such tests are aware of the snag and take it into account. Obviously, though, it would be next to impossible to make sure that nobody at all had any previous practice with Intelligence Tests. The fairest solution to the problem would be to see that everybody who was likely ever to be called upon to take a Test did get plenty of prior training and practice. That would raise the level of performance—but the variations in intelligence would, of course, still be measureable.

With all these factors in mind, then, let us look at the intelligence tests as they are. Although they don't test knowledge as such, but rather the capacity to acquire knowledge, they do take for granted at least the knowledge of how to read and write. Questions to do with the handling of words, in fact, figure largely in all the tests. There is a good reason for this, because experience shows that questions of this sort form the best single indication of intelligence. Indeed it has been found that ability in reading comprehension and extent of vocabulary (as used in normal English teaching) corresponds so closely to intelligence as tested by other methods, that some educationalists place more reliance on these comprehension and vocabulary exercises than on the Intelligence Tests.

It has also been found that speed of performance is perhaps the outstanding factor in determining success or failure in Intelligence Tests. Not always, it's true: speed isn't all that much use, if the person concerned is careless or lacks persistency. But on the whole, this is true. Professor H. J. Eysenck has said that "mental speed" is the "fundamental, inherited basis for intellectual differences between people". This is why, when you come to do the Intelligence Test a bit later on, you will be given a time limit; and why it is important that you keep to it.

This brings us to your I.Q. It's a term that's everywhere these days— and as a rule it's very loosely used. Quite a lot of people don't even know what the letters stand for, and many of those who do know haven't stopped to think what exactly an *Intelligence Quotient* means. The *CONCISE OXFORD DICTIONARY* says quotient is "Result given by dividing one quantity by another". The quantities in this case are mental age and actual age. Mental age is what an Intelligence Test score is meant to find out; and having been found, the mental age has to be looked at in relation to the actual age (in years and months) of the person being tested—and then the I.Q. can be discovered. For example, the mental development of a child of six with a mental age of ten, is obviously different from an adolescent with the same mental age of ten. In effect, the I.Q. is a way of showing this difference—i.e. the six-year-old would have a higher I.Q. than the fifteen-year-old.

✛✛✛✛✛✛✛✛✛✛✛✛✛

The Intelligence Test that follows has been based on one designed by William Bernard and Jules Leopold (in *TEST YOURSELF* published by Corgi Books) so that you can calculate your own I.Q. It's based on the assumption that you are over thirteen years old; and it won't work for anyone less than that. It must be explained that in calculating an I.Q. you have first to decide at what age an individual's intelligence reaches maturity. Most psychologists are agreed that this is between fifteen and seventeen. Bernard and Leopold have fixed fifteen and a half years (that is, 186 months) as the peak age for the purposes of their test (this figure is an average based on a number of the most reputable Intelligence Tests). It is pointed out that the scoring they have adopted may lead to minor distortion in the I.Q. scores of those under that age of 186 months, but that this makes sure that it's more accurate for people above that age (for whom the test is mainly intended.)

HERE, FIRST, IS A SHORT SAMPLE TEST, WITH THE CORRECT ANSWERS AS YOU SHOULD WRITE THEM:

91. MAN *is to* BOY *as* WOMAN *is to*
     (1) lad (2) kid (3) dame (4) girl (5) crowd........ (4)
92. In this series, what number comes next?
     2, 4, 6, 8....................................(10)
93. These words can be arranged to form a sentence. If the sentence is true, write T. If the sentence is false, write F.
     ARE NEVER TREES GREEN............... (F)
     (*The words can be arranged into the sentence* TREES ARE NEVER GREEN, *which is false.*)
94. In this group, which object does not belong?
     (1) pencil (2) pen (3) crayon (4) brush (5) club.... (5)
     (*You can draw or write with pencil, pen, crayon or brush, but not with a club.*)

NOW HERE IS THE INTELLIGENCE TEST ITSELF, AND THESE ARE YOUR INSTRUCTIONS:

In this test, work as fast as you can without sacrificing accuracy. If you wish you may make calculations on the page margins or on a separate sheet of paper. Remember not to work too long on any one question; skip the hard ones and come back to them later if you have time. Make sure to glance at a watch or clock occasionally; or better still, have someone time you. If you work longer than the time allowed, your score will be false.

TIME LIMIT: 45 MINUTES

BEGIN TEST:

1. TRUMPET *is to* PLAY *as* BOOK *is to*
    (1) fun (2) read (3) music (4) words (5) relax...... ( )
2. AUTOMOBILE *is to* WHEEL *as* HORSE *is to*
    (1) leg (2) tail (3) gallop (4) wagon (5) drive...... ( )
3. In this series, what number comes next?
    3, 9, 15, 21, ... ( )

4. COW *is to* BARN *as* MAN *is to*
   (1) stable (2) milk (3) house (4) farm (5) restaurant ( )

5. 1, 2, 3, 4, 5, 6, 7, 8, 9, 10, 11, 12, 13, 14, 15, 16
   Which is the seventh number after the number
   just before 6?.................................. ( )

6. These words can be arranged to form a sentence. If
   the sentence is true, write T. If the sentence is false,
   write F.
   BURN WOOD CAN'T DRY.................. ( )

7. These words can be arranged to form a sentence. If
   the sentence is true, write T. If the sentence is false,
   write F.
   ON FLOAT BOATS NEVER WATER......... ( )

8. In this series, what number comes next?
   1, 3, 5, 7, ... ( )

9. These words can be arranged to form a sentence. If
   the sentence is true, write T. If the sentence is false,
   write F.
   A BAT PLAYED WITH BASEBALL IS........ ( )

10. NEGLIGENT means
    (1) careless (2) cautious (3) unimportant (4) careful ( )

11. John has 10 cents. If he had 3 cents less he would
    have half a much as George. George has how much
    more money than John?
    (a) 7 cents (b) 4 cents (c) 2 cents (d) 13 cents...... ( )

12. HE *is to* HIM *as* SHE *is to*
    (1) me (2) them (3) hers (4) her (5) his........... ( )

13. In this group, which object does not belong?
    (1) radio (2) battery (3) boiler (4) telephone...... ( )

14. In this group, which object does not belong?
    (1) sabre (2) rapier (3) scimitar (4) lance (5)
    cutlass...................................... ( )

15. Only birds have feathers, therefore which is true?
    (1) Birds shed in the spring.
    (2) All feathers are light.
    (3) Snakes don't have feathers................. ( )

16. In this group, which word does not belong?
    (1) architect (2) builder (3) plumber (4) doctor... ( )

17. In this series, what number comes next?
90, 85, 75, 60, 40, ... ( )
18. In this series, what number comes next?
22, 33, 44, 55, 66, ... ( )
19. BOTANIST *is to* SOCIOLOGIST *as* PLANT *is to*
(1) women (2) problems (3) society (4) sociology. . ( )
20. If a person is DISTRAUGHT, he is
(1) ignorant (2) manic (3) shocked (4) bewildered. ( )
21. THREAD *is to* CLOTH *as* WIRE *is to*
(1) stiff (2) radio (3) rope (4) mesh (5) metal. . . . . . ( )
22. SANITATION makes for
(1) water (2) health (3) porcelain (4) godliness. . . . ( )
23. In this series, what letter comes next?
A C E G I . . . . ( )
24. Which number is wrong in this series?
1, 19, 8, 5, 145, 127, ... ( )
25. Print the letter as far from the first letter of the
alphabet as the second I is from the first I in
INHARMONIOUS. . . . . ( )
26. Which letter does not belong in this series?
Z Y X Q W V . . . . ( )

27.
. . . . ( )

28. These words can be arranged to form a sentence. If
the sentence is true, write T. If the sentence is false,
write F.
DESTROY BOMBING CITIES CAN'T AND
MEN. . . . . ( )
29. In this series, which number comes next?
18, 12, 15, 10, 12, 8, ... ( )
30. If A and B are letters write C, unless 5 and 5 add up
to 10, in which case don't write anything but D. . . . ( )
31. These words can be arranged to form a sentence. If
the sentence is true, write T. If the sentence is false,
write F.
TEETH NOT ARE FALSE TRUE TEETH. . . . ( )

32. *is to* *as* *is to*
(a) (b) (c) (d) (e) ( )

33. *is to* *as* *is to*
(a) (b) (c) (d) (e) ( )

34. Which number is wrong in this series?
2, 6, 17, 54, 162, ... ( )

35. In this series, what letter comes next?
A C F J .... ( )

36. *is to* *as* *is to*
(a) (b) (c) (d) (e) ( )

37. In this series, what number comes next?
21, 20, 18, 15, 11, ... ( )

38. SOUTH *is to* NORTHWEST *as* WEST *is to*
(1) north (2) southwest (3) northeast (4) southeast. ( )

39. In this series, which number does not belong?
2, 4, 100, 38, 20, 7, ... ( )

40. In this group, which word does not belong?
(1) sadness (2) melancholy (3) sorrow (4) mourning ( )

41. In this series, what letter comes next?
A C B D F E G .... ( )

42. 1, 2, 3, 4, 5, 6, 7, 8, 9, 10, 11, 12, 13, 14, 15, 16, 17, 18, 19. Print the number which comes as far before 14 in the series above as K comes after F in the alphabet. .... ( )

43. If all men have coats, then big men have
(1) big coats (2) fewer coats (3) coats (4) few coats. ( )

44. In this series, what number comes next?
18, 24, 21, 27, 24, 30, ... ( )

45. Nazis PLUNDERED cities by
(1) guns (2) arson (3) destroying them (4) robbing them (5) knocking them down. .... ( )

46. In this series, what number comes next?
66, 63, 57, 45, ... ( )

47. ⬤ *is to* ◯ *as* ⬛ *is to*

   (a) ⬜ (b) ⚫ (c) ◼ (d) ▣ (e) ◯ ( )

48. In this series, what number comes next?
    2, 9, 6, 7, 18, 5, ... ( )

49. PLANE *is to* SOLID *as* LINE *is to*
    (1) square (2) circle (3) angle (4) rectangle (5) plane. . . . . ( )

50. How many miles can a dog run in 3 minutes if it runs half as fast as a car going 40 miles per hour?. . . ( )

51. A canoe always has (1) paddles (2) canvas (3) water (4) paint (5) length. . . . . ( )

52. In this series what number comes next?
    65, 68, 72, 77, 83, ... ( )

53. How many letters in this line fall next to vowels but after K or R?
    P A U L E G K A T L O I R Q O Z. . . . . ( )

54. In this series what number comes next?
    2, A, 9, B, 6, C, 13, D, ... ( )

55. How many letters in the line below come after the K, but both before R and after T?
    A A B K M X J T T V C R R P L. . . . . ( )

56. 20 men can dig 40 holes in 60 days so 10 men can dig 20 holes in how many days?. . . . . ( )

57. How many letters in this series come just before an odd number and just after a number larger than 6?
    Z, 1, 9, A, 4, B, 3, 14, 19, C, 8, 9, B, 5, D, 12, E, 17. . ( )

58. Suppose Milwaukee leads the league and Pittsburgh is fifth, while St. Louis is midway between them. If Chicago is ahead of Pittsburgh and Cincinnati is immediately behind St. Louis, which city is in second place?
    (a) Cincinnati (b) Pittsburgh (c) Chicago (d) St. Louis (e) Milwaukee. . . . . ( )

59. One series below is in opposite order to the other, except for a certain number. Write the number.
    1, 2, 3   1, 3, 2 . . . . ( )

60. COMPREHENSIBLE advice is
    (1) bad advice (2) comprehensive (3) understand-
    able (4) good advice (5) reprehensible . . . . ( )
61. In this group, which word does not belong?
    (1) the (2) this (3) an (4) it (5) a . . . . ( )
62. Which of these words comes closest in meaning to
    IS?
    (1) to be (2) are (3) lives (4) exists (5) accrusticates ( )
63. A CHASSEUR is a (1) soldier (2) torso (3)
    detective (4) vase . . . . ( )
64. BLEAK *is to* BLACK *as* LEAK *is to*
    (1) white (2) back (3) leak (4) lack (5) water . . . . ( )
65. ADAMANT is the opposite of
    (1) dull (2) unlike Adam (3) yielding (4) stubborn ( )
66. Half a waiter's earnings, and a dollar besides, come
    from tips. If he earns 15 dollars, how many dollars
    come from tips? . . . . ( )
67. Which of these words most nearly corresponds in
    meaning to OPULENT?
    (1) exposed (2) precious stone (3) wealthy (4)
    exposed at one end (5) weeping . . . . ( )
68. If a train is running 3 minutes late and losing 3
    seconds per minute, how many more minutes will
    it take for the train to be running an hour late?. . ( )
69. Which of these words most nearly corresponds in
    meaning to DELETE?
    (1) permit (2) erase (3) rent (4) tasty (5) neat . . . ( )
70. Girls always have (1) sweethearts (2) clothes (3)
    giggles (4) hair (5) figures . . . . ( )
71. A train running 30 miles per hour is in front of a
    train running 50 miles per hour. How many miles
    apart are the trains, if it will take 15 minutes for
    the faster train to catch the slower one?. . . . . ( )
72. PIQUE is most similar in meaning to
    (1) choice (2) decoration (3) elf (4) resentment (5)
    sorrow . . . . ( )
73. A train completes half a trip at 30 miles per hour,
    and the other half at 60 miles per hour. If the whole

trip was 20 miles, how many minutes did the train take to complete the trip? .... ( )

74. Print your answer. A B D *is to* C B A *as* Q R T *is to* .. ( )

75. If 2 is A and 6 is C and 8 is D and 12 is F, how would you spell BEADED, using numbers instead of letters? .... ( )

76. When Aunt Carrie makes soup, she puts in 1 bean for each 2 peas. If her soup contains a total of 300 peas and beans, how many peas are there? ...... ( )

77. No dog can sing, but some dogs can talk. If so, then
   (1) Some dogs can sing.
   (2) All dogs can't sing.
   (3) All dogs can't talk. .... ( )

78. No man is good, but some men are not bad. Therefore,
   (1) All men are not bad.
   (2) No man is not bad.
   (3) All men aren't good .... ( )

79. The Potomac River and the Hudson River have a combined length of 850 miles, and the Hudson River is 250 miles shorter than the Potomac River. How many miles long is the Potomac River? .... ( )

80. Smith and Jones went to the race track, where Smith lost 68 dollars on the first 2 races, losing 6 dollars more on the second race than he lost on the first one. But he lost 4 dollars less on the second race than Jones did. How much did Jones lose on the second race? .... ( )

81. Stockings always have
   (1) sexiness (2) seams (3) garters (4) weight
   (5) sheerness .... ( )

82. In this series, what number comes next?
   9, 7, 8, 6, 7, 5, ... ( )

83. One bunch of bananas has one-third again as many bananas as a second bunch. If the second bunch has 3 less bananas than the first bunch, how many has the first bunch? .... ( )

84.

$is\ to$ ... as ... $is\ to$

(a) ... (b) ... (c) ... (d) ... (e)

...... ( )

85. Birds can only fly and hop, but worms can crawl. Therefore,
   (1) Birds eat worms.
   (2) Birds don't crawl.
   (3) Birds sometimes crawl .... ( )

86. Boxes always have (1) angles (2) shapes (3) wood (4) string .... ( )

87. What number is as much more than 10 as it is less than one-half of what 30 is 10 less than? .... ( )

88. Smith gets twice as large a share of the profits as any of his three partners gets. The three partners share equally. What fraction of the entire profits is Smiths? .... ( )

89. BIRD *is to* FISH *as* AIRPLANE *is to*
   (1) boat (2) whale (3) dory (4) ship (5) submarine. ( )

90. These words can be arranged to form a sentence. If the sentence is true, write T. If the sentence is false, write F.
   ONE IN IS NUMBER THAN MORE BOOKS BOOK .... ( )

THE SCORING

This is a bit complicated, but you'll soon get the hang of it —though you may find that a pocket calculator is a great help.

What you do is this:

1. Having taken the Test as instructed, turn to the Answers at the end of this Chapter. Give yourself one point for each correct answer, and add up your total score.

2. Now go on to the *TABLE OF MENTAL AGES*, and find the Mental Age which corresponds to your total test score.

3. If your age is less than fifteen and a half—you divide your Mental Age by your own age in months. Carry your answer to two decimal points (we said you'd need a pocket calculator!)

4. If your age is fifteen and a half or more—you divide your Mental Age by 186 (that is, the number of months decided on as the peak age). Carry your answer to two decimal places.

5. Now multiply your answer by 100—and the resulting figure will be your I.Q.

HERE ARE TWO EXAMPLES:

Taking a score of 50, which corresponds in the Table to a Mental Age of 195: this is how it works out if, say:

(i) you are fifteen years old (i.e. under the peak age of 186 months). You divide the Mental Age of 195 by your age in months (i.e. by 180). Taken to two decimal places, this gives you 1.08. Multiply this by 100. This will give an answer of 108—and that is your I.Q.

(ii) you are thirty-five years old. You divide the Mental Age of 195 by 186. Taken to two decimal places, this gives you 1.04. Multiply this by 100. This will give an answer of 104—and that is your I.Q.

ANSWERS

1	(2)	31	(T)	61	(4)
2	(1)	32	(c)	62	(4)
3	(27)	33	(d)	63	(1)
4	(3)	34	(17)	64	(4)
5	(12)	35	(0)	65	(3)
6	(F)	36	(c)	66	(8½)
7	(F)	37	(6)	67	(3)
8	(9)	38	(3)	68	(1140)
9	(T)	39	(7)	69	(2)
10	(1)	40	(4)	70	(5)
11	(b)	41	(I)	71	(5)
12	(4)	42	(9)	72	(4)
13	(3)	43	(3)	73	(30)
14	(4)	44	(27)	74	(SRQ)
15	(3)	45	(4)	75	(4-10-2-8-10-8)
16	(4)	46	(21)	76	(200)
17	(15)	47	(c)	77	(2)
18	(77)	48	(54)	78	(3)
19	(3)	49	(5)	79	(550)
20	(4)	50	(1)	80	(41)
21	(4)	51	(5)	81	(4)
22	(2)	52	(90)	82	(6)
23	(K)	53	(7)	83	(12)
24	(8)	54	(10)	84	(d)
25	(I)	55	(4)	85	(2)
26	(Q)	56	(60)	86	(2)
27	(c)	57	(2)	87	(15)
28	(F)	58	(c)	88	(2/5)
29	(9)	59	(1)	89	(5)
30	(D)	60	(3)	90	(T)

Give yourself 1 point for each correct answer. Total points is your score.

TABLE OF MENTAL AGES (IN MONTHS)

YOUR SCORE	YOUR MENTAL AGE	YOUR SCORE	YOUR MENTAL AGE	YOUR SCORE	YOUR MENTAL AGE
2	94	32	157	61	218
3	96	33	159	62	221
4	98	34	162	63	223
5	100	35	164	64	225
6	103	36	166	65	227
7	105	37	168	66	229
8	107	38	170	67	231
9	109	39	172	68	233
10	111	40	174	69	235
11	113	41	176	70	237
12	115	42	178	71	240
13	117	43	181	72	242
14	119	44	183	73	244
15	122	45	185	74	246
16	124	46	187	75	248
17	126	47	189	76	250
18	128	48	191	77	252
19	130	49	193	78	254
20	132	50	195	79	256
21	134	51	197	80	259
22	136	52	199	81	261
23	138	53	202	82	263
24	140	54	204	83	265
25	143	55	206	84	267
26	145	56	208	85	269
27	147	57	210	86	271
28	149	58	212	87	273
29	151	59	214	88	275
30	153	60	216	89	278
31	155				

Now work out your I.Q. (as we showed you in the examples just now), and check your rating on this Table:

I.Q. RATINGS

I.Q.	*Rating*
140 and above	Very high indeed—only a tiny percentage of the population would achieve such a result
130-140	Still very high
110-130	Very good
90-110	Average
70-90	Rather low
70 and below	Decidedly low

We must stress that the result you've just come to is based on one questionnaire only. An I.Q. is normally based on a whole range of such tests—and even then, as we've already said, this method has many limitations.

All the same, we hope you have enjoyed stretching your mind, and seeing how quick-witted you are!

CHAPTER NINE

HOW GOOD IS YOUR MEMORY?

CHAPTER NINE

HOW GOOD IS YOUR MEMORY?

If you haven't got a good memory, it doesn't follow that you are also unintelligent, of course. The proverbial absent-minded professor, for example, is likely in fact to be a highly intelligent individual—while a professional Memory Man who entertains people with his fantastic feats of recall may not be intelligent at all. All the same it's obviously very useful to have a good memory: for one thing it saves a lot of embarrassment if you don't suddenly find, on starting to introduce people to each other, that you've forgotten their names!

The comforting thing, though, is that the memory really can be improved by training. In the case of the professional Memory Man it has obviously been carried to tremendous lengths, by all kinds of exercises and *mnemonic devices*—that is, tricks that help to set up linkages between the various bits and pieces lying about in the mind. For most of us, however, the sort of aids to memory taught to children still stand us in good stead—things like those handy rhymes "i before e, except after c" and "Thirty days hath September, April, June and November" and so on. It's a good idea to brush up these and others like them—and to invent new rhymes for other things you particularly want to remember. You'll find, too, that the exercises and games in this Chapter will be a help.

An important part of all this is—motivation. You've got to be sufficiently interested in the matter in hand to want to remember it. The motivation may be a professional one, but the absent-minded professor probably remembers a very great deal more than a professional performer—but what he remembers is all concentrated on the narrow specialist area he's interested in, and he tends to brush aside everything that doesn't belong to it.

For those of you who are more scientifically-minded, perhaps we can put it in a more scientific way. Here goes then: the term memory means the mental processes whereby past experience is recalled to present consciousness. It depends very largely on the depth of impression made by the original event, experience or fact, and on the strength of the associations surrounding it. Feebleness of impression and association leads to obliviscence (how's that for scientific jargon?), in other words, to forgetting. In fact the particular problem or subject with which our absent-minded professor is concerned has made a deep impression on him—and the associations attending it are sufficiently strong for his purpose—though of course he would probably be more socially acceptable if he took more trouble over matters that lay outside his specialist interest. As for a professional Memory Man, he makes sure that the sort of things he wants to recall for his stage act—the dates and scores of football matches, for instance—enter deeply into his memory by dint of arduous training, and he works very hard with an artificially devised network of associations in order to bring back the facts and figures he needs. All systems of memory training are based on these two special conditions—depth of impression, and strength of associations. Ideally, of course, what is required is (to quote from a scientific treatise): "controlled selective recall of important points in the service of thought"—in other words, remembering what you want to remember when you want to remember it!

There are various factors, though, which can affect memory. We tend, for instance, to repress things we don't want to remember—things that would make us miserable if we did remember them, or which would simply bore us to tears (perhaps this applies to the absent-minded professor). Some psychologists, indeed, think that repression is the explanation of all forgetting—they argue that all experiences (and these may involve facts and figures) which are painful for some reason, or which are in conflict with the accepted standards of society (or with those which the individual has set up for himself) are repressed into the unconscious, and are thus cut off from the associations of conscious memory. There's no doubt that this is often the case; but fatigue, illness, drugs, brain damage, and the natural ageing of the brain also affect memory. In other words, memory is both a physiological and a psychological process.

As a matter of fact, scientists distinguish between two aspects of the term memory. Strictly speaking, they say, it applies first to the individual's recall of his own life-story, to the purely personal happenings in it—and always in a whole context of the original emotion, atmosphere and so on. For example, when you say "I remember the first time I fell in love", you almost certainly remember everything connected with it—how you felt, what you did, what the other person felt and did, where and how it happened, what you and the other person were wearing, what the weather was like, and so on and so on. The second aspect of memory (what the

scientists regard as a looser use of the term) is the recall of knowledge—acquired, it's true, through past experiences, but not necessarily as part of the individual life-story. This kind of memory is entirely impersonal; it concerns items of knowledge that are not set in personal experience. For instance, if you remember how to fix a light-fuse you don't necessarily remember too the first time you did it nor all the circumstances surrounding that occasion. Some people, of course, are better at the first kind of memory—an old person will often be able to recall the past in astonishing detail, but may have forgotten the name of the next-door neighbour.

Scientifically speaking, memory isn't the same as retentiveness; it is based on it, but it's a much more specialized characteristic of mental life. Retentiveness (in the scientific sense) is the retention and continuation of certain features. If, for instance, you were frightened half out of your wits by a savage dog when you were still in your pram, you would probably retain a fear of dogs all your life—although the actual childhood episode that caused the fear had been completely forgotten. In retentiveness, the past is merely carried into the present, and then loses itself in adding to the present. In memory, on the other hand, the past is known either directly for what it was or indirectly by the contribution it has made to the sum of human knowledge. All living organisms show retentiveness—if, for instance, a leaf-bud is bruised, then the leaf itself will show signs of damage when it opens out. But evidence of memory is only found among the higher animals. Some scientists maintain, in fact, that the reproduction of past experience may only be possible for the highly organized and complex nervous system of man (though some of the recent experiments with dolphins, for instance, must have shaken them in this rather sweeping assertion).

But to return to the more general concept of memory; there are, of course, several categories, corresponding to the five senses—that is, you can remember past touch, taste, smell, sound, or sight—or a combination of all of them. It is visual memory, though, that's best for the self-administered tests that follow.

✛✛✛✛✛✛✛✛✛✛✛✛✛

TEST A

Instructions: Have paper and pencil ready. Study the following words for exactly two minutes, writing them down on a scrap of paper if you think this will help you to remember them. Then close the book, throw your notes away, and see how many words (the order doesn't matter) you can then write down.

SCORING AND COMMENTS

Remembering:

20-24 = a very good memory indeed

16-20 = good memory

12-16 = memory is fair

8-12 = not a very good memory

Anything under 8 would probably confirm what you know already—that you have a pretty bad memory!

TEST B

Instructions: Have paper and pencil ready. Examine the diagrams on the black space below for exactly two minutes. Then close the book and see how many of the diagrams you can reproduce (the order doesn't matter) on a blank piece of paper.

SCORING AND COMMENTS

Re-drawing:

12-14 = a very good memory

10-12 = good memory

6-10 = memory if fair

4-6 = not a very good memory

Under 4 would suggest that you have a bad memory!

TWO GAMES WHICH ARE FUN TO PLAY, AND WHICH SHOULD HELP YOU TO IMPROVE YOUR MEMORY AT THE SAME TIME

I. THE CHINESE MEMORY GAME

The ideal number for playing this game is three, though it can in fact be played by any number   or you can play it by yourself. All you need is an ordinary pack of cards (two packs if more than six people are playing) and a largish clear space on the floor or a table.

Scatter the fifty-two cards face downwards and not overlapping each other at all. The object of the game is very simple: to pair up cards which are turned up, memorized and turned down again by each player in turn. It's a bit more difficult than it sounds!

This is how you play. The first player turns up two cards at random, leaving them face up for everyone to see for five seconds, then turns them down again exactly where they were. Everyone, including the player, tries to remember what the cards were and where they are. Each player in turn does the same thing   until sooner or later one player will remember the position of, say, two kings. These will be turned up by that player when his turn comes (and if no one gets them before that), paired, and kept by the player in question. Many times you will find you think you remember exactly where two particular twin cards are only to discover, when you turn them over triumphantly, that you've got one of them wrong. It's all the more annoying when the player following you profits by your mistake, and gets the pair you were after! On making a pair, a player has a second turn. The turning up and pairing continues until all the cards are paired. The player with the largest number of pairs to his credit is obviously the winner - and the person with the best memory!

After playing this game for some time you'll probably find yourself getting much quicker at remembering visually exactly where the relevant cards are to make up the pairs. If not, practise on your own. It is a really useful way of helping to improve your visual memory.

Quite by the way, we must say that—apropos the absent-minded professor and his specialist memory—we have a friend, an English literature specialist, who can out-quote anyone on Shakespeare, but who is absolutely hopeless at this game and never scores more than two pairs—and one of them will probably be sheer chance! So much for the motivation we were writing about earlier.

2. THE MEMORY TRAY

This is a good game for children and adults alike. Someone not taking part in the game lays out on a large tray a selection of widely different objects—anything from an alarm clock to a pair of shoe-laces. The tray is covered over with a cloth. When everyone playing has paper and pencil ready, the tray is uncovered for one minute, and the players examine and try to memorize the objects. The tray is then covered again, and the players are given five minutes to write down as many of the objects as they can remember. The player with the largest number of correct objects listed is obviously the winner.

The game can be made easy—or more difficult. If only very young children are playing, the objects should be fewer and quite big—a doll, a toy engine, an apple, etc. If, however, only adults are playing, then not only should there be many more objects and some of them very small, but additional details can also be asked for—if a book is one of the objects on the tray, for instance, those who can remember the title and the author get bonus points.

This can also be played as a team game. Each of two teams take it in turns to make up a tray, trying of course to get as unlikely a collection of objects as they can—not forgetting that ordinary things are often harder to remember than something really weird and wonderful. The individual scores of the players in a team are added together and the team with the biggest total is the winner.

Another variation is for each team to work as a team instead of as a collection of individuals. Those with better powers of observation and better memories help those who aren't so good—and the score is a team score, instead of a total of separate scores. It can also be a mini-personality test in communal activity!

Now here is another rather unusual way of cultivating your memory.

THE HOUSE OF MEMORY

This is great fun to try out. It's derived from the system of topical mnemonics which was used by the—you've guessed it—Ancient Greeks and Romans. What you do is to build a house in your imagination, with many rooms and having several floors. To each room you assign a particular subject, with a symbol attached. For instance, you might make one room your workshop and label it with a hammer; another the bathroom with a symbolic piece of soap, and so on. Each room should contain various pieces of furniture or equipment—the workshop would have a work-bench with various tools on it, and shelves with the sort of things you would use in your workshop; the bathroom would have a mirrored cupboard, basin, bath, bath mat, etc. The number of objects in each room (and, in fact, the number of rooms too) would correspond to the sub-divisions you make in your own mind for the particular subject or activity represented. The idea behind this method: when you are trying to remember something, you must visualise your imaginary house, and then move from room to room—and when you get to the room with which the forgotten item is associated, your memory will begin to nag at you (if only by making you sure that that's where you've got to look). The thing you are trying to remember may then pop up in your mind; but if it doesn't, you go on into the imaginary room and start looking round. Say you're in your bathroom and you're sure it's something there you're trying to recall; you

start looking round, basin—no; towels—no; soap—no; talc—no; you look in the mirrored cupboard—aspirins—no; cream—no; toothbrush—no; toothpaste—toothpaste! That's it—you were trying to remember to put toothpaste on the shopping list. Well, that's the theory of it, anyway, and it's certainly worth trying.

We've only given the gist of the system, anyway. You can introduce all kinds of elaborations if you feel inclined. The Greeks and Romans were very complicated—they didn't just imagine one house divided up in this way, they went the whole hog and had a town divided into a certain number of districts, each with ten houses. Each of these houses had ten rooms, and each of the rooms was divided into a hundred squares or memory places, some of them on the floor, some on the walls, and some on the ceiling. It sounds impossible, but apparently it worked very well indeed for them, and they were able to skip through their imaginary towns and into their imaginary houses and find whatever they were trying to remember from one minute to the next.

Anyway, for what it's worth, the system survived for hundreds of years after the Romans had disappeared from the historical scene. And before we leave the subject, here is a rather more serious example of the way it might work, Roman style. Say you wanted to fix the date of the invention of printing—A.D. 1436—in your memory. You would go to the first house in the first district of your imaginary town—and that would get the figure 1 into your head. Then you'd go to the fourth room—to fix the figure 4. Then in the thirty-sixth square or memory place in that room you would put some symbol of printing—an open book, for instance. And so, hopefully, you would have embedded the date 1436 in your memory for ever. When you wanted to recall the date, you'd work the other way round—starting with the symbol of the open book (because it's easier to visualise a small specific picture) and then work back to the rest of the figures of the date from there. Try out the more elaborate system for yourself—making use of a drawing in the first instance. You could begin with just the house and then go on later to

construct the imaginary town to which it belongs. It can be great fun, and will very likely improve your memory as well, though you may find it a bit tiring to begin with!

OBSERVATION TEST

A good memory is usually closely linked with good powers of observation. We want you to examine the following picture for two minutes exactly. Then cover it up completely and do the observation and memory exercises relating to it which come after it. Don't look at the picture again until you have done all the exercises.

The first two exercises are just for limbering up.

EXERCISE A

Write down, as quickly as possible, eight different objects you noticed in the picture.

EXERCISE B

Now write down five objects or details relating to men: five relating to women: and five relating to children.

Now here comes the really difficult test.

EXERCISE C

Answer the following questions about the picture. (Warning: not all of the questions necessarily relate to the picture. Some are meant to catch you out).

1. How many uniformed people did you see?
2. What are their jobs?
3. Who is (or are) sitting in the left-hand seat?
4. Describe what the person or persons sitting there are wearing, and what luggage or personal possessions are present.
5. Describe what the person or persons sitting there are doing.
6. How many people are sitting on the middle seat? Describe them.
7. How many air lines feature in the picture—and what are they?
8. How many queues are there in the picture—where are they—and how are they made up?
9. Are there any children's toys in the picture? If so, how many, and what are they?
10. Are there any musical instruments in the picture? If so, how many, and what are they?
11. Are there any pieces of sporting equipment in the picture? If so, how many, and what are they?
12. Are there any newspapers or magazines shown in the picture? If so, how many, and what are they?
13. Are any books shown in the picture? If so, how many—and what are their titles?
14. How many of the men in the picture are wearing hats? How many are wearing top coats? Describe them, and say where they are.
15. How many of the women in the picture are wearing hats—and how many are wearing coats? Describe them, and say where they are.
16. Are any of the toys shown in the picture connected with transport? If so, describe them.

17. Do the skins of animals figure in any of the women's coats? If so, describe them.
18. Is there any evidence in the picture of close personal contact between any of the passengers? If so, what is it, and who are involved?
19. Is there a book stall in the picture?
20. Are there any non-white people in the picture? If so, describe them.
21. Are any of the men bearded? If so, describe them.

SCORING AND COMMENTS

As A and B were limbering up exercises, they didn't stretch you very far, and you shouldn't congratulate yourself too heartily if you did well at them! Probably you should have got all the answers right, if you pride yourself on having a good memory, and a quick eye. If you only wrote down four (or less) different objects for A, and a total of five or less (out of a possible ten) for B, it was probably an ominous pointer to your showing on Exercise C!

This is obviously a much more exacting test of your powers of observation and memory. As some of the questions involve a number of details, and some of them are false leads, you should work out the score like this: each answer must be correct to score a point.

1. Two uniformed people: 1 point.
2. One pilot, and one stewardess: 1 point.
3. One elderly lady: 1 point.
4. The elderly lady is wearing:
    a check coat: 1 point.
    a hat with a feather: 1 point.
    she has an umbrella: 1 point.
    she has a customs shop bag: 1 point.
      it contains a bottle of whisky: 1 point.
      and a carton of cigarettes: 1 point.
      Bonus for number of cigarettes (100): 1 point.
Possible total: 7 points.

5. The elderly lady is reading a book: 1 point.
   Bonus for correct title *YOU!*:   1 point.
                                Possible total: 2 points.

6. Three people: 1 point.
   one woman: 1 point.
   one man smoking a pipe: 1 point.
   an Indian wearing a turban: 1 point.
                                Possible total: 4 points.

7. Two air lines: 1 point.
   They are: Air France   1 point.
             and Lufthansa   1 point.
                                Possible total: 3 points.

8. Two queues: 1 point.
   one at Air France counter: 1 point.
     consisting of three men: 1 point.
                    three women: 1 point.
                    two children: 1 point.
   other queue at Lufthansa counter: 1 point.
     consisting of two men: 1 point.
                    one woman passenger: 1 point.
                    one stewardess: 1 point.
                                Possible total: 9 points.

9. Yes—one: 1 point.
   a toy petrol tanker: 1 point.
                                Possible total: 2 points.

10. Yes: 1 point.
    a violin: 1 point.
    and a guitar: 1 point.
                                Possible total: 3 points.

11. No: 1 point.
    But deduct one point for every item
    mentioned which isn't there!

12. No: 1 point.
    Deduct one point for every object
    mentioned which isn't there!

13. Yes: 1 point.
    Five books: 1 point.
    Bonus for spotting *YOU!*   1 point.
                                Possible total: 3 points.

14. Four men wearing hats (including one turban): 1 point.

   The pilot: 1 point.

   The Indian's turban: 1 point.

   Man at Air France counter wearing a trilby: 1 point.

   Man at Lufthansa counter wearing a
      peaked cap: 1 point.

  Two men wearing top coats: 1 point.

   One of them at Air France counter: 1 point.

   The other at Lufthansa counter: 1 point.

                   Possible total: 8 points.

15. Four women are wearing hats: 1 point.

   Stewardess wearing uniform cap talking
      to pilot: 1 point.

   Woman with beret type hat at Air
      France counter: 2 points.

   Another woman at Lufthansa counter: 2 points.

   Elderly lady, wearing hat with feather: 2 points.

  Three women wearing coats: 1 point.

   Elderly lady: 1 point.

   Woman with dark coat at Air France
      counter: 1 point.

   Woman with leopard skin coat at
      Lufthansa counter: 1 point.

                   Possible total: 12 points.

16. Yes—the little boy is playing with a
   petrol tanker: 1 point.

17. Yes, one of the women is wearing a leopard
   skin coat: 1 point.

18. Yes, man and woman on middle seat: 1 point.

   The woman has her arm through the man's: 1 point.

                   Possible total: 2 points.

19. Yes (you can see a bit of it near the
   elderly lady):   1 point.

20. Yes—one Indian: 1 point.

   He is wearing a turban and is bearded: 2 points.

   He is sitting on the middle seat: 1 point.

                   Possible total: 3 points.

21. Two men are bearded: 1 point.
    One of the musicians (in addition to the
        Indian): 1 point.

Possible total: 2 points.

Possible grand total: 69 points.

SCORING AND COMMENTS

65 points or over—your powers of observation and recall are remarkably good.

60 to 65:	very good indeed.
55 to 60:	very good.
45 to 55:	good.
35 to 45:	fairly good.
25 to 35:	fair.
15 to 25:	weak.
Under 15:	very weak.
Under 5:	very weak indeed!

❖❖❖❖❖❖❖❖❖❖❖❖

There are, of course, a good many more exercises, tricks and devices for sharpening the memory, and you may have already worked out some for yourselves. In any case, though, don't forget to give these a try!

CHAPTER TEN

YOUR PERSONALITY

CHAPTER TEN

YOUR PERSONALITY

The title of this chapter is much too grand, and you mustn't take it too seriously. Your personality, whoever you are, is rich and varied and complex, and to assess it at all satisfactorily would demand a whole range of scientifically devised questionnaires, closely related according to a carefully co-ordinated plan, and scored with reference to a series of complicated scientific scales. Each of these questionnaires, in order to meet the proper scientific requirements, would be too long for a single chapter in a book like this. In fact it would be easy to devote a whole volume to each aspect of your personality, and even then, so mysterious is the human psyche, it might only touch the fringes and would certainly not offer the more or less precise and objective kind of measurement that can be applied (within the limitations we've already indicated) to your intelligence or to such measurable aptitudes as a good head for figures.

To a large extent, then, this chapter is primarily for entertainment. But provided you don't jump to too many conclusions about yourself after doing the questionnaires or try to make drastic changes in your personal life as a result of them, your answers may help you to understand yourself better and perhaps even to modify certain aspects of your behaviour in ways that will be more fulfilling for yourself and for others. There are scientists, of course, who assert that it's all in our genes and that there's little if anything we can do to modify our inherited characteristics. And there are others who argue that it's all a matter of environment—that we are conditioned by our early circumstances, upbringing and so on. There are some, though, who accept the existence and influence of both hereditary and environmental factors without robbing the individual of some freedom of choice and some power to change the direction of his life. We believe strongly that change is *always* possible, at any age and in any circumstances. The results of psychoanalysis and of religious experience both provide ample justification for such a belief, and so, very likely, does your own life story.

The first questionnaire, in fact, is designed to show you whether you take a pessimistic or an optimistic view of life. As with most questionnaires it impinges on other qualities as well, such as sociability, shyness, self-confidence and so on and you will find that some of the questions crop up again, in slightly different forms, in some of the other tests.

QUESTIONNAIRE A

Answer YES or NO. Try and be as honest as you can in your answers (after all if you aren't you'll only be cheating yourself!).

Do you:

1. consider that you generally suffer from poor health?
2. have a poor appetite?
3. suffer from a feeling of physical inferiority?
4. sleep badly?
5. have disagreeable dreams?
6. suffer from mysterious aches and pains?
7. have frequent spells of dizziness?
8. suffer from nervousness?
9. suffer from persistent headaches?
10. experience a persistent feeling of tiredness?
11. worry a great deal?
12. frequently feel irritable?
13. experience a strong sense of loneliness?
14. frequently feel bored?
15. feel you have no real friends?
16. suffer from extreme shyness?
17. suffer from lack of self-confidence?
18. frequently find your mind wandering?
19. suffer from all kinds of foolish fears?
20. experience frequent spells of guilt or remorse?
21. hate being criticised?
22. feel you are frequently being humiliated?
23. feel that you are continually being misunderstood?

24. feel that you always have bad luck?
25. frequently complain of unfair treatment?
26. feel that your life has been one long failure?
27. have a sharp sense of the insecurity of life?
28. feel that life is on the whole a futile business?
29. torment yourself continually over all the wickedness that exists in the world?
30. find that you take little pleasure in life?
31. feel that no-one can really be trusted?
32. usually feel depressed when you wake up in the morning?
33. often feel that you don't really care what happens to you?
34. often feel miserable for no real reason?
35. get unduly bothered by noise?
36. often think that people don't really care what happens to you?
37. feel that the world's in such a mess that it would be unfair to bring a child into it?
38. often get the feeling that you are somehow outside it all?

❖❖❖❖❖❖❖❖❖❖❖❖❖

SCORING AND ASSESSMENT
QUESTIONNAIRE A

Well, there are some very obvious questions there! The conclusions are pretty obvious too. If you had to answer YES to all those questions you really would be an out and out pessimist—or at any rate you'd be in a truly black mood when you answered them. If you answered NO to all of them, on the other hand, you're probably one of those sunny individuals it's a real pleasure to know. The odds are, though, that your score falls somewhere between the two extremes. A reasonable scale would probably be as follows: Answered NO:

35 and above—very optimistic indeed, with a markedly positive and trusting attitude towards life.

30-35	—very optimistic.
25-30	—still decidedly optimistic.
18-25	—still predominantly optimistic.
13-18	—certainly on the pessimistic side, but not seriously so.
9-13	—definitely pessimistic.
5- 9	—very pessimistic.
Under 5	—seriously pessimistic.

The bother with that kind of questionnaire, of course, is that the qualities it tests are so broad. It's rather like a rake with widely separated prongs—it drags in all kinds of other material as well as its main objectives. The next questionnaire, though, is a little finer-toothed (though you'll find that there's some overlap of questions from the one you've just done).

❖❖❖❖❖❖❖❖❖❖❖❖❖

QUESTIONNAIRE B. NOW ANXIOUS ARE YOU?
Answer YES or NO

Do you:
1. often have unaccountable dizzy turns?
2. get sudden racing sensations in your heart, even though you know it's sound?
3. Are you often quite suddenly short of breath, even if you haven't been exerting yourself?
4. Do you tend to break out into a sweat even if you haven't been taking exercise, and when in good health?
5. Do you tend to wake up after a bad dream soaked in sweat?
6. Are you rather prone to attacks of diarrhoea and other stomach upsets, although in quite good health?

Do you:
7. suffer a lot from headaches?
8. sleep badly?
9. get in a panic if you sleep badly?
10. often wake up in the middle of the night worrying over some problem?

11. worry a great deal about your health?
12. Are you away from work a great deal because of your health?
13. Do you quite often take tranquillisers?
14. Do you sometimes stutter or stammer?
15. If you are having a row with somebody do you find your body and voice trembling almost uncontrollably?
16. Are you more prone than most people to little accidents and mishaps?

Do you:

17. worry a great deal about money, even when there's no real need?
18. worry a great deal when you are about to buy some expensive item, whether you can afford it or not?
19. tend to take articles back to the shop because you think they are sub-standard?
20. get into more of a state than most people you know when you have to appear in public in some capacity?
21. worry a great deal about the future?
22. find that when one worry has been removed another always takes its place?
23. Are you subject to sudden, inexplicable saggings of the spirit?
24. Are you painfully shy?
25. Do you get frightened on lifts, tube-trains, in tunnels, or on aircraft?
26. Do you feel apprehensive when the telephone rings or when you hear the postman arriving?
27. Are you nervous, for no reason, in the presence of policemen, bank managers, and persons in authority?
28. Do you often feel unaccountably anxious at the cinema or theatre?
29. If you are watching a very exciting film, play or television programme do you need to pass water a great deal?
30. Do you sometimes feel that you cannot possibly cope with your difficulties?
31. When you were a child were you unusually afraid of

the dark?

32. Do you frequently (and for no real reason) get a feeling that there is something important which you have neglected to see to?

33. Do you worry over little things almost as much as over big ones?

34. When you are sitting or lying down, do you find it very difficult to relax?

35. If you make some social blunder, do you go on brooding over it for weeks after?

36. If someone appears unexpectedly do you tend to jump out of your skin?

Do you:

37. panic if some small hitch occurs in your plans?

38. go to pieces in an emergency?

39. get tense over quite small problems?

40. lie awake worrying at nights?

41. tend to wake up convinced that the house is on fire, or that a burglar has broken in?

❖❖❖❖❖❖❖❖❖❖❖❖❖

SCORING AND ASSESSMENT
QUESTIONNAIRE B

It's obvious enough that YES answers score on the side of anxiety, and NO answers point to lack of it. The following would probably be a reasonable assessment:

YES Answers

30-35 —You are a very anxious and nervous person indeed.

25-30 —You are a decidedly anxious person.

20-25 —You are quite an anxious person.

15-20 —You tend to be an anxious person, but not unduly so.

10-15 —You don't often suffer from anxiety.

5-10 —You are enviably free from anxiety.

Under 5 —You are quite remarkably free from anxiety!

That questionnaire should give you strong indications as to whether you suffer from anxiety or not. But like most such questionnaires it can only take you so far. It doesn't show you, for example, what you do with your anxiety if you are a victim of it. The anxious person (like anybody else with a handicap) can cope with his or her anxieties with courage and determination—or without them. If, for instance, you had to answer YES to the majority of the questions above, but were nevertheless able honestly to put a NO against number 12 ("Are you away from work a great deal because of your health?) and number 38 ("Do you go to pieces in an emergency?"), and if in addition you found yourself answering YES to some of the questions but adding such mental reservations as "I do worry if some small hitch occurs in my plans—but I carry on just the same", then the likelihood is that you are refusing to give in to your anxieties and that you would be justified in adding courage among your personal qualities. It must be added, though, that the very anxious person rarely lacks this quality, and the excessive anxiety is often the result of over-conscientiousness and the setting of impossibly high standards of attainment. If you had to put YES to nearly all the questions, though, it may be that you need specialist help.

If the first two questionnaires have suggested to you that you are both optimistic and comparatively free from anxiety, you may still want to know how much confidence you have in yourself. Here is a questionnaire which may help you to decide.

❖❖❖❖❖❖❖❖❖❖❖❖

QUESTIONNAIRE C
HOW SELF-CONFIDENT ARE YOU?
Answer YES or NO

Do you:
1. often feel that your job is too demanding?
2. often wish that your colleagues would give you more encouragement?

3. worry a lot about whether or not other people like you?
4. Are you often worried about making a fool of yourself?

Do you:

5. spend a lot of effort trying to get approval from other people?
6. often worry that people will misjudge you?
7. feel strongly that you lack someone with whom you can discuss personal matters.
8. feel that people·expect too much of you?
9. Are you easily embarrassed?

Do you:

10. sometimes feel insecure in your surroundings?
11. feel uncomfortable when you enter a room with several people already there?
12. worry that people may be talking about you behind your back?
13. keep looking at yourself in a mirror?
14. feel you are a bad mixer?
15. hesitate to join in conversation?
16. Have you got the feeling that you can't do things as well as other people?
17. Are you dissatisfied with your achievements to date?
18. Do you feel dejected if you are asked to tackle an unfamiliar task?
19. Do you often wish you were in somebody else's skin?
20. Will you go to great lengths to avoid having to make a speech?
21. Are there a lot of things about yourself you wish you could change?
22. Do you think you are unpopular with other people?
23. Do you lack confidence in the decisions you have taken?
24. Are you envious of the success of others?
25. Do any of your relations make you feel you are not good enough for them?
26. Are you generally disappointed in photographs of yourself and feel they don't do you justice?
27. Do you get a shock of disappointment if you hear a recording of your voice?

28. Do you very much resent criticism?
29. When people pay you compliments, do you tend to suspect their sincerity?
30. Do you tend to think that other people will let you down?
31. Do you sometimes keep your opinions to yourself because you are afraid that people might scoff at them?
32. Are you dissatisfied with your appearance and your dress sense?
33. Do you feel you have to introduce your achievements and qualifications into a conversation with strangers?
34. Do you rely a great deal on club ties, college crests and other insignia of status?
35. Are you doubtful about your attractiveness to the opposite sex?

SCORING AND ASSESSMENT
QUESTIONNAIRE C

You will of course have spotted that it is the NO answers which point to self-confidence. Generally speaking the following scale would be reasonable:

NO Answers

30-35   —You have very considerable confidence in yourself and your abilities. You are very rarely troubled by feelings of under-achievement or personal unworthiness. You take it for granted that most people will like you. You don't find it in the least necessary to be suspicious of other peoples' opinions of you. Without being vain or conceited you approve of yourself quite a lot.

20-30   —You have strong self-confidence. The moments of doubt or disappointment in yourself, although you do have them, don't affect the forward-moving currents of your life. You are probably more modest about your achievements than the top scorers.

15-20   —You are only reasonably self-confident, and have quite strong moments of self-doubt.

10-15   —You are decidedly lacking in self-confidence. You are more likely to assume that your plans will fail than succeed. You have a poor opinion of yourself, and jump to the conclusions that other people don't like you, and that you are a rather unattractive person.

Under 10 —Your valuation of yourself is so low that it can be said that you are a typical victim of an inferiority complex.

A healthy self-confidence is one thing, an over-assertive, aggressive, and domineering personality quite another. The following questionnaire may help you to spot whether you have tendencies in this direction—and perhaps help you to correct them!

QUESTIONNAIRE D
ARE YOU INCLINED TO BE OVER-ASSERTIVE, AGGRESSIVE AND DOMINEERING?
Answer YES or NO (Adults only)

1. Are you nearly always the one to start an argument in your marriage or among your friends?
2. If you overhear strangers arguing do you usually wade in?
3. Do you approach an argument as if it were a fight to be won at all costs?
4. If an argument is going against you, do you tend to get angry?
5. Are you ready, in order to win an argument, to introduce facts and figures you know to be dubious?
6. Do you go on insisting on your opinion, even when other people are tired of the argument?
7. Do you prefer the hard-hitting kind of debate to the more carefully reasoned one?
8. When you are outmanoeuvred in an argument, do you tend to react strongly—for example, by going red in the face, shouting, leaving the room, or bursting into tears?

9. Do you find it difficult to suffer fools gladly?

10. When you are in your car do you tend to be always on the look-out for misdemeanours or mistakes by other drivers?

11. If you think someone has done you a bad turn do you immediately think of ways of paying him back?

12. If you disapprove of the behaviour of a friend would you immediately tell him so?

13. If someone is rude to you do you flare up at once without pausing to see if perhaps you were mistaken?

14. Do you tend to be "agin the government", whatever kind it may be?

15. Do you tend to think that your political opponents are always wrong, deluded or dishonest?

16. If someone is smoking near you, and you yourself are a non-smoker, do you immediately ask them to stop?

17. If someone gets in front of you in a queue do you tell him to get back sharply rather than politely?

18. If you were in a cinema or theatre with plenty of vacant seats, and someone sat in front of you who obscured your view would you tell him to move rather than move yourself?

19. If you are sold sub-standard goods, do you always complain?

20. If you are poorly served in a restaurant, do you always complain?

21. If you found a burglar in your house and you had a gun, would you shoot first and think about the consequences afterwards?

22. Do you regularly find something in the newspapers to make you angry?

23. Do you believe that it is always necessary to fight for your rights?

24. Do you find it difficult to forgive people who have let you down?

25. Are you usually the one to make the decisions?

26. If you are serving on some committee, do you expect to be elected to one of the jobs on it?

27. Do you prefer giving orders to taking them?

28. When you enter a lecture-room, do you find yourself automatically making for the front seats?

29. Do you get rid of persistent salesmen quickly?

30. Do you tend to be impatient of such notices as *Keep off the Grass, Trespassers will be Prosecuted*, etc.?

31. Do you tend to be on the offensive with people in authority?

32. Do you tend to agree with the idea of every man for himself?

33. Are you good at bluffing your way out of tight corners?

34. Can you usually think up a good excuse if circumstances demand it?

35. When you play games are you more concerned about winning than setting an example of sportsmanship?

36. Do you prefer violent, physical games to the more skilful but less energetic ones?

37. When you are playing tennis, do you tend to go in for hard drives rather than the more delicate strokes?

38. Do you get a kick out of playing games like squash in which you can belt the ball with all your might?

39. Do you like watching the more violent television programmes?

40. Do you regularly watch the wrestling bouts on television?

41. Do you feel disappointed if during a football match you are watching there isn't a punch-up of some kind?

42. If you had the chance, would you like to watch an execution?

43. Have you ever genuinely felt you would like to really kill somebody?

44. Do you find it extremely difficult to understand the point of view of the genuine pacifist?

45. Do you sometimes pick a fight with someone who has greatly annoyed you, or at least feel strongly tempted to do so?

46. If you encounter someone who is rather obstreperous do you gleefully accept an opportunity to take him

down a peg or two?

47. Do you ever grind your teeth, either consciously or without realising it?

48. Do you sometimes get so angry with someone else that you shout or swear?

49. Do you ever get into such a paddy that you throw things about?

50. Do you often emphasise the points you are making by banging your fist in your hand or on the table?

This is a longer questionnaire than the others, because in order to bring out the tendency towards over-assertiveness and aggressiveness, it's useful to have a kind of build-up by way of questions which bear on *much milder* manifestations of these qualities—because of course a measure of self-assertiveness is healthy and necessary.

❖❖❖❖❖❖❖❖❖❖❖❖

SCORING AND ASSESSMENT
QUESTIONNAIRE D

It is of course the YES answers which point to the over-assertive, aggressive and domineering characteristics.

YES Answers

50-40   —YES answers would probably suggest that you do possess these characteristics to an uncomfortable degree—uncomfortable at any rate for those around you! You would certainly need to think hard about ways in which you might modify your behaviour.

40-30   —Would still suggest that you are decidedly bossy!

30-25   —Would probably indicate that you are bossy, but pretty well aware of it, and that you make efforts to correct the tendency.

25-30   —Would probably argue that you have a strong, self-assertive character, with marked flashes of bossiness, but not to any extreme degree. It's likely that you would be unpopular with some people who resent your slightly authoritarian tendencies, but respected by many others for your strength of character and qualities of leadership.

20-15 — Would probably still indicate forcefulness of character and a healthy desire and ability to register your beliefs and opinions.

15-10 — Would probably suggest that while you are rightly aware of your own value, you tend to be uncertain of yourself, mild in manner and rather too inclined to dodge trouble or argument whenever you can.

Under 10 — Would probably suggest that you tend to subscribe too easily to the doctrine of "anything for a quiet life" — though even a few YESES probably indicate that you have within you the seeds of self-assertion, and perhaps that you could suddenly prove that you are the worm that turns!

❖❖❖❖❖❖❖❖❖❖❖❖

You are no more likely to get the best out of life if you are terrified of its possible risks and dangers than if you are foolishly rash. Here is a questionnaire that may help you to decide whether you veer too much in one or other of these directions, or whether you strike a happy mean between them.

QUESTIONNAIRE E: HOW CAUTIOUS ARE YOU?
Answer YES or NO.

1. If something exciting were happening outside your house in cold weather, would you dash outside without stopping to put on something warm?
2. Do you forget to go to the doctor for a health check?
3. Do you shrug off worries about your financial situation?
4. Do you easily ignore an outstanding debt?
5. Would you choose a job involving variety, travel, etc. — but not a great deal of security — in preference to an absolutely secure stay-put one?

6. Would you take a job that really interested you even though it didn't have a pension scheme?

7. Can you envisage any circumstances in which you might give up a secure and pensionable job?

8. Do you spend surplus money when you have it rather than saving it?

9. Would you ever contemplate giving up your present job before you were quite certain that you had a new one to go to?

10. Do you think you are spending too much money on your insurances?

11. If you had a good chance (say 70:30) of making a lot of money on the Stock Exchange would you sell or greatly increase the mortgage on your house in order to raise the necessary sum, to play the market?

12. Have you ever bought shares in a new enterprise that hadn't yet proved itself?

13. Do you ever gamble on horses, dogs, results of general elections and so on?

14. Do you enjoy a card game more if you are playing for money?

15. Would a life without any risks be too dull for you?

16. Do you always lock up your house at night and when you go out?

17. Do you neglect to read through the guarantee when you are buying something?

18. Are you rather slack about reading the small print on contracts?

Do you:

19. tend to catch trains, etc., by the skin of your teeth?

20. tend to be late for appointments?

21. tend to prefer playing games with some element of risk, to the quieter kind?

22. cheerfully accept your children taking part in rough games?

23. go for speed-thrill rides when you are at a fair-ground?

24. enjoy fast driving?

25. often neglect to wear a safety-belt when driving a car?

26. disapprove of driving tests?

27. often dash across the road leaving your more careful companions still on the other side?

28. If you went to a new swimming pool would you dive in straight away?

29. When you are swimming in the sea do you ever go out of your depth?

30. Do you enjoy heights?

31. If you were offered a free trip in a glider would you accept?

32. If you were climbing a mountain and had nearly reached the top when you noticed dark clouds gathering, would you nevertheless press on?

33. If you are a car owner, do you only get the essential repairs carried out?

34. Do you consider having a fire-extinguisher in your home an unnecessary luxury?

35. If you were offered a place in an expedition along the Amazon, setting out in a fortnight's time, would you accept?

++++++++++++++

PRELIMINARY EXERCISE

It's pretty obvious that it's the NO answers which point in the direction of caution. But it's obvious too that some of them involve sensible doubts, and others a tendency towards too much timidity. Before looking at the Answer section, *tick* those questions which you think involve sensible doubts, and mark with a *cross* those you feel reflect too much timidity. You don't need to mark all the questions, of course. You will find the suggested correct assessment to this little exercise after the Scoring and Assessment for this questionnaire.

SCORING AND ASSESSMENT
QUESTIONNAIRE E

NO Answers

30-35   —would suggest that you are over-cautious to the point of timidity, and to the detriment of your full enjoyment of life.

25-30   —would also suggest that you are much too cautious in your attitude to life.

15-25   —would probably suggest that you are sensibly cautious where it is necessary, but that you are open to new experiences and have a healthy appetite for adventure.

10-15   —would probably indicate a tendency to be rather too free in taking unnecessary risks.

5-10   —would almost certainly indicate a strong element of rashness in your approach to life.

Under 5 —would almost certainly suggest that you are incautious to the point of foolhardiness!

NOW FOR THE PRELIMINARY EXERCISE

It would be reasonable to tick questions 2, 8, 16, 17, 18, 19 20, 25, 26, 31, 32, 33, 34; and cross questions 1, 3, 4, 5, 7, 15, 21, 22. The questions which have been left unmarked are those which are most likely to involve contradictory considerations or a good deal of controversy.

✦✦✦✦✦✦✦✦✦✦✦✦✦

We all like to think that we get on with other people and that we are popular with them. This does not mean that popularity among a wide range of people is essential to happiness or that you aren't liked if you don't happen to be a great social mixer. After all, it may be much more valuable to be loved or very much liked by a few people than to be popular with a large number and there are some very popular people who don't necessarily attract really deep liking. It doesn't necessarily follow, either, that because you are rather a retiring person who doesn't much like parties and so on you are going to be any less liked by those with whom you do come into contact. *So please bear these points in mind* when you come to do the next questionnaire.

QUESTIONNAIRE F: ARE YOU POPULAR?

1. Do you feel you always have to preserve your dignity?
2. Are you always on your guard in case someone plays a trick on you, and so makes you a laughing stock?
3. Are you concerned that other people might not respect you?

Do you:

4. feel most of the time that you are under scrutiny by others?
5. talk at length about your current interest or latest hobby to all comers?
6. encourage other people to talk about their interests, even if you're not particularly interested?
7. like hearing about other people's jobs?
8. If you hear someone making a mistake over some fact during a conversation do you tend to point it out?
9. When you are asked to join some committee do you usually accept the invitation?
10. If you are voted off some committee do you accept the decision good humouredly?
11. Are you touchy—always tending to suspect insults?
12. If you are on your own (single, divorced, widowed, etc.) do people still often invite you to their parties, etc.?
13. If someone is holding forth in a witty and amusing way, do you tend to try and match his/her witticisms?

Do you:

14. tend to interrupt other people a lot?
15. always try and fit in with the mood of the company?
16. readily make small loans to your friends, when you are in a position to do so?
17. feel it's a good idea to help your friends because a time may come when you need *their* help?

18. Are you annoyed if your good turns to other people aren't appreciated?

Do you:

19. believe that it's better to have others depend on you than for you to depend on others?

20. believe you should always make an effort to be approved of?

21. If you are at a party and someone starts telling a joke which you have already heard, do you tend to stop them?

Do you:

22. tend to persuade your friends to do what you think is best for them, rather than what they really want to do?

23. find that practically everybody you meet has something really interesting about him or her?

24. When you are in company do you tend to ignore those of the opposite sex who don't strike you as physically attractive?

25. Do you nearly always find old people boring?

26. Is it a great nuisance to you to visit a friend when he or she is sick?

Do you:

27. always take your turn at standing rounds of drinks?

28. tend to hesitate when you are asked to contribute to some collection?

29. Do people often come to you with their troubles?

30. Do people younger than yourself often seek your advice?

Do you:

31. enjoy talking to and playing with children?

32. enjoy entertaining other people?

33. rather often cancel appointments with your friends?

34. tend to be late in keeping appointments with your friends?

35. turn to your friends when you want cheering up?

36. tend to play practical jokes on your friends?

37. At a party or social occasion, do you make a point of talking to a lonely stranger?

38. Can you usually let yourself go at a party?

39. When you are introduced to someone at a party and fail to catch their names, do you ask your host or hostess to repeat them?

40. Do you make an effort to remember peoples' names?

41. As a rule do you easily make new friends with members of your own sex?

Do you:

42. quite often make contact by letter or telephone with friends you haven't seen for a long time?

43. try and answer friends' letters as promptly as possible?

44. make a point of congratulating your friends when they have achieved some success?

45. drop your friends because they appear suddenly to have taken against you?

❖❖❖❖❖❖❖❖❖❖❖❖

ANSWERS AND COMMENTS
QUESTIONNAIRE F

1-4 —Should be NO in each case. The spontaneous person, who is open and unguarded, who never stops to think about his dignity, and who can take a joke against himself is of course likely to be popular. Such a person, moreover, is likely to generate his own kind of dignity and to receive respect, largely because he never thinks about it!

5 —should be NO, because you should be quick to stop talking about your latest hobby or craze as soon as you see that glassy look coming into your listener's eyes!

6 —YES is the required answer here; we love being asked about our interests, and if someone listens to us patiently we are bound to feel well disposed towards him.

7 —YES is needed here too—the person who is full of eager and spontaneous curiosity about how other people live and work is usually both likeable and liked.

8   —We hope you said NO! Pointing out peoples'
           mistakes in public will certainly *not* make you
           popular!

9-10   —YES is the answer hoped for. People who are
           willing to help in this way, but who can accept
           rebuff or rejection gracefully and with good
           humour are bound to attract respect and
           admiration.

11   —NO, it's to be hoped. Touchiness is a common,
           but not very endearing trait—though those who
           know you well may be very understanding
           about it!

12   —YES would be a very promising answer. People
           are usually so keen to have couples to their
           gatherings, in order to get the numbers and
           sexes balanced, that they often overlook their
           single friends (as many a divorced or widowed
           person has sadly discovered). If in spite of being
           in this category you do often get invited out, the
           likelihood is that you've got a great deal to
           offer your friends and that they gratefully
           appreciate it.

13-14   —NO. You won't endear yourself to people if you
           try and steal their thunder or interrupt them
           before they've finished what they wanted to say.

15   —NO would probably be the best answer, because
           people want you to be yourself and not just fit
           artificially. Besides, the mood of the company
           may need changing!

16   —A ready YES would certainly help to make you
           popular!

17-18   —NO to both these questions would indicate that
           there's no element of calculation in your atti-
           tude, and it's the person who does a good turn
           spontaneously without thinking whether it's
           appreciated or likely to stand him in good stead
           one day who is, quite naturally, most liked.

19   —YES, that's the best way round, because it would

suggest that you really like helping people. The over-dependent person is often a bore anyway.

20 & 21 —NO to both these questions. Making an effort to be liked seldom succeeds—your response must be spontaneous. As for that old joke—it would obviously be kind to let the narrator finish it—and to summon up a laugh at the end, if you can do it naturally!

22 —NO—you may have good intentions, but this is a sure way of being accused of bossiness! Offering sound advice, and pointing out the pros and cons of a particular course of action is a different matter.

23 —If you can honestly say YES you have the eager, generous interest in other people that makes for great popularity.

24-26 —If you can say NO to these it would suggest that you are considerate and thoughtful—and obviously these are likeable qualities.

27 —YES! There's nothing more likely to make you unpopular than to be always forgetting when it's your turn!

28 —NO, it is to be hoped. Next to getting out of standing your turn for a round of drinks there's nothing more likely to make you unpopular than hanging back when the collection box is going round.

29-32 —A YES to all these questions indicate a generous, giving and truly sympathetic nature. If people come to you for advice it's because they trust you. The face of someone who is really enjoying the company of children is in itself a pointer to a loving, and loveable, nature. To like having people around you in your home is also frequently a sign of warmth and spontaneity (though of course everybody likes to be alone sometimes).

33 & 34 —Hopefully NO. To keep cancelling arrangements

with your friends or to be continually late with your appointments with them is bound to look like lack of real concern for them—especially if you don't come out with the real reasons and offer lame excuses instead!

35   —YES is the required answer, because the capacity to take as well as to give is necessary in any genuine relationship, and your real friends enjoy giving something to you as much as you enjoy giving it to them.

36   —NO would be the better answer. An occasional practical joke may be fun, but to make a habit of it would make you a bore, and would smack of inconsiderations and even a tendency towards cruelty into the bargain.

37-40   —If you can answer YES to all these questions you have staked a considerable claim to genuine popularity. To try and set a stranger at ease is clearly a loving action; to try and make sure of peoples' names shows respect and considerateness—and to be able to enter into the spirit of a party is a great social asset. But remember that the over-persistent 'life and soul of the party' can be an awful bore!

42 & 43   —YES answers would be further indications of true considerateness towards friends.

44   —YES. Generous recognition of and pleasure in a friend's success are obviously endearing characteristics.

45   —Hopefully NO, because liking shouldn't be seriously affected by what the other person does; a reluctance to take offence and a readiness to forgive are obviously desirable qualities.

✦✦✦✦✦✦✦✦✦✦✦✦✦

SCORING AND ASSESSMENT
QUESTIONNAIRE F

40-45. —Correct answers would probably suggest that you are very well liked indeed—popular in the fullest and most genuine sense of the term—and also more than usually adaptable and successful in your social relationships. You would be likely to have a generous and loving nature. In fact you'd be someone we'd very much like to meet!

30-40 —Correct answers would probably have much the same significance, though not perhaps to such an unusual degree.

20-30 —Correct answers would still probably suggest that you are on the whole both liked and genuinely likeable. Perhaps you are subject to occasional moods of irritability towards your fellow-men and women, or are not always unselfish, and perhaps, too, you aren't a great social mixer. But nothing at all to worry about.

10-20 —Correct answers would probably still indicate that you have loving and out-going instincts, but that you don't perhaps always follow them. It may be, too, that you have spells of disliking both your fellow-men—and yourself.

Under 10 —Correct answers would probably indicate that you do not possess many of the qualities that make for popularity and perhaps that you tend to be anti-social in your attitudes. It may also indicate that you don't much like the human race and prefer to keep yourself strictly to yourself. But note that even a very low score would still suggest that you had the potentialities of loving and being loved. Even a single one of these potentialities can bring about a transformation!

In order to be loving and to be loved, one of the qualities we must possess, perhaps above all others, is tolerance. Indeed it could be argued that tolerance is one of the most important aspects of love. Here then is a questionnaire which may help you to see how truly tolerant you are.

QUESTIONNAIRE G: HOW TOLERANT ARE YOU?

Answer YES or NO

1. Is it difficult for you to listen to people who hold different views from your own?

Do you:

2. try to avoid discussion with people who hold such views?
3. think it is asking for trouble to compromise on certain issues with political opponents?
4. find it extremely difficult to be on friendly terms with people who hold opposite views to your own in politics or religion?
5. Are you convinced that under no circumstances would you change the opinions you hold at present?
6. At a General Election do you always decide in advance which way you are going to vote?
7. Do you consider it a complete waste of time to listen to party political broadcasts?
8. Do you think that those who hold religious beliefs are completely deluded?
9. If you belong to a particular form of religion yourself, are you convinced it's the only one that really embodies the truth?
10. Do you tend to scoff at those who claim the existence of paranormal phenomena? (i.e. telepathy, E.S.P., etc.).
11. Are you against equal pay for women?

Do you:

12. feel strongly that women should not be allowed to pilot aircraft?

13. feel strongly that women should not be ordained as priests?

14. believe that the place of all women, under all circumstances, should be in the home?

15. want to see the opposite sex subordinated to your own?

16. reject the idea that your psychological make-up contains components normally associated with the opposite sex?

17. think that homosexuals should not have the same civic rights as other people.

18. believe that other races are inferior to your own?

19. Does it upset you to realize that, if an inhabitant from another planet arrived on earth in order to take back two representative specimens of the human race, he would, on a statistical basis, have to choose a Chinese and an Indian?

20. Do you tend to think that coloured people are intellectually inferior to yourself?

21. Would you be very upset if a coloured family came to live next door to you?

22. If a coloured family did live next door to you, would you be reluctant to get on neighbourly terms with them?

23. If your son or daughter announced an intention to marry someone of a different colour, would you adamantly refuse to accept the idea?

24. Do you believe that early marriages are under all circumstances to be frowned on?

25. If your daughter announced that she was going to have an illegitimate baby, would you be more shocked than if your son announced that he had fathered one?

26. Would you find it very difficult to forgive your daughter if she had an illegitimate baby?

Do you:

27. believe that the relatively new sexual freedom means that people now lack all moral standards?

28. believe that those younger than you are worse than you were at their age?

29. believe that sex outside marriage must, under all cir-

cumstances, be immoral?

30. In interviewing anyone for a job, etc. would you tend to turn down anyone with a hippy-type appearance?

Do you:

31. believe that drop-outs are mainly motivated by laziness?

32. bring pressure on your teenage children to conform to your own standards of dress and appearance?

33. believe that the old ways were always the best?

34. always have very decided ideas as to what is right and wrong?

35. always stick to any decision you have made?

36. seldom question your own moral standards and behaviour?

37. tend to believe that sexual transgressions are always the worst ones?

38. get into a temper if somebody stubbornly refuses to admit that he is wrong?

39. believe that strikers in an industrial dispute are invariably in the wrong?

40. believe that trade unions should be abolished?

41. If you were an employer would you always refuse to employ anyone who had a prison record?

Do you:

42. believe that disobedient children should always be punished.

43. believe that all drug takers should be put in prison?

44. Have you come to the conclusion that all politicians are either dishonest or talk nonsense all the time?

❖❖❖❖❖❖❖❖❖❖❖❖❖

SCORING AND ASSESSMENT
QUESTIONNAIRE G

The YES answers point in the direction of intolerance. But note that some of these questions involve matters on which differences of opinion are natural · and inevitable. For example, you might believe that women oughtn't to become priests, and have some perfectly good, and not necessarily anti-feminist, arguments to advance in support of your opinion. It is the *accumulation* of YES answers that would be significant—and the following scale would probably be fair:

YES Answers

44-40 —would suggest a very intolerant nature indeed, accompanied by great dogmatism, self-righteousness and rigidity of thought.

40-30 —would indicate a high degree of intolerance, with little ability to see other points of view and a dangerously inflexible approach to life, but accompanied perhaps by occasional flashes of insight and an occasional suspicion that you might be wrong.

30-25 —would still indicate large areas of intolerance and narrowness of thought in your nature—but without too much self-righteousness or too absolute a conviction that you are always in the right.

25-20 —would suggest a reasonable balance between your pet ideas and prejudices, and an over-all instinct of self-criticism and tolerance.

20-10 —would probably indicate a very tolerant, understanding and self-aware approach to life, together with the ability to be more conscious of that Biblical beam in your own eye as much as the mote in the other person's.

10-5 —would probably suggest an unusually tolerant and forgiving nature.

Under 5 —would also indicate unusual tolerance, but possibly veering too much in the direction of pliability and permissiveness.

LOVE AND MARRIAGE

Most of the positive qualities touched on in the previous questionnaire are, of course, relevant to a satisfactory relationship between the sexes. It is easy enough to make such generalised pronouncements, but when it comes to the actual sexual relationship it is a very different matter. It would be ridiculous to pretend that any cut and dried or, conclusive *tests* can be applied to something so personal, intimate and complex. Success or failure may depend on all sorts of factors unique to the individual or to the couple concerned. Those factors which would make for success in one case, would make for failure in another. Each sexual pairing to a large extent stands alone. Not one of them is exactly like another.

The most that could be claimed for the questions and answers that follow is that they may provoke you to stop for a moment and think about your own unique love life—and possibly help you to make the kind of adjustments you may think necessary in your own particular and individual case.

The first questionnaire is designed to help you decide whether you have the qualities and attitudes that are likely to make for a happy love relationship.

QUESTIONNAIRE H: ARE YOU LIKELY TO BE A GOOD LOVER?

Examine the following statements and answer TRUE or FALSE.

1. There are some people entirely lacking in sexual attractiveness.
2. Sexual attractiveness is entirely a physical or biological matter.
3. Sexual attractiveness contains the potentialities of true love.

4. Love between members of the opposite sex is impossible without the physical relationship.

5. Sexual attraction is all that is necessary for a satisfactory relationship between the sexes.

6. Friendship between members of the opposite sex is impossible without a physical relationship.

7. In the finest human relationships the physical element is entirely absent.

8. The man should always make the running in the early stages of a relationship with a woman.

9. A man should always play the dominant role in a sexual relationship.

10. Women always mean *Yes* when they say *No*.

11. Women like to be treated with a certain amount of roughness.

12. A man never needs encouragement in sex.

13. Women always admire a very manly man.

14. Unless some physical contact takes place at the first meeting between two people who are mutually attracted, the relationship is not likely to go further.

15. Conversation on serious subjects in the preliminary stages of a relationship is a waste of time.

16. A lot of what the books call fore-play in love-making is a waste of time.

17. Nowadays people are sensible if they go for their sexual pleasures where they can find them.

18. It is ridiculous to suggest that absolute fidelity to one's partner of the moment is necessary.

19. Success in love-making is impossible if both people are inexperienced.

20. Abstinence from sex before marriage is a ridiculous expectation.

21. If a couple have sex before marriage their married life will suffer.

22. All religious teaching on sex is nonsense.

23. Love doesn't enter into it when you get down to the actual business of sex.

24. In an intimate relationship, it is quite natural to find

some parts of the other person's body ugly or disgusting.

25. It is quite natural to find certain aspects of sex disgusting.

26. It is quite natural to object to having certain parts of one's body touched.

27. Mutual orgasm is always essential to a happy sex relationship.

28. It is quite natural in these enlightened days for a couple to accompany each other to a blue movie, a sex orgy, etc.

29. It is quite natural to have hostile feelings towards one's sex partner.

30. One should never tell one's partner the intimate kind of things that give one particular pleasure.

31. In a sexual relationship, the most important quality is tenderness.

32. It is natural for a man to concentrate on his own pleasure in love-making.

33. Your relationship is in danger if, while you are with your partner, you are attracted to someone else.

34. It is best to work out a love-making routine in advance.

35. It is natural for a man to suspect a woman who makes the first advances.

❖❖❖❖❖❖❖❖❖❖❖❖❖

ANSWERS AND COMMENTS
QUESTIONNAIRE H

1. FALSE The mysteries of sexual attraction are endless, and everyone is pleasing to somebody.

2. FALSE Physical and biological factors enter into it, of course—but human beings are complex creatures, and all kinds of cultural, social, and psychological elements play their part and perhaps other more mysterious ones we know little about.

3. TRUE In a normal, mature person it is the next to impossible to experience sexual attraction without at least a flickering of tenderness and some realisation of the possibility of love.

4. FALSE Love in any profound sense of the term does not depend exclusively on sex, though of course it is in sex that it seeks its natural outlet. There are all sorts of circumstances in which sex may not be possible, but in which love may survive as strongly as ever.

5. FALSE It may be all that is necessary for a transitory sex relationship, but for a deeper and more lasting one other elements are needed as well. In real love it is the *whole person* who is valued. Without the realisation of this mutual valuation, and periodic assurances that it does exist, a really satisfactory relationship is impossible.

6. FALSE It frequently happens.

7. FALSE Or almost entirely false. Nearly all human relationships, including those between friends and those between parents and children, contain an awareness of physical presence. That is why some sort of physical contact nearly always takes place—the caresses exchanged between parents and children, for example, or the hand clasping in a friendship between two men, or the kisses exchanged between women friends. If one has a friend of the opposite sex it would be most unusual to be totally unaware of his or her sexual presence. Usually there is some element of mutual attraction, some recognition of the possibilities of a closer relationship if circumstances were different. These elements add a special flavour to the relationship which is usually absent when the friendship is between members of the same sex. *But one of the lessons that experience teaches is that while this element is something to be valued, it is not always necessary to act on it!*

8. FALSE Why should he? Such an expectation implies an outdated belief in male superiority.

9. FALSE In a successful relationship there may be a good deal of interchanging of roles. The man who

strongly believes that he must always dictate the course of events is liable to be the domineering type with an immature concept of what constitutes true masculinity.

10. FALSE It may be true sometimes—but no more of women than of men. The assumption behind this belief—still only too common—is again the immature one of bogus masculinity.

11. FALSE It is another of the assumptions of the crude or immature male, and may also indicate a neurotic attitude to sex—a secret fear and dislike of it and a hidden hostility towards women. Women do indeed like *decisiveness* in their men, but that's a very different matter from roughness, which implies a lack of considerateness and a devaluation of the woman concerned.

12. FALSE One of the false assumptions about a man is that he is always at the ready. He is subject to moods of inconfidence just as much as women. There may be times when he needs coaxing too.

13. FALSE Or rather, false if by a "manly man" is meant the old stereotype of the he-man. True manliness, by any worth-while measure, involves tenderness, protectiveness, gentleness, etc., as well as some of the more traditional qualities.

14. FALSE Quite often the overt signs of mutual attraction don't appear until much later in a relationship. Indeed quite often the mutual attraction itself isn't recognised at once.

15. FALSE Of course—such an attitude would only be possible in the crude or the superficial.

16. FALSE It may not always be essential, but it usually is, and it usually adds immeasurably to the mutual satisfaction of the partners. Dogmatically to assert the contrary would suggest a greedy, selfish, aggressive and immature attitude towards sex.

17. FALSE Promiscuity is not the best way of obtaining

sexual fulfilment, which belongs only to a strong and gradually deepening relationship. It is well known among psychologists that the promiscuous are often sexually immature or insecure, often with quite serious psychological hang-ups.

18 FALSE It may not always happen, and an act of infidelity doesn't necessarily or inevitably destroy a relationship, but the suggestion is by no means ridiculous. On the contrary, attachment to one person makes for greater sexual satisfaction in the long run. Sex between two people is something that should get better and better as the relationship grows and deepens. Superficial sex may give relief—but the relief is at a pretty primitive level.

19. FALSE Of course. Loving sex is a matter of mutual discovery, accompanied by understanding and tolerance. The self-styled sex expert is usually a cold fish, whose sex is mostly in the head and the will.

20. FALSE It may not happen very often nowadays in the western world, but it was an expectation in the past that probably produced no more distress than the problems raised by the permissive society—and it's an expectation that still exists in many parts of the world. This isn't to sit in moral judgment on the matter—only to point out that there are all kinds of ways in which the human race have arranged their sexual affairs. It isn't at all impossible that the young of another generation may react against permissiveness and again subscribe to ideas which now strike us as impossibly old-fashioned.

21. FALSE And particularly so, of course, in our kind of society. In others, pre-marital sex might produce all kinds of social and economic problems which would make the marriage more difficult. But it would take more than that to destroy a

genuine love relationship!

22.   FALSE   Some religious teaching on the subject may be rigid and narrow-minded, but even then it contains *some* rationality. Religious leaders don't all take an out-and-out prohibitive attitude— and all of them are at least concerned about the *value and dignity* of human sexual relationships.

23.   FALSE   Spontaneous passion, of course, must be there, but if it is the expression of love it makes for greater satisfaction. Love is the charge that carries it further and deeper. Everyone who has experienced it knows, for example, that an orgasm fuelled by love is infinitely more satisfying than any other kind.

24 & 25.   FALSE   Those who do feel this are either deceiving themselves about their love for their partners, or they haven't yet come to terms with their own sexuality, or they are suffering from some other psychological hang-up.

26.   FALSE   Preliminary shyness is natural enough, and must be respected; but it is not natural among partners of long standing to place taboos on certain parts of their bodies.

27.   FALSE   It is the best thing of all in a sex relationship, of course, but it doesn't *always* happen, and when it doesn't it isn't the end of the world!

28.   FALSE   It would be *un*natural for a couple to feel the need of such stimulation, and would probably indicate immature or abnormal elements in their sexual make-up.

29.   FALSE   It does happen often enough, but only in those whose sexual natures are in some way immature.

30.   FALSE   Some people may very well find it difficult in the early stages of a relationship, but if such a reluctance were to continue too long, it would spell trouble. Mutual frankness in such matters is essential to happiness. In love making, it's true, one expects the other person to find out

some of the things one likes, but there are usually quite a few where the other person needs guidance.

31. TRUE   It's the basic and most important of all the elements of love.

32. FALSE   Or at any rate false to a large extent. Any lover should be aware of his partner's own needs, and to concentrate exclusively on one's own is greedy and selfish. On the other hand, there is a moment for both partners when each of them has to let go without any restraint.

33. FALSE   It is perfectly natural to continue to be attracted to members of the opposite sex. But—as we've said before—you don't have to *do anything* about it!

34. FALSE   Sex must be spontaneous, not planned and scheduled!

35. FALSE   Why shouldn't she? If a man despises a woman because she shows that she is attracted towards him, then he doesn't deserve her!

SCORING AND ASSESSMENT
QUESTIONNAIRE H

35-30   —Correct answers would suggest that your attitudes towards the love relationship are outstandingly mature, and that you have the qualifications for making a really good mate for somebody.

30-20   —would suggest that you are rapidly developing the qualities that are needed to make a good lover, and that your basic attitudes towards love and sex are very sound.

20-15   —would suggest that you still have a great deal to learn about the right balance in a relationship between the sexes and the place of sex within it, but that you possess the capabilities to do so.

15-7   —would suggest that you are only partially aware of what is needed to make a mutually rewarding relationship between the sexes, and that you have a lot of growing up to do.

Under 5 —would probably indicate that you are so un-enlightened and immature in your attitudes towards love and the opposite sex that you haven't really even begun to develop normally.

❖❖❖❖❖❖❖❖❖❖❖❖

Although any of the questions in that questionnaire could be applied to married couples, as well as other partnerships, you might also like to look at a selection of questions specially chosen for married people. There's no claim that they could tell you more about your marriage than you already know, either consciously or in your heart of hearts; or that if your marriage has gone wrong they would show you how and why; or what you ought to do to put it right. But they may give you food for useful thought, remind you of some things that are easily forgotten, and even indicate some areas where you might make adjustments.

QUESTIONNAIRE J: HOW'S YOUR MARRIAGE?

Answer TRUE or FALSE

1. It's always comforting to reflect that if things don't work out it's easy enough nowadays to get a divorce.
2. If a married couple go to a marriage guidance coun-sellor it's a sign that their marriage is already past saving.
3. You can't expect a marriage to succeed if the husband and wife have entirely different interests.
4. Happy marriage is impossible without economic secu-rity.
5. A marriage in which the wife goes out to work is bound to get into difficulties.

6. A marriage comes under strain as soon as children start arriving.

7. A woman should get back to her job as soon as she has recovered from her confinement.

8. A woman should encourage her husband to share in every stage of the children's upbringing.

9. A woman has every right to expect her husband not to stray while she is in the late stages of pregnancy.

10. It is only natural that a husband should find his wife unattractive during pregnancy.

11. A woman is never as passionate sexually as a man.

12. The sexual attraction between a husband and wife is bound to weaken as they get older.

13. A woman can't enjoy sex after the menopause.

14. A husband and wife cannot be close friends in the real sense of the term.

15. Unless the sexual attraction between a husband and wife persists their marriage is bound to fail sooner or later.

16. If either husband or wife are unfaithful at any time the marriage will never recover.

17. A marriage between partners of widely differing ages can never be successful.

18. For either husband and wife to be frequently attracted to members of the opposite sex means that the marriage is heading for disaster.

19. There is no reason why sex in marriage should ever become boring.

20. In marriage it is best to arrange set times for love-making.

21. The happiest marriages are those in which one partner is always ready to give way to the wishes of the other.

22. The more a married couple stick to their home the happier their marriage will be.

23. A good marriage doesn't need the presence of outsiders.

24. Husband and wife should occasionally spend a portion of their holidays apart.

25. It's allright if husband and wife sometimes spend their spare time apart.

26. A marriage is likely to fail when a wife who goes out to work achieves greater success than her husband.

27. A marriage in which the bulk of the money belongs to the wife is likely to fail.

28. A husband or wife should keep their professional affairs to themselves.

29. A marriage won't succeed if either the husband is a hopeless handyman, or the wife can't cook or keep house.

30. A husband and wife must continue to take pains with their personal appearance.

31. A wife should not treat her husband like a baby, and should discourage any tendency he may show to behave like one.

32. There's nothing wrong if a wife likes to be treated like a little girl.

33. It is quite normal for the sexual side of a marriage to be sometimes temporarily in abeyance.

34. It is a good idea for married couples to get away from their families occasionally.

35. Too great a concern with one's grown-up children can be damaging to a marriage.

36. It is not necessarily a bad sign if husband and wife go to a sexy film or show together.

37. Wife-swapping isn't likely to harm a marriage.

38. It's only natural if a wife often finds her husband's sexual attentions rather a nuisance.

39. It's ridiculous for older married people to enjoy being naked together.

40. The arts of love-making (for man or woman) are just as important in marriage as they were before it.

ANSWERS AND COMMENTS
QUESTIONNAIRE J

1. FALSE   Or at least it shouldn't be comforting, unless the marriage is already in considerable difficulties. Sadly some marriages do go wrong, but it's unwise to dwell on the possibility that yours might be one of them when there's no real need to.

2. FALSE   The very fact that a married couple take this step is a sure sign that all is not yet lost and that they have the desire to straighten things out. Many marriages have been salvaged by marriage guidance counsellors and turned out very happily afterwards.

3. FALSE   Community of interests isn't essential. There are many happy marriages in which the partners have quite different interests.

4. FALSE   Economic security is very pleasant to have of course, but it would be ridiculous to suggest that it's essential. Indeed the mutual struggle to make ends meet often forges even closer bonds.

5. FALSE   It can cause difficulties sometimes, of course—in which case husband and wife should try and find out why. In some cases the wife might be well advised to give up her job—but *not* if it means a serious curtailing of her own personal fulfilment.

6. FALSE   All the statistics prove the contrary.

7. FALSE   Or at any rate, false in the absence of special circumstances. In its early years an infant needs its mother's presence for its own development. If the father is a good and responsible one he will know this, and if his wife insists on going back to work he may resent it because he feels his child is being neglected.

8. TRUE   A husband can easily feel left out of it if he's at all insecure, while if he's fully mature he will have a strong instinct to be involved with his children.

9. TRUE   No doubt a loving wife can forgive her husband for such behaviour, but that doesn't alter the fact that it's a pretty shabby trick, and one that a really mature man who genuinely loves his wife isn't likely to play.

10. FALSE   It would be quite *un*natural. A normal husband enjoys the sight and fact of his wife's pregnancy. Her attractiveness is just as strong even if it may be of a different kind.

11. FALSE   A marriage which accepts this premise is likely to be in trouble.

12. FALSE   Or at any rate, it's false until quite an advanced age. There's no rule as to the age at which sex urges fade in people, and they vary enormously in this respect. Which reminds us of the old lady of 76 who, asked by a researcher when her sex life had ended, said with surprise "Oh, I'm afraid you'd have to ask someone older than me."

13. FALSE   Many women enjoy sex far more after it, because the risk of unwanted pregnancy has been removed. There is no reason why a woman who is healthy—mentally as well as physically—should find her sex life affected by the menopause.

14. FALSE   The deepest kind of friendship grows up between a happily married couple.

15. FALSE   There are plenty of instances where illness or some other cause prevents a sex life without impairing the happiness of the marriage.

16. FALSE   A soundly based marriage can survive such trials, and sometimes be better than ever afterwards. There are hundreds of wives and husbands who have obtained divorces in such circumstances—perhaps because their pride was hurt—and have lived to regret it bitterly. But of course it's sensible to avoid anything that imposes emotional suffering and strain on a marriage.

17. FALSE   There are plenty of instances to prove the

contrary.

18. FALSE It is perfectly natural for husbands and wives to go on being attracted to members of the opposite sex. It's what each does about it that counts.

19. TRUE If the sexual side of your marriage *has* become boring, it would be wise to set about altering the situation.

20. FALSE This is one of the ways in which sex *can* be made boring. One should be spontaneous in one's sex life, and enjoy the element of surprise and unexpectedness.

21. FALSE Such a marriage is more like a bondage than a happy and mutually fulfilling partnership.

22. FALSE To cling to the home like a limpet is a sure way of introducing boredom into it. It's wise to resist the temptation, at all stages of one's life   though this doesn't mean that married couples don't sometimes want, and need, to be on their own.

23. FALSE No relationship can exist in isolation. A marriage is stimulated and freshened by contact with other people. Happily married people usually have many friends. Happiness attracts.

24. TRUE It's wise for husband and wife to be apart occa-
& 25. sionally. Everybody sometimes craves for time and space in which to look inside themselves. Such absences renew a marriage rather than damage it.

26. FALSE It does happen sometimes, of course, but not if there is mutual trust and if both are mature adults.

27. FALSE Again, it can happen, but there are plenty of examples to the contrary.

28. FALSE It helps a marriage if a husband and wife can share their interests and worries with each other.

29. FALSE It is certainly very pleasant for both partners if the husband can do the odd jobs about the house and the wife is a wonderful cook, but plenty of

marriages have succeeded without those bonuses!

30.   TRUE   The reasons surely are obvious!

31.   TRUE   In a really happy marriage each partner is concerned to help the other reach maturity and fulfilment.

32.   FALSE   There are plenty of women, of course, who tend to cling to the role of daddy's girl (just as there are many men who continue to be mummy's darling). But obviously it's a tendency that doesn't make for a fully mature married relationship.

33.   TRUE   The sexual side of one's nature has its ebbs and flows, and it's wise to take heed of them.

34.   TRUE   Naturally a married couple wouldn't want to leave their children if they were very young or if there was no one suitable to look after them, but an occasional break from family cares can only do good to a marriage.

35.   TRUE   It's bad for the children and it's bad for the married couple. We must nourish our own personalities and not try to live through our children. An over-concern for the children who have left the home, on the part of husband or wife, is probably one of the commonest causes of a marriage losing its vitality in middle age. A certain distance from our children makes them respect us—and usually leaves them free to come back in their own good time!

36.   TRUE   But with this reservation—a thoroughly satisfactory marriage doesn't need external stimulation. But if the visit is just for the hell of it it's not likely to do much harm.

37.   FALSE   Surely this is a sick way of treating a marriage? It suggests the need to flog up failing sexual appetites, and a tendency to treat one's partner as a merely sexual object. It's difficult to believe that a marriage in which it takes place is in really good shape.

38. FALSE Naturally a wife may not always want her husband to make love to her—and it's a false assumption that the husband is always in the mood for it. In a really happy marriage the wishes of either partner in such matters are conveyed easily and gently, and if the decision is a negative one, it's accepted with good humour. If either partner find the other's advances a nuisance it suggests some lack of love or a dislike of sex in general.

39. FALSE This is an area where a couple may absolutely please themselves—at any age.

40. TRUE In fact it's a truism that two of the commonest reasons for the withering of the marriage relationship is taking it for granted and allowing love-making to become a matter of routine and mere habit.

❖❖❖❖❖❖❖❖❖❖❖❖

SCORING AND ASSESSMENTS
QUESTIONNAIRE J

It must be emphasised that there's nothing scientific and exact about the scoring suggested here. It's merely offered as a purely subjective guess on the part of the authors. We say again that *every marriage is unique, with its own laws of being*. Actions and attitudes which would destroy one marriage may have little or no effect upon another. No outsider can know for certain the subtle and complex reactions and interactions within a particular marriage. Only *you* can really know which of the questions and answers above are truly relevant to your partnership, and whether the suggested scoring is applicable to it. Anyway, here are our tentative suggestions:

40-35 —Correct answers: Would probably point to an unusually stable and mature marriage, and one that is still vital in every respect.

35-25   —Would also probably suggest a highly satisfactory
          state of affairs.

25-20   —Would probably indicate a generally satisfactory
          marriage relationship, but one in which some
          areas perhaps need re-examination and renewed
          care.

20-15   —Would perhaps imply that although there is
          nothing seriously wrong with the marriage, there
          are a number of danger points.

15- 5   —Would present a picture which, at any rate to
          the outsider, looked unpromising.

Under 5 —Would perhaps suggest that the marriage is, for
          the moment at any rate, in rather a bad way.

CHAPTER ELEVEN

CARDS ON THE TABLE—THE TAROT

THE FOOL

CHAPTER ELEVEN

CARDS ON THE TABLE—THE TAROT

So far we've been dealing with ways in which, on your own, you can look into the various mirrors we've been holding up, and perhaps get to know your Self better. In the following chapters, we shall be describing other ways in which—with outside help like cards, crystal ball and even mechanical gadgets, and very likely with another person involved—you may also find out more about yourself. And first we are going to explore a very ancient and respected method of reading a rather special sort of card—the Tarot.

As with every other method of trying to know your own personality and divine likely future events in your life, you have to be willing to believe that it is possible to do so. And that may not be so difficult; there may not be any scientific laws which apply to the connection between a person's future and, say, the random dealing out of cards but . . . no less a man Carl Jung (one of the other great psychologists of Freud's time) came to believe, after years of study and research, that the ancient and so-called unscientific studies of alchemy, astrology and even the I Ching (a way of reading personality and future from arrangements of small sticks) were each in their widely different and not strictly scientific ways aiming at a process of psychic integration—something which Jung felt was very close to what he called the process of individuation—that is, becoming increasingly aware or conscious of the self and of society; a process which leads to a greater sense of wholeness for the individual—in other words, to maturity.

Now, although Jung himself didn't include the study of the Tarot cards in his investigations, it is perhaps no coincidence that the Tarot system also represents this search for maturity as a quest (as all the old myths and fairy-tales do), a continuing adventure with dangers and set-backs and perhaps magic help, with the hero or heroine—your Self, in other words—winning through in the end. Jung saw the search for self-knowledge as something which could and should go on all through life—a search which fell into two distinct parts; the first of these we have got to experience, since this is mainly the natural process of growing up physically (knowing the self outside); the second part takes courage and a conscious decision to experience, since this is the process of inner development and greater self-awareness (knowing the self inside).

It seems likely that the Tarot cards deal with these two processes—each of the major (or Trump) cards, for instance, represents a different stage of life, and these stages are divided quite clearly into outer and inner development. By laying out the cards in various ways and reading their meanings, it is claimed that it is possible to see the way ahead and that—by understanding and accepting this— the individual may follow the direction his or her life was meant to take, and therefore to develop the self further in some way.

There does not seem any reason to us why, properly read with the help of authentic interpretations, the Tarot cards should not indirectly help (as Jung believed that such so-called unscientific methods could help) the individual towards greater understanding of the Self and the events of that Self's inner and outer life. So don't reject the Tarot before giving it a fair and reasonably serious trial!

❖❖❖❖❖❖❖❖❖❖❖

Tarot cards are believed to have originated in Italy and France—and there are some very old and beautiful sets of them still in existence, one in particular was hand-painted in 1415 for a young Duke of Milan. There are some people who believe that the origins lie much farther back—that, for instance, the name comes from two Egyptian words *tar* (a path) and *ro* or *ros* (royal) which being combined could mean the royal path of life. And an eighteenth century writer claimed that the ancient Chinese had a series of pictures which closely resembled the Tarot. Whatever may be the truth, it seems likely that though there are some major changes among the characters, there has been surprisingly little alteration in the basic designs of the cards for hundreds of years.

What follows are the generally accepted meanings or hints to be gathered from each of the cards of the Tarot pack. We obviously haven't the space to show you what each card looks like, even in general terms, but we have asked our illustrator to draw some of the twenty-two Trump cards, and just a few of the fifty-six suit cards. It might be a good idea at first—until you become sufficiently familiar with the meanings of all the cards—to write them out on a separate sheet to have in front of you while you deal and read the cards; perhaps all the Trumps on one sheet and each suit on another. Anyway, you'll probably be able to work out your own best method—because as you'll have already gathered, everything about reading the Tarot cards has to be very personal to you.

❖❖❖❖❖❖❖❖❖❖❖❖❖

THE TRUMP CARDS
These represent the various stages of life—and since the cards may appear right way up or upside down, the meaning for both positions are given for each card.

THE FOOL (the only unnumbered card)—symbolically representing the child starting out on life, the innocent spirit following the butterfly of sensory experience.

right way up: unexpected influence; important decisions to be made; can indicate start of new cycle of destiny; can refer to the creative dreamer.

upside down: troubles ahead following wild, chaotic impulses.

I. THE MAGICIAN—represents emerging self-awareness of the child; he holds the intellectual and physical power to come to terms with his surroundings.

right way up: will-power, expansion of personality, initiative, versatility; can mean vigorous events coming.

upside down: weakness of will, nervousness, running
away from reality.

II. THE HIGH PRIESTESS—the feminine force linking conscious and unconscious minds (the two pillars); language of her book of ancient mysteries has to be
learned.

right way up: intuitive solutions to problems; influence
of wise woman; can mean inspiration to
creative person.

upside down: bad influence of a woman; warning
against emotional instability.

THE HIGH PRIESTESS

THE LOVERS

III. THE EMPRESS—figure of plenty, the good things of the
earth and of the body.

right way up: domestic stability, motherhood, ample
comfort; good connections with nature;
sensual pleasure; growth.

upside down: indifference from outside world; domestic
disturbances; mother trouble; privation.

IV. THE EMPEROR—figure of ruler; throne and other signs of majesty; representing the power of reason.

right way up: authority; ambition; vigour, action; powerful influence for good in worldly matters.

upside down: loss of good position; being done down by person in authority; sign of weakness, insecurity.

V. THE POPE (or HIGH PRIEST)—represents moral authority, upholder of accepted code of behaviour (the pillars are of established religious building), also carries inspiration from the other world.

right way up: good sensible advice; inspirational guidance, even religious influence.

upside down: bad counsel; twisted influence; presence of someone apparently good but using evil influence.

VI. THE LOVERS—represents the adolescent break with parental control; the struggle between loyalty to parents (particularly the mother) and the lover; between tradition and independent action; Cupid helps by shooting arrow of decision.

right way up: important choice to be made; intuition not reason must guide; a step towards maturity.

upside down: holding back from making important decision; muddle by trying to hold on to everything; inability to let past relationship go.

VII. THE CHARIOT—figure representing someone who is winning through; psychic energy and physical instincts harnessed.

right way up: achievement through personal effort; overcoming of difficulties; strong personality.

upside down: too much strength; suggestion of someone who forces others down; success at the cost of others.

VIII. JUSTICE—typical signs of worldly justice, scales, etc;
progress so far being weighed and measured; law of
life to be followed.

right way up: a time of coming to terms, of accepting
conditions, and abiding by the law.

upside down: legal trickery; danger of getting caught in
unfairness; or being unfair to others.

IX. THE HERMIT—a lonely truth-seeking figure, walking
away from worldly life—the light on the card represents intuition.

right way up: time to stop and think things out, and to
listen to inner voice; perhaps advice from
wise friend; time to be quiet.

upside down: turning away from obvious help and
advice; determined refusal to listen to
self or others.

X. WHEEL OF FORTUNE—represents turning point of an
individual's life; the animals on the wheel are parts of
the self moving round, particularly of the unconscious
coming up.

right way up: a whole new cycle of personal events;
influences outside one's control moving
one's life; a good sign.

upside down: the end of a cycle of events; outside forces
beyond one's control changing one's life.

XI. FORTITUDE—gentleness defeating strength on this card;
consciousness holding back wild instincts.

right way up: overcoming bad impulses; chance to act
with courage; making friends with an
enemy.

upside down: giving in to bad impulses; fear of action,
loss of opportunity.

XII. THE HANGED MAN—represents deliberately going head
first into the depths of the unconscious; the hanged
man is tied to the tree of life by a foot, so is safe and still
in touch, still living.

right way up: willingness to go along with unexpected
events; ability to turn things upside down

to find truth of situation; listening to the inner self.

upside down: difficult inner struggle; losing out to the dictates of outer world; too great a reliance on material things.

XIII. DEATH—signifies death of old self; the skeleton is cutting away what is no longer needed.

right way up: the losing of something or someone by outside forces which clears way to better life; removal of things within one's self that are no longer necessary.

upside down: something taken away against one's will; being held back by some loss; the missing of new opportunities.

XIV. TEMPERANCE—the figure is bridging gap between outer and inner worlds; pool can be seen as the unconscious; the cup is being filled with new life.

right way up: careful handling of people and situations leading to progress; good relationship possible.

upside down: good opportunities wasted by clumsiness; difficulties created by lack of care.

TEMPERANCE

JUDGEMENT

XV. THE DEVIL   representing the collective evil of the unconscious; very primitive and dangerous—and as the
picture indicates, only loosely held down.

right way up: need to recognize and redirect lower instincts; conscious attempt to meet hidden
forces.

upside down: warning of bad instincts trying to take
over; temptation to use situation for bad
purposes; beware of trying to pretend
evil impulses don't exist.

XVI. THE TOWER—can be seen as the carefully built structure
of person's life so far being struck by brilliant light of
greater (cosmic) understanding; life itself is always
flexible and changing, being broken down and built
up, so individual life must be the same.

right way up: personal disaster caused by world events;
universal upheaval bringing unfair, unexpected personal suffering.

upside down: disaster brought about by one's own
doing; unnecessary suffering; "asking for
trouble."

XVII. THE STAR—representing faith ("steadfast as a star");
the waters can be seen as the conscious and unconscious
flowing together.

right way up: something good on the way; a feeling of
hopefulness and energy coming appar-
ently from nowhere.

upside down: lack of trust; refusal to raise one's eyes
from the ground and see new chances
being offered; doubt.

XVIII. THE MOON—traditionally connected with solitude,
mystery, silence; the animals in the picture represent
the instincts, the crayfish the unconscious, the gates
an experience.

right way up: problems to be solved only by one's self;
some sort of crisis arising; intuition not
logic can carry self through.

upside down: danger of sticking to where you are instead of stepping out boldly; fear of the unknown.

XIX. THE SUN   representing wholeness, the union of conscious and unconscious (the figures dancing together).

right way up: success in spite of everything, linked with strong imagination and creative ideas; "getting home safe and dry" after a successful adventure, inner and outer.

upside down: failure through trying phoney means to success; or through day-dreaming instead of doing; likelihood of being "shown up".

XX. JUDGMENT   trumpeter sounds for the rebirth of the whole self (the child rising); the two halves of the self have come through, fully mature now.

right way up: real achievement; great pleasure in success; a new lease of life; good health.

upside down: punishment, from self and from outside world; failure; loss.

XXI. THE WORLD —represents the whole self, dancing in the circle (the symbol of psychic wholeness); circle is also an egg, with new self waiting to be born again.

right way up: successful climax of affairs; the harmonious coming together of several events; end of a series of circumstances.

upside down: energies misdirected; running round and round in a circle, getting nowhere; inability to break out of rut and use energies properly; failure to "pull one's self together"

THE FOOL—to be looked at again at the end of the quest; a happy "whole" being, "innocent" of disharmony and ugliness of spirit; the sort of person often called a fool because he seems not to care for ordinary worldly things (the dog biting him is being ignored) but skips along in the sunshine (the light of the spirit) following the butterfly, the very spirit of Life.

❖❖❖❖❖❖❖❖❖❖❖❖❖

Before we go on to give brief indications of the cards in the four suits, we want to stress that both these and the meanings of the trump cards above are very short summaries of the full implications of each card. If you believe the Tarot cards can help you in your search for your self and for greater maturity, or even if you have become interested in Tarot as a fascinating subject, you would certainly need to study the subject further.

The four Tarot suits are Batons (or sticks), Cups, Swords, and Coins. There are fourteen cards in each suit (king through to ace, with one extra court or picture card included). As with the trump card meanings, we are giving a brief summary for each card, in each of the two positions in which it can be turned up:

KING OF BATONS

QUEEN OF CUPS

BATONS

	(right way up)	*(upside down)*
KING	strong, loyal, domestic	strict, narrow-minded
QUEEN	loving, fond of nature, sociable	bossy, over-maternal, vain
KNIGHT	quick, active, a traveller	disturbing, destructive

KNAVE	stimulating, faithful	gossipy, superficial
TEN	forceful, too successful	liar, interferer
NINE	strong, brave, safe in life	stubborn, suspicious
EIGHT	change, journeys, good news	impetuous action, too hasty
SEVEN	difficulties to overcome, success with courage	hesitation and loss
SIX	hopes come true, good news	no news, fears of future
FIVE	need for energy and courage	beaten by troubles
FOUR	cultural success, good ideas work out	artificiality, bad ideas
THREE	artistry, inventiveness succeeds	schemes come to nothing, impracticability
TWO	well-earned riches, authority	over-ambition, empty success
ACE	new beginnings, upsurge of energy	greediness, imagined power

CUPS

	(right way up)	(upside down)
KING	leader; clever, ambitious	no morals, treacherous
QUEEN	artistic, romantic	easily swayed, untrustworthy
KNIGHT	ideas man, easily bored	a fraud, false with a fair face
KNAVE	painstaking; a student	selfish, scheming
TEN	peacefulness, harmony	anti-social, selfish
NINE	affection, steadiness	complacency, sentimentality
EIGHT	change in affections	abandoning good relationship
SEVEN	time for choice	opportunity lost
SIX	the past brings good	looking back instead of forward

FIVE	need to pull things together	back luck, worry, anxiety
FOUR	emotional happiness; family made	too much of a good thing; sick and tired
THREE	creation of love, fertility	selfishness, sensuality
TWO	happy agreement, reconciliation	trust betrayed; separation
ACE	fertility, love, marriage	infertility; love lost

TEN OF SWORDS

KNIGHT OF COINS

SWORDS

	(right way up)	*(upside down)*
KING	clever, "with it", versatile	cold, cruel, ruthless
QUEEN	quick, intelligent, self-reliant	too sharp, underhand
KNIGHT	courageous, fights well	danger of being "bull at a gate"
KNAVE	diplomatic; good negotiator	a nosey parker, vindictive
TEN	worst is over, can only improve	false hope, worse to come

NINE	despair, failure, violence; must hold on	no help from anybody
EIGHT	difficult times, every effort needed	hard work leading nowhere
SEVEN	danger, great care needed; can overcome	throwing in the towel too soon
SIX	moving away from trouble	don't try to avoid problems
FIVE	temporary defeat, don't complain	watch out for treachery
FOUR	well-earned rest, breathing space	being shut away, locked up, depressed
THREE	big clear-out; upheavals	quarrelling; general chaos
TWO	good coming out of bad; friendship when needed	stirring it up for no good reason; betrayal
ACE	"all systems go", success certain	going off at half-cock; failure, injustice

COINS

	(right way up)	(upside down)
KING	slow, but steady; loyal	dull, plodding
QUEEN	lives well, open handed	miserly, materialistic
KNIGHT	honourable, virtuous	priggish, old-fashioned
KNAVE	dutiful, money saver	too fussy, self-important
TEN	inherited money, family strong	loss of property, theft
NINE	orderliness, material success	good things going to end
EIGHT	talents and energies will succeed	trying to make "a fast buck"; dishonesty
SEVEN	keep at it—don't sleep on the job	chances missed
SIX	prizes, solvency, charitableness	throwing too much money around
FIVE	hard times but don't give up hope	present course is disastrous
FOUR	financial power, law, order, stability	greed, rush of power to the head

THREE	skills rewarded, business success	too cocky, taken down a peg
TWO	movement, change, bringing joy	reckless action, over-indulgence, drunkenness
ACE	stability, comfort, the good life	fears, greediness, death; too worldly

There are, of course, many ways of laying out the Tarot cards for a reading, and we shall only be giving you three of the simpler arrangements, followed by a brief outline of how to read them. In getting a pack of Tarot cards, try to avoid one in which the trump and court cards are double-headed (i.e. like ordinary playing cards) if you want to use them for readings, because one of the most important things in Tarot is that the cards can be turned up either right-way up or upside-down—the meaning being very different indeed according to which way up a card appears. You will understand what we mean by looking at the drawings of the cards.

Anyway, assuming that you've found yourself a good pack of Tarot cards (which will consist of 78 cards altogether), here are a few simple rules (based on ancient practice) which should be followed if the cards are really to reveal anything to you:

1. Always treat the cards carefully, coming to feel that they are very particularly yours and no one else's. Make yourself familiar with each card and its meaning, and get to know all the details in the pictures.

2. Keep the pack wrapped in a large silk square, and keep it inside a box. Put the box away somewhere safe—and don't let other people handle either it or the cards themselves. This is to make sure that the personal connection between you and your cards is not broken.

3. Always lay the cards out on the silk square, so that they are not in contact with anything else.

4. If you are reading the cards for yourself, you should face east. If you are reading them for another person (when you feel experienced enough to do so, that is), he or she should sit facing north, and you should sit opposite, facing south.

Before you lay them out, the cards should be shuffled very carefully, making sure you reverse some of the cards as you shuffle, so that there will be a good mixture of cards the right-way up and upside-down. You are now ready and, we hope, in the right frame of mind to lay out the cards and discover some meaning from them.

LAYOUT NO. I—THE CIRCLE

This gives a forecast of the year ahead, starting from the day on which you're doing the reading. Beginning (on an imaginary clock face) at nine o'clock and going anti-clockwise, lay out twelve cards face up, ending with a thirteenth card face up in the centre of the circle, like this:

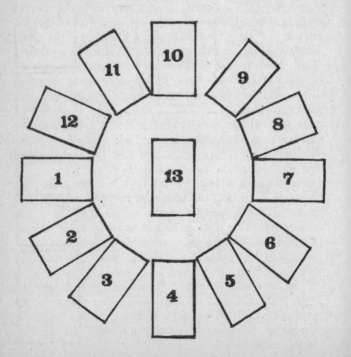

The thirteenth card is the most important, as it will indicate the general trend of the whole year—e.g. hopeful, troubled and so on. So read this card first. Then read the other cards, starting at 1 and moving anti-clockwise round the circle. The *first card* refers to *the month to come*; the *second to sixth cards* each tell you what to expect in *the month they represent* (i.e. second, third, etc.); the *remaining cards* will be *general indications of progress*, and events likely to take place.

✦✦✦✦✦✦✦✦✦✦✦✦✦

LAYOUT NO. 2—NINE CARDS

For this arrangement, nine cards are dealt from the top of the pack, face down, as shown in the numbered diagram below:

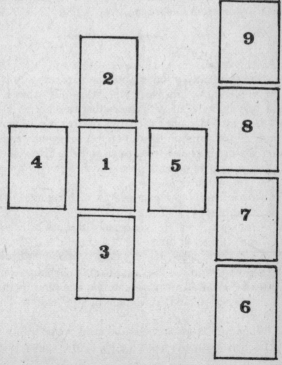

Starting with No. 1, turn the cards up one by one in numerical order, interpreting each in the following connection:

No. 1 is the most important factor about your present circumstances.

No. 2 shows the best you can do at the present time.

No. 3 indicates the background to the present.

No. 4 shows what caused the present situation.

No. 5 indicates what is most likely to happen if things continue as they are, and provided nothing important occurs to change the course of events.

Nos. 6-9 show, in a very general way, what progress you may make in the near future. Reading No. 6 as referring to events nearest to the present and each succeeding number as referring to events further and further away from the present.

❖❖❖❖❖❖❖❖❖❖❖❖

LAYOUT NO. 3

The third way of laying out the cards does not have, as far as we know, any particular title—but it has been used for very many years with interesting results:

Start by taking out a card from one of the suits to represent yourself (or someone else, if you feel sufficiently experienced to read for anyone else). A rough guide to help you choose is:

a *cup* card represents people with light brown hair and fair complexions.

a *baton* card represents people with blonde or red hair and blue eyes.

a *sword* card represents people with dark brown hair and grey, hazel or blue eyes.

a *coin* card represents very dark people with brown eyes.

If these categories are too vague to make a choice, you can use instead the old Tarot representation of a man by the trump The Magician, and a woman by the trump The High Priestess.

When you've picked out the card representing yourself (The Personal), place it face up in the centre of the silk.

Shuffle and cut the rest of the pack as usual, and deal cards as follows:

Turn up the FIRST CARD

and put it over The Personal card, saying "This covers me". Whatever it is, it will represent your present environment (what is most influencing you at the present time).

Turn up the SECOND CARD,

put it horizontally over the first card, saying "This is my obstacle". If it happens to be a favourable card, it will be good in itself, but not to you at present.

Turn up the THIRD CARD,

put it above the head of the Personal Card, saying "This crowns me". It will represent either the best you can do, or the ideal you'd like to achieve; what you want but haven't yet achieved.

Turn up the FOURTH CARD,

put it below the feet of the Personal Card, saying "This is beneath me". This will represent what you have to work with and can use.

Turn up the FIFTH CARD,

put it to the side the Personal Card is facing away from saying "This is behind me". This will represent what has happened already; maybe the past from which you are moving away.

Turn up the SIXTH CARD,

put it to the side the Personal Card is facing towards saying "This is before me". This will represent the influence or current which is coming to bear on the present situation.

Leave these six cards where they are, and turn up the NEXT FOUR CARDS, putting them face up one below the other on your right-hand side.

The first signifies yourself, your attitude and connection with the situation.

The second represents your house, your surroundings; the influence, people and daily life.

The third represents your hopes and fears.

The fourth will show what is to come.

This last card is obviously the most important of the lot, and you must learn to concentrate very hard on it. With practice and thorough understanding of the cards and their meanings, it is surprising how much can be learnt from such a reading. To give you a better idea of how to interpret the cards which come up, we decided to take the Tarot pack, deal a simple horseshoe layout which is used to answer a particular question, and to interpret them briefly. This is how the cards should be dealt, face upwards, starting with the card numbered 1 and dealing anti-clockwise round to No. 7. Each card will deal with a different aspect of the questioner's life, and these aspects are given below, with our interpretations:

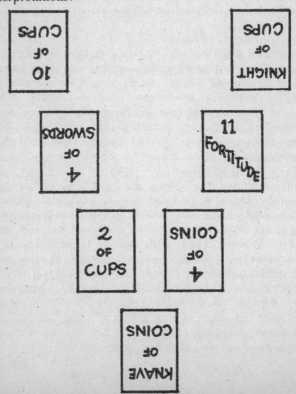

As you will see, the cards are shown here in words rather than pictures, which would obviously have been too small to read clearly. The question asked was "Am I going to achieve success with my creative work?".

CARD NO. 1—PAST INFLUENCES

TEN OF CUPS *(upside down)*: this suggests that the questioner has acted in the past out of self-interest and has, perhaps as a result, suffered disruption of an orderly routine at some time.

CARD NO. 2—PRESENT CIRCUMSTANCES

FOUR OF SWORDS *(upside down)*: this indicates that right now the questioner may be shut up inside, isolated, possibly depressed; and will have to break out before anything can happen.

CARD NO. 3—FUTURE CONDITIONS

TWO OF CUPS *(right way up)*: this is a good card, and foretells a happy agreement, a coming-together, which could mean a reconciliation between warring parts of the questioner's self (it's easy to argue with one's self as we all know). This could mean a harmonious atmosphere for the questioner, which would obviously have an effect on creative work. This card could also reflect, of course, particularly good and happy relationships with others in future.

CARD NO. 4—THE BEST POLICY TO FOLLOW

KNAVE OF COINS *(upside down)*: this is rather a difficult card to interpret, since it suggests self-importance, fussiness, enjoyment of power for its own sake. A positive interpretation could be that the questioner must be careful, and only use power for altruistic reasons. It could also be a warning not to be too fussy and self-important—these qualities could certainly stand in the way of creativity.

CARD NO. 5—ATTITUDES OF THOSE AROUND THE QUESTIONER

FOUR OF COINS *(upside down)*: this again has to do with the misuse of power, and with greed, and suggests that the questioner has made companions of people who are trying to be too bossy and grab hold of everything.

CARD NO. 6—OBSTACLES IN THE WAY OF AN ANSWER TO THE QUESTION

TRUMP CARD XI—FORTITUDE *(right way up)*: this card is representative of consciousness overcoming wild instincts, and it suggests a struggle with selfishness and greediness (which have appeared in previous cards here) before, perhaps, artistic success could be achieved. It could also mean a chance to act courageously, to overcome hostility from others by being friendly and non-aggressive.

CARD NO. 7—THE ANSWER

KNIGHT OF CUPS *(upside down)*: this shows a fraud, someone with a charming exterior but a false heart. The interpretation here again is not easy; it could be that the questioner will have to beware of someone who appears to be helping towards creative success but is in fact not doing so. It could also be that the questioner has to beware of falsity within. A further interpretation might be, of course, that success itself is something that appears good and worth having, but when achieved seems somehow empty and worthless. Success, in fact, may be the fraud pictured here. This rather surprising conclusion may, indeed, be the Tarot's answer to the questioner who should perhaps take it to heart and stop hankering after worldly success!

As you will see, it is quite a complicated business making a good, meaningful reading—for yourself, and most particularly for anyone else. It's probably easier, we think, to start with a simple layout of cards which you try reading for yourself; then, as you begin to learn the different meanings and understand the various messages of the cards, you can try a more complicated layout, again reading for yourself. Eventually, and if you feel yourself to be an intuitive, sensitive person, you might like to try a reading for a friend. You'll find you have to concentrate very hard indeed, soaking up the meanings of the cards as you turn them up, and thinking—or perhaps feeling would be the better word —for and about the person for whom you're reading the cards. And we would again stress that this chapter is only an introduction to the Tarot. If you are genuinely interested in it, we would strongly advise you to study the whole subject thoroughly—and there are details of the books which we feel will be most helpful at the back of this book.

Finally, always remember that— as with any other means of divining character and the future—Tarot has to be believed in, entered into, and used with sincerity and humility before it will yield genuine and meaningful results.

CHAPTER TWELVE

CROSS THE PALM WITH SILVER

CHAPTER TWELVE

CROSS THE PALM WITH SILVER

As the title suggests, this chapter covers some of the methods of reading character and destiny which are perhaps more usually associated with fair grounds or those little booths on the piers at the seaside. Most of us probably approach them more for fun than with any serious belief—although, since we've nearly all still got remnants of the superstitious belief in magic that was so strong in our primitive ancestors we may have a sneaking feeling that there just *might* be something in it.

And perhaps there is. Quite a few serious investigators have re-examined some of these very ancient practices, for the light they may throw on various aspects of the human psyche. So let's start by looking at the character and destiny that may lie in your hands.

PALMISTRY—or CHIROMANCY
(to give it its fancy name)

This is the ancient belief that the palm of the hand contains a map of each individual's life, which can reveal the inner workings of his character and even predict his destiny. You may be surprised to know that this is *not* only believed in by the gypsies and the fairground fortune tellers. A number of psychotherapists, in fact, take prints of the palms of their patients' hands (usually by getting them to lay them palm down on a pad soaked in Indian ink and then pressing the palms on to a sheet of soft paper or tissue which easily takes the imprints) and study them at leisure together, of course, with the results of various other diagnostic tests. Dr. Charlotte Wolff, for example, has declared that "The hand is a visible part of the brain", and she has studied hands as one of the possible means of forming a psychological diagnosis. Indeed, even the great C. G. Jung wrote of the more modern approaches to palmistry ". . . the findings and knowledge are of essential importance for psychologists, doctors and educationists. It is a valuable contribution to character research in its widest application."

So obviously chiromancy can't be dismissed as complete nonsense. It is, however, a pretty complex subject and all that we can do here is to indicate some of its basic elements, as believed and practised by many professional palmists. If, however, you want to become an expert at reading hands yourself, you would, of course, have to devote a good deal of study to it.

THE HANDS

As a matter of fact it isn't only the palms you would have to study. A great deal can be learned from the hands themselves.

1. HANDSHAKES

You can begin by noticing the ways in which people shake hands.

A firm hand-clasp generally indicates a firm, positive and friendly character—unless it is too hard and prolonged, which may indicate a desire to impress.

A weak, flabby, wet fish type of hand-shake rather obviously suggests a weak and flabby character.

A limp, perfunctory hand-shake may mean that the person concerned is too full of a sense of his own importance to be bothered to think much about you.

A quick, sharp squeeze may point to someone who is always in too much of a hurry to pay attention to you, and who is impatient of the small details and niceties of life.

If this kind of short, sharp hand-shake also gives you a sensation as if a soft pad of flesh had been momentarily pressed into your hand, it may indicate a sensual, luxury-loving nature—and it can be a form of sexual invitation.

A hard, dry hand-shake is traditionally associated with nervousness, irritability, self-centredness, and a rigid control of the emotions.

The moist hand is sometimes said to denote the opposite quality—an insufficient command of the emotions.

2. HAND HABITS

You can probably learn quite a lot, too, from the way people hold their hands and what they do with them. If, for example, the hands are laid in the lap or along the arms of a chair in a relaxed manner, then their owner too is probably relaxed, patient, and has an unfretful attitude to life.

If, however, a person is constantly fidgeting with the hands or biting at them, it is probably a sign of anxiety or nervous tension.

If someone continually waves his or her hands about in talking, drawing imaginary pictures in the air, making all kinds of gestures, etc., then the person concerned is usually voluble, talkative and perhaps too prone to "spill the beans".

But if you see someone who usually keeps his hands fairly still suddenly gesturing with them you can be pretty sure that you have touched on a topic that has aroused great emotional interest. If the gestures are notably graceful it may be that the interest is an artistic one of some kind. Musicians, painters, sculptors, etc., often make these arabesques with their hands.

The person who continually puts one or both hands in his pocket, or in the case of a woman, who takes every opportunity to hide the hands, by tucking them under the arms, or drawing them up into the sleeves of a dress or a coat, by sitting on them, etc., is inclined to be either secretive or self-conscious.

3. HAND SHAPE, SIZE, COLOUR AND SPREAD

An expert would usually begin a reading by asking you to hold up your hands, backs towards him. This is because a great deal can be learned from hand shape and size. There are five basic shapes:

(a) *The Square hand:* i.e. the hand in which the distance from below the fingers to the beginning of the write is much the same as that across the hand. Usually this kind of hand also has rather short, squarish fingers. Generally speaking this is the hand of the practical, common-sense, down-to-earth kind of person, who hasn't much imagination but a great capacity for hard work.

(b) *The Cone-shaped hand:* usually this kind of hand is rounded at the base, and has rounded, tapering fingers. It's said to be predominantly a female hand, and to denote an appreciation of art and beauty and the kind of friendly, outgoing disposition that makes a highly successful hostess. If the fingers are very smooth their owner, though quick-witted (and very likeable) may not have much intellectual staying-power; but if the fingers are rather knotty at the knuckles more mental stamina is indicated.

(c) *The pointed hand:* usually a very graceful hand, with long, pointed fingers, belonging to the very sensitive and intuitive—and often to those with psychic powers. If the fingers are very smooth, there is a certain lack of energy and hence of achievement; but if the fingers are knotty, there is a good chance of success in the world of arts or entertainment, or in professions like hair-dressing and beauty culture.

(d) *The spade-shaped hand:* this kind of hand is narrower at the base than at the top. Usually the fingers are broad, and spade-shaped at the tips. This is supposed to be the hand of the individualist who is fond of activity and travel (but not perhaps very reliable as a love partner); of the scientist and engineer; and of those with a strongly inventive or mechanical bent.

(e) *The mixed hand:* i.e. the hand containing a mixture of the characteristics noted above. Palmists say it's the hand of the versatile sort of person who combines creativity and practicality, and who is often to be found on the business or organising side of the creative arts.

SIZE

Generally speaking those with small hands think and act quickly, but tend to be reluctant in carrying out their ideas themselves, especially if the hands are also smooth.

Generally speaking people with large hands have a thoughtful disposition, a tendency towards careful analysis of a problem or situation, and (especially if the joints of the fingers are knotted) they like to implement their own ideas.

COLOUR

Pale hands denote a lack of vitality (probably accompanied by a poor circulation), and a cool temperament.

Yellowish hands point to a cautious, pessimistic approach to life.

Red hands indicate an over-active and aggressive nature.

Pink hands are apparently ideal, pointing to health of body and mind, and an energetic, enterprising nature.

SPREAD

When a palmist asks a sitter to hold up his or her hands (the backs facing him) he is making deductions from the way in which the fingers are held. Here are the six main telltale signs:

(a) *If the fingers are held closely together* the owner is very conventional and rather touchy.

(b) *If all the fingers are separated* the deduction is that the owner is generous, freedom-loving, and highly unconventional not to say bohemian.

(c) *A space between the first (i.e. index) and second fingers* is said to indicate the person with a strongly independent turn of mind.

(d) *If the third and fourth (or little) fingers are held apart* the assumption is that the owner values his or her freedom of action above everything else, so that he or she would be utterly unsuited to a conventional kind of marriage.

(e) *If all the fingers bend or curl slightly inwards towards the palm* the usual deduction is of a tenacious nature, possessive in personal relationships, and very careful in money matters.

(f) *A wide gap between the thumb and the first finger* is said to indicate a generous, frank and outgoing nature.

(g) *If the fingers are strongly knuckled*—that is if the finger joints can easily be seen when the backs of the hands are held up (and provided this is not the result of rheumatism or arthritis) the person concerned is someone who thinks carefully and sensibly before taking action, and who is not subject to impulse.

But needless to say none of these indications should be taken too seriously in isolation: the conclusions derived from them would need to be held in reserve, to be checked in the light of the reading as a whole.

MORE ABOUT THE FINGERS

The study of the fingers—and of the little pads of flesh beneath them, where they join the palm—would take a book in itself. But here are some of the basic points about them, sufficient at least to enable you to make some deductions.

Long fingers (long, that is, in relation to the rest of the hand): generally denote a capacity for abstract thought and exactitude.

Short fingers: usually mean quickness of thought, but impatience with detail.

Long, very slim fingers: suggest that the intellect is very much in control.

Short, strong fingers: suggest that the emotions and the physical nature are predominant.

Thick fingers: are supposed to show emotional drive and energy (and the same applies to thick hands).

Thick fingers which are also noticeably protuberant and plump as they join the palm: are said to denote a great relish for good food and other luxuries.

The index (i.e. first finger) if it's longer than the third finger, a commanding authoritative nature is indicated; and if it's a good deal longer, the owner is likely to be distinctly domineering.

If it's a little shorter than the third finger, a rather reserved nature is suggested.

If it's a good deal shorter, a person unwilling or unable to accept responsibility is indicated.

If straight, a good type of character is implied.

If crooked, the owner may be expected to suffer from a very low opinion of himself.

The middle (or second) finger:

If long (stretching beyond both the fingers on either side) it's a sign of extreme caution, or of a serious outlook on life, often with many cares and responsibilities.

If short, an over-hasty temperament is indicated, and if very short, a lack of inner strength.

If straight and in reasonable proportion to the other fingers, a prudent but tolerant attitude to life is indicated.

If crooked, a tendency towards morbidity of temperament may be present.

The third (or ring) finger:

If long (i.e. if it's as long, or nearly as long, as the middle finger) it's supposed to be a pointer to the love of money and excitement.

If short, a tendency to gambling and speculation is indicated according to some palmists, though others apparently see it as a sign of strong ambition, and of a materialistic nature.

If straight and well formed, it's said to be a sign of strong artistic leanings.

If crooked, it's supposed to be a pointer to the money grubber.

If leaning towards the middle finger, the owner is emotionally immature, with an unrealistic attitude towards love.

The little (or fourth) finger:

If long, it's supposedly an indication of considerable financial success.

If short, the opposite.

If straight, the diplomatist and opportunist.

If crooked, a tendency to miss out on opportunities owing to a lack of vision.

If leaning inwards towards the middle finger, a shrewd business sense.

THE NAILS

Large = another indication of a good business brain.

Small = a cynical attitude towards life.

Filbert shaped = a loving nature.

Square = a quarrelsome disposition.

Round = tendency to fault-finding, and irritability.

Pink = vitality, health, and a warm disposition.

Red = passion and aggression.

White = mental alertness.

Hard = good health.

Soft = delicacy of constitution.

Fluted (i.e. with vertical grooves) = a tendency towards skin ailments and disorders of the joints.

Dented = signs of past illnesses.

Half moons = strong heart and good circulation (though some palmists claim the opposite!).

Absence of moons = the sign of the inveterate bachelor; or in women, of a humdrum marriage.

White spots = a sign of exhaustion and a run-down state of health—time you had a good holiday!

THE THUMB

Many Indian palmists claim that the whole of a person's character and life-story can be deduced from the thumb alone. Others say that as the thumb plays such a vital part of gripping, guiding, manipulating—and therefore in all technological developments—and has done since the beginning of man's evolution, it must therefore be one of the most important keys to character and destiny. Here are some of the conclusions drawn by palmists from the study of the thumb.

(a) SIZE

If a person has good control and direction over his life, the thumb should be at least long enough to reach the first joint of the index finger (when laid close to it), and its nail section should be longer than that of any of the fingers.

The larger the thumb, the greater the moral force, self-control and intelligence of the owner.

Small thumbs indicate a weak and highly impressionable nature.

(b) ANGLE

If, when the hands are held out, the thumb is naturally held at a wide angle from the rest of the hand this suggests a generous, independent nature. If the angle is exaggeratedly wide, though, the owner may be too independent minded—to the point of being selfish and anti-social. If the thumb is held close to the hand, however, it may be that the owner not only lacks independence of spirit, but is selfish, cold, and close with money into the bargain.

(c) SET

The higher the set of thumb (in relation to the rest of the hand), the more selfish and the less intelligent the owner is likely to be.

The lower the set of the thumb the better the co-ordination of the owner, and the higher his degree of physical skill and dexterity.

(d) FLEXIBILITY

Flexible thumbs are a sign of alertness, sharp observation and adaptability.

Over-flexible thumbs, though, may indicate a person too easily swayed by others.

Stiff thumbs are said to indicate caution, rigidity of mind, but also reliability.

(e) SECTIONS

Palmists divide the thumb into three sections. The top, nail section is taken to represent will power—and its degree can be determined by the size of this section.

The second section is said to represent reason and again size shows the amount.

The bottom section (traditionally known as the Mount of Venus) is the fleshy area at the base of the thumb (encircled by the life-line on the palm), and as it is said to represent our love lives, our capacities for friendship, and our appreciation of beauty and the good things of life it is considered of great importance by palmists. Here are some of the basic deductions made from the Mount of Venus:

(a) If this fleshy pad is strongly pronounced but firm—and particularly if in addition it has upward-pointing lines across it you are likely to be warm and outgoing in temperament and to have a strong capacity to both give and receive love—and probably to be highly sexed.

(b) If it is high and rather soft an excitable, rather changeable nature is indicated.

(c) If it is small, narrow and flat, then the owner is too self-contained and detached.

(N.B. There are all kinds of other signs which palmists look for on the Mount of Venus—and also on the pads at the bottoms of the fingers—but these are too complicated for a preliminary survey like this.)

READING THE PALM

Before we go into the detail of the palms themselves, these are the basic rules which are usually followed by professional palmists.

BOTH HANDS NEED TO BE STUDIED—because in palmistry the left hand is regarded as the hand depicting our inherited constitution and characteristics—in other words, the destiny we are born with. The right hand shows what we do, or are capable of doing with these inherited characteristics—in other words, how we can exercise control over our own destinies. For those who are left-handed, it's the other way round—i.e. the right hand is the hand of destiny, and the left hand shows what you are actually doing with your lives.

IT HAS LONG BEEN A DOCTRINE OF PALMISTRY THAT FIRM CONCLUSIONS MUST NEVER BE ARRIVED AT FROM A SINGLE LINE. The final reading must be based on a mixture of lines and signs.

THE MAIN LINES

Begin by carefully studying this "map" of the palm, and if you are looking at your own hands, experiment to find the position which shows the lines on the palms most clearly.

(a) THE LIFE LINE

This line begins at the edge of the palm, between the thumb and index finger, and it encircles the fleshy pad at the base of the thumb (the Mount of Venus).

A long, clearly marked life line, with very few breaks in it, is taken as a sign of a healthy constitution and a long life.

A double life line is a further indication of strength and vitality.

If the life line is thicker at the base than elsewhere, it is yet another indication of a long, healthy life.

When the life line sweeps outwards, across the palm, it is much more likely to point to drive and vitality than if it comes straight down.

A chain effect (like tiny links) along the life line, is usually an indication of poor health, especially spinal trouble or a tendency to allergies.

When there are sharp breaks in the life line, it may mean the occurrence of serious illnesses or accidents.

When crosses appear on the life line, they may indicate troubles past or to come.

If the crosses come at the end of the line, towards the base, they are often interpreted as pointing to serious troubles early in life, such as the loss of parents.

The appearance of an island (a little enclosed space) indicates that this point in your life is a time of rather

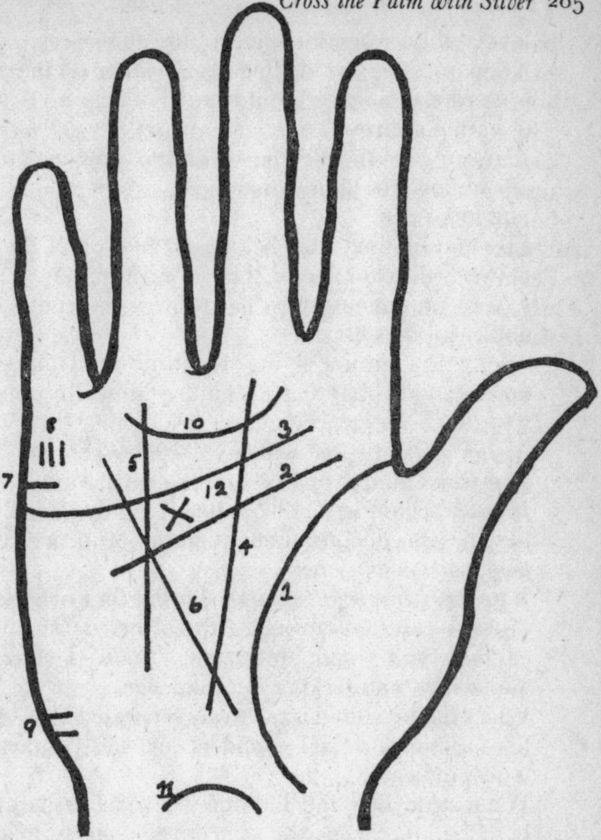

KEY

1. LIFE LINE
2. HEAD LINE
3. HEART LINE
4. FATE LINE
5. FORTUNE LINE
6. HEALTH LINE
7. MARRIAGE LINE
8. CHILDREN
9. TRAVEL LINES
10. SENSITIVITY LINE
11. INTUITION LINE
12. SPIRITUALITY

low vitality, when it is best to take things easy.

A square along the life line (as elsewhere on the palm), is a protective sign– an indication of help from outside or within the psyche.

Lines crossing the life line are said to show the presence of emotional or family anxieties.

(b) THE HEAD LINE

Like the life line, this begins on the side of the hand between the thumb and the index finger.

A very prominent, deep head line is indicative of the ability to concentrate.

A long, straight line shows organising ability, an eye for detail, and probably a strong drive towards obtaining wealth, power or prestige.

A short straight line will usually show common sense, shrewdness and probably business capacity.

If at its beginning the head line is lightly joined to the life line, this denotes thoughtfulness, prudence, and an avoidance of extremes.

If the head line is joined to the life line for a considerable distance (say half-an-inch), the owner is usually very cautious and timid, under the thumb of elders and authorities, and lacking in confidence.

When the head line is narrowly separated from the life line, a more original confident and independent outlook is indicated.

When head line and life line are widely separated in both hands, the person concerned is likely to be extremely impulsive, reckless and unable to stick at anything for long.

When there is a double head line, the probability is that the owner has some interest in life which is as important as the career actually entered.

When the head line curves down, a strongly imaginative and intuitive nature is indicated.

If there is a wide fork at the end of a sloping head line, too much imagination and versatility may be indicated, together with an inability to concentrate.

When the line is split into several branches at the end, there is probably a tendency to muddle-headedness.

When the head line is very lightly marked and wavering, a difficulty in concentrating and a general lack of purpose in life are suggested.

Little links or islands on the head line, point to spells of anxiety and tension.

A break in the headline may point to some kind of breakdown but if the break is enclosed by a protective square, or if the line overlaps, full recovery is indicated.

A number of small lines crossing the head line would show worries, probably accompanied by headaches.

If a line reaches up from the head line to join the heart line (see the map of the palm) there is a strong likelihood of a very unhappy love experience or marriage, and probably of a much more successful turn of events after it is over.

Note that many people have one of the above indications on the one hand, and quite a different one on the other. This is a common symptom of the kind of conflict in which one side of the nature is pulling against the other.

(c) THE HEART LINE

This starts at the opposite edge of the palm to the thumb, under the little finger, and runs towards the thumb side of the palm.

In some cases the heart line is missing from the palm. Usually this is taken to mean that it has been absorbed by the head line, so that the person concerned, while capable of the most tremendous concentration on any goal, and nearly always achieving it, has to pay the price of emotional aridity.

A long, clear heart line, denotes the possession of high ideals and a warm, loving nature.

A short heart line is usually said to indicate selfishness, passion without love, and a very reserved nature.

A thin, faint heart line without branches, is also indicative of a reserved nature, which cannot go out to meet others.

When, in a normal heart line, there are small branches, rising upwards, affectionate long-lasting friendships are indicated.

But if the branches dip downwards, disappointments in love and friendship are indicated.

A chained heart line—i.e. with many tiny links— denotes a good deal of changeability and fickleness.

When the heart line runs from the edge of the palm, right across it, and on to the pad beneath the index finger, the owner is probably extremely jealous and possessive in love.

When the line stops short under the second finger, a person who is incapable of any subtlety in love is indicated. If this feature is present in both hands, selfishness and greediness in love are indicated. But if the left hand has a long and curved heart line, it is usually a safe deduction of an over-repressive childhood.

An upward curve of the heart line, to finish between the index and second finger, is a very hopeful sign for a good and happy marriage, as the owner can be relied on to be tolerant and loving.

When the heart line crosses over the pad beneath the index finger, and then plunges downwards to join the head line, disappointments in love are indicated— together with a tendency to have poor judgment in the choice of lovers.

A narrow space between the heart line and the head line, suggests narrowness, and often selfishness, of outlook.

A wide space between these two lines, on the contrary, suggests breadth of mind and vision.

Crosses and breaks in the heart line are pointers to emotional sorrows, including possibly the loss of a lover or friend, or the end of a love affair.

A complete break in the heart line is usually the sign of a nature that demands too much in love.

(d) THE FATE LINE

This usually begins at the bottom of the hand, near the

wrists, and then climbs up the palm to the base of the second finger. Sometimes, though, this line starts higher up the palm. It is not uncommon for it to be altogether absent. When this happens, the person concerned is usually aimless, changeable and irresponsible, and is not likely to have an exciting or purposeful life.

A long, strong fate line, is an indication of a life of variety, colour and considerable success.

But if the line is so heavy that it is almost like a cut across the hand, then it may suggest a marked tendency to get in a rut.

Faint, wavery lines, in the position of the fate line, may indicate indecisiveness and lack of achievement.

When the line branches off in another direction, some change in career or way of life is to be expected.

When the fate line starts inside the life line, help and loving concern from the parents in the earlier years of life are indicated.

When it is joined on to the life line at the beginning, close family ties are usually present—and you may be called upon to sacrifice yourself for your parents at some stage in your life.

When the fate line begins on the pad of flesh on the far side of the palm, opposite the thumb, the owner usually has a need for public approval, and may well become an actor, entertainer or politician.

When the fate line runs from the bottom of the wrist to the pad of flesh below the middle finger, the owner is likely to be a hard, steady worker and one who will always go for a secure job—or perhaps for an unexciting but steady marriage.

When other lines cross the fate line, they indicate obstacles to be overcome.

Branches which drop downwards and away from the fate line, are signs of reversals in life.

Branches which rise upwards, and away from the fate line, however, denote successes in a whole variety of endeavours.

A double fate line is an even more hopeful sign of success and good fortune.

Breaks in the fate line, denote important changes in life, though these are not always necessarily for the good. But if the lines overlap at this point, then the change will definitely be successful.

Islands along the fate line aren't hopeful signs, because they usually denote troubles and uncertainties.

Squares on the fate line are (as elsewhere on the palm) signs of protection -and assure you that you can overcome the blows of fate.

When a branch runs from the fate line to the third or ring finger, it points to success in artistic undertakings.

(e) FORTUNE LINE

This line is situated to the left of the fate line (see palm map).

When it begins right down at the base of the palm, and then climbs up to the third finger, fame and fortune as an artist, entertainer or politician are predicted.

A clear fortune line without any marks cutting across it, is said to point to wealth or at least very comfortable means, without any financial worries.

Some people have a double fortune line, and this denotes that the wealth will come from a variety of sources.

A break along the line, indicates a serious loss of wealth, but if the line continues strongly after the break, then the person concerned will again become wealthy, either by recovering the lost fortune, or by gaining a new one! If the fortune line crosses the life line, a common interpretation is that members of the family are likely to squander some of the wealth. If, however, it runs alongside the life line, a large inheritance is forecast.

When a separate line joins the fortune line to the fate line, the wealth will be derived from a highly successful business partnership.

Quite often, though, this line doesn't start until fairly high up the palm.

If it starts at the head line, wealth will only arrive after many years of hard work and careful investment.

When it starts above the heart line, fulfilment (and sufficient means to enjoy it) belong to a later period of your life.

Lines crossing the fortune line, point to obstacles that have to be overcome in order to attain wealth.

A star or triangular shape at the top of a long fortune line, redoubles the fame and public acclaim attending the owner's career.

A square at any point along it, is a sign of protection against any serious check to a public career.

(f) THE HEALTH LINE

This line begins below the little finger and runs across the palm towards the base of the thumb.

If you can't find this line on your palm at all, don't worry in fact you should cheer, because its absence is said to be a sure sign of sound and unbroken health.

If you do have such a line but it is clear and straight and without breaks, that too shows that you will have sound health, and financial success in your business, whatever it may be, as well. But, if it joins the life line, and is stronger than it at this point, this indicates a critical period of ill health.

When the health line is crooked or wavering, there is said to be a tendency towards a variety of illnesses.

A number of little breaks in the line are, in the view of palmists, an indication of digestive problems of various kinds.

Little chains or islands along the line, suggest periods of serious illness.

Small lines crossing the health line, indicate a proneness to headaches.

If these small lines are also notably red, there is also a tendency to feverish types of illness.

A square along the health line is, once again a sign of protection.

N.B. In order to obtain some idea when periods of illness indicated on the health line are likely to occur—the portion of the line (starting under the little finger) before it touches the first of the more or less horizontal lines across the palm, belongs to the earlier years of life; the space between the first two horizontal lines represents the middle years; and the rest of the line belongs to one's later life.

(g) THE LOVE AND MARRIAGE LINE

This is a small line (or lines) which begin on the far side of the hand, just below the little finger.

If the line is fairly long (reaching, say, midway or more across the base of the little finger) and is also clear-cut, a long and happy marriage is indicated.

When there are two or more lines, all of them clearly marked, more than one marriage (or deep attachment) is implied. The lower these additional lines are, the earlier in your life the marriage or serious attachment was. If one of these additional lines is to be found very close to the base of the little finger, a marriage late in life is indicated.

A number of very light lines, points to a number of affairs, but none of them sufficiently serious to lead to a lasting attachment.

When the line begins with a fork, a long courtship before marriage is to be inferred.

When it ends in a fork, the implication is that the married partners go their own ways, and are in effect separated—even if not legally so.

An upright line at the end of the marriage line, is said to denote the end of the marriage by divorce or death.

A small line very close to the marriage line (either below or above it), points to an affair either just before marriage, or during it.

A break in the marriage line, shows a break in the marriage—but if the line then continues, the couple will be reunited.

(h) CHILDREN

According to some palmists the existence and number

of these are shown by tiny lines running down into the marriage line. But others look for this indication in the lines round the joint of the forefinger.

(i) TRAVEL LINES

These lines appear on the edge of the palm, opposite the base of the thumb. They really denote the individual's desire to travel, general restlessness and spirit of adventure. The implementation of the desire will depend on other factors, including the necessary opportunities—and the necessary cash!

Assuming these to exist—many lines indicate many journeys, and deep lines indicate that the journeys are of considerable importance to the individual concerned. When the life line forks at its base, and one of the forks points towards the travel line or lines, there is a strong possibility that the person concerned will eventually settle in a country other than his own.

(j) THE SENSITIVITY LINE

This is the curved line (known in chiromantic lore as The Girdle of Venus) above the heart line.

If it is small it shows a highly sensitive nature.

If it is long and very clearly marked it can be a bad sign, pointing to all kinds of disappointments and failures.

If it is broken, an over-anxious, over-tense attitude to love is suggested, together with difficulties in giving expression to feelings. There are some palmists who prefer not to find this line at all, seeing it as almost invariably a sign of misfortunes.

(k) THE INTUITION LINE

This is a semi-circular mark sometimes found at the curved, lower end of the palm, above the wrist and roughly opposite the lower end of the life line.

If it is absent, the person concerned lacks intuitive qualities.

If it is deep and clear on both hands, very strong intuitive powers are to be inferred, and probably a highly developed sixth sense which opens the possessor to psychic influences.

If the line appears on one hand only, the conclusion generally is that the psychic power is present, but has not yet been properly recognised or acted on.

(l)   LINES OF SPIRITUALITY

According to ancient chiromantic lore, a mark known as The Mystic Cross, (sometimes to be found in the centre of the quadrangle between the head line and the heart line) is a sure sign of the person who is deeply involved (sometimes indirectly, through someone very close) in the spiritual life—or in occultism.

(Another mark, known as The Ring of Solomon is sometimes found in conjunction with The Mystic Cross. It is a line encircling the base of the index finger, and running from between the index and middle fingers to the outer edge of the palm. It is traditionally regarded as a sign of wisdom.)

SOME MINOR LINES

A series of lines under the joint of the thumb, is said to be another prediction of riches and honours.

A number of lines round the joint of the index finger, is regarded as a good luck sign, and may denote an inheritance.

Lines round the joint of the middle finger, are often taken as a sign of general unhappiness.

A line rising from the base of the third (ring) finger and running through all the joints, indicates the high-minded person who is destined to achieve wealth and honour.

If lines run round the joint of this finger, the path to fame won't be an easy one.

A number of rings round the last joint of the little finger, indicate an indecisive and inconsistent kind of person.

With the help of the map you should now be able to make a rough reading of your own or somebody else's hands. But remember that if you want to go beyond the party fun stage, you would need to study the subject much more deeply.

THE CRYSTAL BALL

Crystal gazing is another of the very ancient methods of divination. It probably originated in Egypt some six thousand years before the birth of Christ, and a number of beautiful ancient Egyptian crystals have been found by archaeologists. It was much in use among our old friends the Ancient Greeks and Romans, and spread to many parts of the world. It is still frequently used—for example in Japan, where a crystal ball is found in many homes, to be consulted on all important occasions.

But before you dismiss crystal gazing as a lot of super-stitious nonsense only likely to be practised in the mysterious Orient and other faraway places it's worth bearing in mind that many perfectly hard-headed western scientists make use of it in psychological experiments or in psychotherapeutic diagnosis and treatment. It is, for example, one of the aids employed in helping patients to revive early memories. This works in two ways: first, the actual act of gazing into a crystal ball can create a relaxed and dreamy state—it's similar to hypnosis in this respect: and second, the crystal can serve as a focus round which distant memories can begin to gather. In some cases, however, these memories either appear to be actually projected into the crystal, or the shadows or movements which the gazer sees (or imagines he sees) in the crystal, take on the shapes of the memories he is trying to recover in some form or other.

This matter of focus is of essential importance in approaching all these devices—whether it be the crystal ball, an arrangement of cards, the tea leaves at the bottom of a cup, or whatever. From the strictly psychological point of view, the various devices help the concentration and free play of imagination, memory and fantasy—and so provide a kind of channel through which the forces of the unconscious may find their way.

The ancient practitioners of crystal gazing (and many of its modern adherents) also believed, of course, that more mysterious psychic forces, including those that relate to our future destinies, may also reach up towards the surface. You don't necessarily have to believe this in order to take an interest in crystal gazing. But whether you approach it from a strictly psychological point of view, or as a believer in extrasensory perception, or, if it comes to that, as an unashamed believer in magical forces, it is always helpful to bear in mind this idea of focus.

Whatever your approach, it doesn't do to dismiss out of hand all the ancient rules and traditions surrounding the practice of crystal gazing. For the purposes of this chapter it seems reasonable to omit the elaborate rituals, (the magic circle surrounding the crystal and so on) which were considered essential in the past, and which are still employed in many parts of the world. But the inclusion of some of the ancient lore is justified—because it is a further important aid to the process of focusing, providing a kind of framework or funnelling for it.

Here are some hints from the experts about the crystal and how to set it up.

1. First get your crystal! It should be of perfect shape and clarity. Ideally it should be four to five inches in diameter, and in any case not less than one and a half inches (about the size of a medium orange).
2. It doesn't matter whether the crystal is held in the hands or placed on a pedestal of some kind. If it is held, a piece of black velvet should be placed at the bottom of the crystal, to avoid dirt or sweat getting on it. If it's put on a table, the table should be covered by a white linen cloth, and a piece of black material—preferably silk—should be arranged round the crystal, in order to exclude reflections.
3. This matter of excluding reflection is important. Ideally the Gazer should sit with the light from a single window or a lamp falling over the shoulder on to the crystal. As a matter of fact a candle gives the best kind of light—though some of the serious practitioners prefer moonlight. You can crystal-gaze by daylight though—provided the light isn't too brilliant.

4. The room in which you place your crystal shouldn't contain mirrors or pictures whose glass might throw reflections. If possible, too, clear out ornaments, bright colours, anything in fact which might distract the eye. In particular, of course, the background to the crystal should be a plain dark one.

5. Before placing the crystal on the table (and on its pedestal if you have one) it should be warmed by being held in front of a fire or close to the body for a few minutes.

HOW TO CONDUCT A CRYSTAL GAZING SESSION

1. Talking between the Gazer and the person for whom he is making the reading should be in quiet voices.

2. Anyone else in the room must keep as quiet as possible.

3. Although anyone may look into the crystal, the only people allowed to touch it should be the Gazer and his subject. The ancient theory behind this is that handling by anybody else mixes the magnetisms in the crystal, and so weakens or destroys its sensitivity.

4. In fact if possible a crystal should be the exclusive personal property of the Gazer, and he or she should take every step to keep it so, carefully wrapping it up after use and locking it away. The more strictly these rules are obeyed—the more, that is, the crystal becomes impregnated with the personality of its owner—the more sensitive, the experts say, it will become.

5. In the old days, magical passes with the left hand were made over the crystal, and these are still used today by most practitioners, ostensibly to increase the crystal's sensitivity.

6. You should sit back and relax as much as possible before you look into the crystal, closing your eyes and trying to get into as calm a frame of mind as possible.

7. Ancient practitioners stressed the point that the frame of mind must be good; they believed that evil thoughts in the minds of either the Gazer or his subject inevitably led to some form of punishment.

8. When you open your eyes, force them to stay fixed on

the crystal, and do not allow them to wander.

9. As you gaze don't hesitate to wish for the kind of things you want to see. These may either be answers to requests or questions addressed to you by your sitter, or they may be prompted by the feelings and intuitions you've picked up from your sitter.

10. Don't continue your gazing for more than five minutes on the first few occasions and don't be disappointed if nothing happens at the first few attempts. It's rare for a Gazer to see visions the first time, and it's generally recognised that here, as everywhere else—and no matter how intuitive or psychic you may be—practice gradually improves performance.

11. Performance is, in any case, variable. Even those with very strong psychic powers (or intuitions—or whatever more rational term you want to use) don't always get results, and may go through quite long spells in which the crystal is utterly unresponsive.

12. A single session is of limited value. Ideally, the sittings should take place daily for about five days and always at approximately the same time. Over this period the length of the sitting should gradually be increased from five minutes to a maximum of half an hour. The theory here is that the crystal acts as a kind of medium through which the thoughts of the sitter are transferred to the Gazer, and the Gazer's own psychic vibrations, together with the influences to the good which he wishes to exert on his sitter, are in their turn conveyed back to him. And this is a process, of course, which demands time and a gradual build-up.

WHAT MIGHT HAPPEN

1. What you hope to have, of course, are what are most easily described as visions—though you may prefer to use more down to earth language.

2. Before a vision appears, the crystal clouds over, and seems to be turning a milky grey colour.

3. Some Gazers never get beyond this clouding stage; others have had the experience of seeing the milky grey turn to red, and then—radiating from the centre of the crystal—to all the colours of the rainbow.

4. When this clouding appears, you should stay absolutely still, taking special care to beathe slowly and deeply and go on gazing into the crystal patiently and passively, without anxiety of any kind.

5. Then the visions should usually begin to appear. At first they will be jumbled and confusing, but gradually they will clarify, as the stream of cosmic truth (as the practitioners believe it to be) pours into the crystal.

THE TYPES OF VISION

Visions of all sorts can appear in the crystal including scenery, still pictures, events in motion, or even pieces of writing. These visions are commonly divided into eight main categories:

1. The most common kind are projections of the Gazer's own imagination. These are really a form of day-dreaming. But the day-dreaming has been started up by the concentration of the Gazer upon his sitter, through the medium of the crystal, and by whatever psychic currents may be passing between them.

   Therefore it would be unwise to dismiss visions obtained in this way as of inferior value, because they have been placed in the Gazer's imagination as a result of his close contact with his sitter, and if the Gazer is sufficiently sensitive and intuitive he can make positive use of them by wise and careful interpretation.

2. Other visions appear to be the product of current events known to both the Gazer and the sitter, the Gazer having picked up with his psychic antennae the fact that these are specially important to the sitter.

3. Sometimes, though, the current event which shapes the vision in the crystal is not known to the Gazer, and seems to be put into his mind from that of his sitter by some sort of thought transference.

4. Sometimes the current event is known to the Gazer but not to his sitter, and is projected into the crystal because the Gazer knows intuitively that this is a significant event for the sitter in some way or another.

5. Sometimes the event is unknown to either the Gazer or his sitter, in which case it seems to enter the crystal by some other process which is at present a mystery to us.

6. Another type of vision, produced by past events in the sitter's life, of which the Gazer has no conscious knowledge, may be important because they could make the sitter aware of the significance of these past events.

7. Other visions may be caused by suddenly revived memories of the Gazer's past life, which for some reason would be helpful to his sitter. The concentration on the crystal opens up the Gazer's subconscious mind—not unlike the free-association and other methods used by the psychoanalyst. The deeply buried memories may however be those of the sitter, entering into the Gazer's consciousness through the medium of the crystal.

8. Finally there is the type of vision (which practised crystal gazers say is by no means uncommon) that appears to reveal the future. Some scientifically-minded people, of course, will reject this claim as complete nonsense. Others, perhaps, wouldn't venture to be so dogmatic.

INTERPRETING THE VISIONS

There are a number of traditional rules for interpreting the crystal visions. You don't necessarily have to believe that these have a positive value in themselves. But you may feel that they can help you to concentrate and organise your intuitive or psychic powers. Here are what the most important of them are said to indicate:

1. *White clouds*—either the presence of benevolent influences, or an affirmative answer to a question addressed by the sitter to the Gazer.

2. *Black clouds*—unpleasant events.

3. *If the cloudiness is red, orange, or yellow*—a warning of

danger, illness, sorrow, loss, slander, deception or an unpleasant surprise of some kind.

4. *If the cloudiness is blue, green, or purple*—a sign of approaching happiness and fulfilment.

5. *If the clouds appear to be descending*—a negative answer to all the sitter's questions.

6. *If the clouds seem to be moving to the left*—a sign that the sitting must be brought to an end.

7. *If the clouds seem to be moving towards the right*—spiritual beings are present at the sitting.

8. *Visions which are seen in the background of the crystal* are taken as belonging either to the remote past or to the fairly distant future.

9. *Those which appear at the front of the crystal*, however, belong to the present or the immediate future.

10. *A vision which appears to the right of the Gazer*—is symbolic.

11. *A vision appearing to his left*—is an actual representation of an event.

12. *When a piece of writing appears in the crystal* (which apparently happens quite frequently)—it must be taken at its face value (no trying to read between the lines).

All you have to do now is to get your crystal! You may begin by treating it as a joke or a party game—but you may be in for surprises which will change your mind.

None of the things mentioned above may happen to your crystal. But don't throw it away. You may not get occult visions—but you may find that the crystal will help to liberate your fantasy life, sharpen your awareness and intuitions—and possibly awaken psychic powers you never knew you possessed or even believed to exist.

❖❖❖❖❖❖❖❖❖❖❖❖

YOUR DESTINY IN A TEA OR COFFEE CUP?

This really does seem to be scraping the bottom of the barrel . . . to mix our metaphors! It would be difficult to think of anything which smacks more of the party game or frivolous pastime. All the same, this is also an ancient method of divination.

Let's begin by postponing any discussion as to whether there might, after all, be something in it, and see instead what you have to do.

PREPARATIONS

You begin by pouring the tea leaves or coffee grounds from the drinker's cup into a white china cup. Shake the cup well, so that the leaves or grounds cover as much of the inside surface of the cup as possible. Then turn the cup upside down so that any loose leaves or grounds fall into the saucer.

It's the particles left inside the cup which you need for the patterns you are going to try to read.

Note that it's better to tip the tea-leaves or coffee grounds into a fresh white cup, rather than let someone bring you the cup they've just been drinking from. In fact it's not a bad idea to have a special cup for the purpose, which you take with you if you think you're going to be called upon to perform!

One other preliminary point—you may think it's daft, but one of the present writers finds that, to establish a rapport with someone who wants a reading, it helps to hold hands for a moment, or to hold some personal object of his or hers.

It all depends now on the free flow and fertility of your imagination and intuitions in interpreting the patterns which you see in the cup. All we're going to do is outline the kind of shapes gypsy fortune tellers traditionally look for, and leave the rest to your individual fantasies! Not that you'll ever find anything exactly like these shapes, but that doesn't matter: all you have to do is to see something roughly similar. But whatever you do, only use these as the basic patterns: you must look for variations, as well as letting your imagination spot anything else it wishes.

Here, then, is a list of traditional patterns recognised by professional readers:

ANCHOR: Near the bottom of the cup—an emblem of hope and prosperity, especially in business affairs. Near the top of the cup, not too closely hemmed in—long lasting love and fidelity. If it's crowded out and partly obscured by other leaves or grounds—broken love and possible divorce.

BIRDS: Appearing in any part of the cup—a sign that financial and other worries will soon be over for the Reader. Appearing in the midst of a thick, cloud-like cluster—an already prosperous way of life is going to get even more lush. Attended by a lot of dots—a long sea voyage, or some other long trip, in the near future.

BUSH: The Reader has many helpful and generous friends. If the bush is rather bare—fortune may not be quite so kind. A well-covered bush, standing clear—then the Reader may expect to receive an unexpected sum of money from some source or other.

CHILD: Towards the top of the cup, and standing clear—a carefree love affair taking place in the near future. If the child pattern shows in a cloudy mass—the affair will be more serious, and may involve one of the parties in a considerable sum of hush-money. Both cloudy and near the bottom of the cup—a child will result from the affair, causing a good deal of worry and expense.

CLOUDS: Standing apart and somewhat speckled—success in a current enterprise and a good deal of happiness in store. Dots surrounding the pattern—success is assured, but only if too many risks are not taken. If the cloud is dark or heavy—a change in profession or direction is to be recommended.

CLOVER LEAF: This, of course, is a good luck symbol. At or

near the top of the cup—the good luck should arrive quite soon. Near the middle or at the bottom of the cup—the good fortune is going to be considerably delayed. Very clear-cut shape, standing alone—tranquil and unruffled happiness is in store. Clouds round the shape—the good fortune has some unpleasant circumstances round it.

COFFIN: As might be expected this symbol denotes death or at least a very serious illness. But a very clearly defined coffin near the top of the cup means a less serious illness, a long life to come, and a nice fat inheritance from a relative.

CROSS: This is a symbol of misfortune—and one that nearly always affects the Reader rather than the person for whom the reading is being made. At or very near the top of the cup—the misfortune won't be too serious and should pass quickly. In the middle or at the bottom—the Reader is in for a very bad time, and even more so if the symbol is cloudy. Specks or dots with the cross—recovery from misfortunes will be complete, and into the bargain the Reader is likely to be awarded a large sum of compensation in a law suit!

DOG: Near the top of the cup and clearly marked—a symbol of great devotion and fidelity. Surrounded by a lot of leaves or grounds—some of your sitter's apparently loving friends or relations are two-faced. Near or at the bottom of the cup—either you or your sitter have to tread warily with your acquaintances, if some kind of hurt is to be avoided.

FISH: This is another symbol relating to the Reader and not to the sitter. It denotes some important forthcoming event which will be very lucky, especially from the financial point of view. If the symbol is rather thick and clouded —there may be obstacles in the way, but ones that can easily be surmounted. If specks or dots accompany the symbol—caution and patient effort will be needed to help bring about the favourable outcome.

FLOWERS: Wherever they appear in the cup these are always symbols of success. The more clear-cut they are, the greater the success and the more quickly it will arrive.

GARDEN: This is supposed to be a pointer to a party or some other joyful gathering of close friends. If the symbol is clouded—someone will be present at the occasion whose professions of friendship can't be trusted.

HEART: This symbol denotes happiness and joy, especially if it is in the clear. Surrounded by specks —money is also to be expected. Two hearts— the sitter will soon be engaged to be married. If a letter of the alphabet accompanies the twin hearts—it will be the initial of the first name of the prospective partner.

HORSEMAN: This is invariably a good sign. Clear-cut—a letter or some other exciting good news from abroad, or perhaps the unexpected offer of an exciting new job. When clouded—the marvellous good news is only going to take a little longer to arrive!

HOUSE: Another message for the Reader. Near the top of the cup—great success is on the way. In the middle or below— a warning to be on guard with professed friends or business associates, because someone has malicious intentions.

KNIFE: Again a symbol for the Reader. Standing clear and pointing in Reader's direction—a warning that someone has harmful intentions. If it's cloudy—the danger is the greater.

Knife pointing away from Reader—the harmful or revengeful intentions are in the Reader himself/herself.

LETTER : This symbol is always taken to mean that news of some sort is on the way. Clear and unclouded—the news will be very good. Clouded —the news will be very bad. Clear and also surrounded by dots—money or something else of value is on the way. With a clearly shaped heart nearby and the letter also clear— a very encouraging love message is to be expected. If the heart is clouded—the love message will be distinctly disappointing.

LILY : Wherever this symbol appears, provided it is clear and standing alone—a sign of a long and happy life. At or near the top of the cup—a message—usually for the Reader—that he or she has, or will eventually have, a very happy marriage. Near the bottom of the cup, and if also clouded or thick—a great deal of anger is present, and many troubles are in store.

LION : (Or any other wild, fierce animal). Near the top of the cup—great prosperity and the attainment of a position near the top of the social ladder. At or near the bottom—any attempt at social elevation should be avoided, because someone would become extremely jealous and exert a harmful influence.

MOON : On the whole, a good sign for the Reader. Near the top of the cup—certain riches and honours. Near the bottom—great good fortune is to be predicted over the course of a life-time. Noticeably thick and cloudy and near the bottom—many disappointments are in store, but even then good fortune and happiness will eventually prevail.

MOUNTAINS : Clearly marked, and wherever they appear— the possession of realiable and influential friends, who will always do their best to help. Thick and apparently surrounded by clouds —powerful enemies are indicated.

MOUSE: This symbol is usually addressed to the Reader. It's a warning of robbery and dishonesty. If the sign is by itself—harmful effects can be avoided with a little care. Thick and cloudy— great determination and cleverness needed to avoid losses.

PEDESTRIAN: This symbol denotes successful business ventures, new and helpful friendships, a trip or holiday (possibly abroad), and in some cases the recovery of business losses, or stolen goods. A particularly good omen for a woman, because it indicates an unusually good and understanding husband.

RING: A common symbol, of course, of marriage. If clearly seen near the top of the cup—a very happy one. Cloudy and near the bottom— either the projected marriage won't take place, or if it does it won't last long.

ROAD: Clearly seen—dramatic and highly favourable changes. Cloudy—financial reverses and ill health. Specks surrounding the road—a long and productive life, attended by very comfortable circumstances.

ROD: Associations of aggression here, a fight within the family as the result of an inheritance. Dark and cloudy—the inheritance is going to be lost to another person, and further difficulties, including illness, are liable to arise.

ROSE: A very favourable sign all round. It's an assurance of happy love, marriage, and family life—with happy children to enrich it. It is also said to be an assurance of great success to artists and scientists.

SACK: This can mean a burden that has to be shouldered. Clearly marked, open at the top and spilling its contents—fruitfulness and riches. Clouded and hemmed in—a warning that someone close to you may squander your money.

SCYTHE: The scythe is a common symbol, of course, of Time (the Great Reaper). Very thick and cloudy—and especially if accompanied by something that looks like an hour-glass—a warning of imminent danger of a serious kind. Fairly clear, accompanied by a lot of dots—a great love disappointment is to be inferred. Very clear and apart—a good sign, devotion in love, and/or a long and happy marriage.

SNAIL: Sometimes said to denote security and self-sufficiency, and sometimes, especially if surrounded by dots or specks, a life of constant harrassment.

SNAKE: This symbol is addressed especially to the Reader, but can be applied to the sitter as well. It's a warning to be on the look-out for a lying and malicious enemy. Near the top of the cup—not such a bad sign because the hostile intentions of the enemy can be prevented by taking great care. Near the bottom —the danger is greater because the enemy is someone quite unexpected. Cloudy looking— the enemy's plots, though initially successful, will fail in the end. A letter of the alphabet appearing near by—a clue to the identity of the enemy. In all cases, the sign of a snake is to be taken seriously.

STARS: The traditional predictors read a great deal into this symbol. Near the top of the cup, clear and standing by itself—great happiness. Cloudy or surrounded by a mass of leaves or grounds—a long and healthy life, but with many worries and difficulties. Surrounded by spots—a good sign, denoting wealth, much success and honour in life, and great respect from one's fellow men. More than one star— the birth of many children is predicted. Several stars together surrounded by dots or specks—a danger that these children may be a source of sadness and worry when they grow up.

SUN: By itself and near the top of the cup—a very happy sign, with good fortune in everything. Obscured by a cloud-like mass of leaves or grounds—an indication of many illnesses. Surrounded by dots or specks—an illness is coming very soon, but it won't be a serious one.

TREE: This symbol, too, has traditionally been rich in interpretations. A single tree, clearly marked and standing by itself—a sign of life-long good health. Two or more trees, clearly separated— signposts to the fulfilment of plans and desires. Separate trees surrounded by specks or longish flecks—good fortune is assured, but it may take a long time to mature, and will call for careful thought and planning. Small specks surrounding the trees—wealth, especially as the result of wise investments. A group of trees very close together, especially if cloudy— warning of misfortunes, which can only be avoided by great care and much hard work.

UMBRELLA: Generally speaking this is taken as a symbol of protection, especially if the umbrella is open and in the clear. Closed—the restoration of something lost, including a lost friendship.

WOMAN: Near the top of the cup—an indication of a happy and successful courtship. Surrounded by dots or specks—the woman concerned is both wealthy and fertile. Thick and rather cloudy—the relationship will be somewhat spoiled by jealousy.

WORMS: An odd symbol, but one frequently used. Near

the top of the cup—a sure sign of good luck in both business and marriage. In the middle or towards the bottom of the cup—a warning of dangerous rivals in business or love, some of whom may be those who are apparently close friends.

YACHT: Or any other boat with sails. This symbol is usually taken as an indication of long journeys to foreign parts, or of some close connection, through love or business, with them. If the sails are set—success is predicted. If furled—either the journey will not take place for some time, or it has taken place in the past. Surrounded by cloudiness or a mass of leaves or grounds—warning of trials and difficulties to be overcome, but the conclusion usually is that even then the enterprise will be successful in the long run.

❖❖❖❖❖❖❖❖❖❖❖❖❖

There you have a pretty good preliminary dictionary of symbols. One interesting point about them you will have noticed—that a number of them really apply exclusively to the person who is reading the tea or coffee cup. In practice many practitioners use them for their sitters as well, but it does mean that you can tell your own fortune from your cup.

If you memorise all the symbols and their interpretations we've given you, you will undoubtedly have as much as you need to give a really good party turn. You may, of course, find it hard to take anything so apparently trivial as tea leaves and coffee grounds at all seriously. But before you relegate the whole business to the category of party tricks it's worth considering the following points:

1. The shapes and patterns we've given you in our short dictionary of predictions will only rarely, of course, appear absolutely clear-cut and recognisable. Usually the inside of a tea cup ready to read looks something like this:

The formation of these symbols depends to a very large extent on the exercise of your own imagination.

2. This means that you have to bring a good deal of yourself to your reading. As with all these methods, the interpretations can only be as good as the interpreter. It is, therefore, at least possible that if you have unusual perceptiveness, sensitivity, intuition, and perhaps psychic power (if you like to think in such terms) you might find these symbols as useful a channel for these gifts of yours as any other. Note, too, that you don't have to be slavishly bound to these traditional and time honoured symbols though they deserve respectful consideration. You might very well invent some of your own that would serve the purpose equally well—provided they genuinely proceeded from your own unconscious, in contact with that of your sitter (if you are making the reading for someone else). The main value of any set of symbols is that it provides a preliminary framework or discipline.

3. The point we made earlier in this chapter about the value of a focus for intuitions is also relevent here. There's no real reason why the dots, specks, patterns, etc., made by tea leaves or coffee grounds shouldn't provide a perfectly good focus.

4. It is interesting, too, to note that the patterns made by tea leaves and coffee grounds have some similarities to the ink blot patterns used by Hermann Rorschach and his followers in stirring up and assessing various emotional responses. These are made by putting some ink on a piece of paper, which is then folded, producing a symmetrical blot, rather resembling a butterfly—like this:

It must be stressed that the Rorschach Test, is a thoroughly worked out scientific process. Ten standardised blots, some plain and others with colour, are used; carefully chosen questions are addressed to the sitter as he looks at the blots; the answers are scientifically scored, rated and assessed, and so on. But the basic underlying principle is that the blot patterns stimulate the flow of fantasy and of forces from the unconscious—and it could be argued that the arrangements of tea leaves and coffee grounds might also do this.

So maybe there's something in it after all! *In fact the really important concluding point that must be made, is that any method, device or approach which may release people's emotions and hidden thoughts and desires must be treated with a strong sense of responsibility and some respect.*

CHAPTER THIRTEEN

WHAT'S IN YOUR STARS?

CHAPTER THIRTEEN

WHAT'S IN YOUR STARS?

A good many of us probably get our ideas of astrology from the popular star-gazer columns of newspapers and magazines, which are a lot of fun but obviously haven't the space or time to go into what is a complicated and fascinating subject. Astrology has been defined as a system of thought, a way of closely relating everything in nature—animal, vegetable, mineral, human, planetary, cosmic—and using this relationship not only to detect facts about individual human beings and their characters and future lives, but also to predict the continuing evolutionary changes of the whole race. In astrological terms, the past is divided into Ages, each something over 2,000 years long; thus the Age of Taurus ran from 4220 B.C. to 2160 B.C., followed by the Age of Aries which stretched up to A.D. 1 when the Age of Pisces —our present Age—began. Actually, at this date we are on what astrologers call the cusp (that is, the dividing line) between Pisces and the next Age, that of Aquarius, which is due to begin in A.D. 2160. In previous Ages man has dealt successively with himself and his outside world (when he was learning to light fires, make tools, build, etc.), with himself and other people (learning to live in communities, cities, civilizations); now in the Age of Aquarius he will have to learn to deal with himself and his inner world. As one leading astrologer (Alan Oken) puts it "we are learning the painful truth that we have got to get on together or perish—and that to get on with people, we've got to know and understand a lot more about our inner selves individually . . .", and he goes on to say "Selfconsciousness is a priority for the Aquarian Age man and woman. The greater the awareness of self, the greater the consciousness of the potential energies available to a human being, the greater the possibility for evolutionary development." The argument of the astrologers is that there's no reason why astrology —properly studied and understood—should not help us in its own way towards such greater awareness and under-standing of self. According to the great psychologist Jung, who researched astrology extensively, all events happening at a certain moment of time have the particular qualities of that moment of time in them. That is, the moment of a person's birth is linked with all other natural happenings at that moment. This could include the positions and be-haviour of the sun, moon and planets, and suggests that a horoscope—which is a picture of the heavens from a parti-cular point on earth carefully drawn for the time and place of an individual birth—could give a trained astrologer some insight into the character and possible events in the life of that person.

As we've just said, astrology is a complicated subject—far too complicated in fact to go into in any depth here—so we shall try to give you the bare outlines and general pointers.

Before we go into even the basic essentials, though, we might as well find out your general attitude towards all sorts of unseen factors which may possibly make up and influence your character:

QUESTIONNAIRE

1. Do you sometimes touch wood for luck?
2. Do you avoid walking under a ladder propped up across your path?
3. Do you literally cross your fingers when wishing your-self or someone else good luck?
4. Do you believe that an unborn baby may be affected in some way by something happening to its mother—for instance if she is badly frightened?
5. Do you think that a mother's state of mind and body at the time of baby's birth—i.e. happy, frightened, co-operative, unwilling—might affect the baby and its own reactions to life?
6. Do you believe that there are unseen influences, in-tangible forces around us—the sort of atmosphere which animals and children (and a few hyper-sensitive

adults) seem to pick up, so to speak, but which can't be recorded and photographed?

7. Are you aware of being definitely affected, mentally and physically by the weather—i.e. slowed down by a dull grey cloudy day, or exhilarated by a stormy wind?

8. Do you ever feel weather coming—e.g. get a headache before thunder?

9. Have you ever had a genuine experience of premonition —something you suddenly "felt" was going to happen, and it did?

10. Do you believe in telepathy and extra-sensory perception?

11. Do you believe (whether or not you follow a religion) that there is some force or forces beyond ourselves and our material world, which plays some part in the universe?

❖❖❖❖❖❖❖❖❖❖❖❖❖

ANSWERS AND COMMENTS

If you have answered YES to:

8 or more of these questions, it's highly likely that you are open to the idea that astrology may genuinely help you to know yourself, and even to predict the sort of events likely to happen in your life.

7-4 suggests that you half-believe this.

3 or under –you see yourself as a hard-headed realist who takes nobody's word for anything, and who has to have genuine "this really happened to me" experiences before you'll believe—anything.

To begin at the beginning, the Zodiac is the name given to the area of space in which the sun, the moon and principal planets lie. It is divided by astrologers into 12 parts—or signs—through which the sun passes. The names given to these signs and to the planets are very old indeed, because studying the stars and relating human life and events to them is one of the oldest human activities, going back thousands of years.

It isn't enough, however, (even though it may be ego-stroking) to pick out your birthday sign and leave it at that. In fact, to learn anything about yourself or your future from astrology, your individual horoscope has to be drawn up and for that not only your date of birth is needed, but also the place and, if possible, the time of birth too. This is because the planets and in particular the sun have an influence on you and, since they all (including the earth) move round in relation to each other, it's obvious that each of them will be in a different position in relation to a particular spot on earth (i.e. the place where you were born) and that position too will vary according to the time of day or night (i.e. the time you were born). All the planetary influences, in fact, have to be taken into account in making anything like an accurate horoscope.

Let's take an example—that of a person born, say, on 26th June—i.e. when the sun was in the Zodiac sign of Cancer. Now the position of the moon happens to be particularly important in the horoscope of anyone born under Cancer, since it is the ruling planet of that sign (we'll be listing all the ruling planets shortly). As the moon, however, moves into a different sign (part of the sky) approximately every forty-eight hours, it's obvious that not all Cancerians will have the moon in the same position in their horoscopes, and that it will exert a different influence according to that position. Let's say that when our imaginary Cancerian was born, the moon was in Taurus. This would make him or her a Tauran/Cancerian, with different characteristics from, say, a person born with the moon in Libra, who would be a Libran/Cancerian. This explains why all general horoscopes can seem wildly wrong—people born under the same sign are subject to so many different influences that their characters are bound to be very different.

To go back to our imaginary Cancerian. The next influence to consider is that of the sign rising over the horizon at the time of birth. Now each part of the sky, or sign, takes about two hours to pass over the horizon (incidentally, if you've ever done any star-gazing or gone to one of those fascinating planetariums, you'll know how the whole vast sky-full of stars and planets is moving and changing position all the time   and, we hope, you'll know what we're now talking about!). So suppose we say that when this Cancerian of ours was born, the sign of Aries was coming up over the horizon. This makes our example a Tauran/Arian/Cancerian. And this process is carried on right through all the planets; their positions, the signs they are in, their relation to each other, all adding something to the horoscope being drawn up. It's becoming obvious, in fact, that there is a lot more to the making of an astrological horoscope than sometimes meets the eye! And that learning to take into account all the different influences around you at birth could help you to draw an in-depth character study of yourself   a picture which would help you to better understanding and acceptance of yourself.

It's all very well, you may be thinking, to talk about the position of planets at different times and places, but how on earth am I expected to know that. The answer is in an ephemeris   a book of tables giving the position of the planets on any given day (going back to the year dot)   and this is, as you can see, really essential if you're to get anywhere at all with your horoscope. (At the end of the book we give details of this and other useful books.)

To make things sound more complicated than ever, we show you below how each sign, in addition to having a ruling planet, is connected to one of the four elements of Earth, Air, Fire or Water, and is also said to be either male or female. We are also setting out the brief divinatory meanings of the planets themselves, and what the elements and the sex of each planet indicates. All these influences will contribute their own particular characteristics to the sign in question.

	RULING PLANET	ELEMENT	SEX
ARIES	Mars	Fire	male
TAURUS	Venus	Air	male
GEMINI	Mercury	Air	male
CANCER	The Moon	Water	female
LEO	The Sun	Fire	male
VIRGO	Mercury	Earth	female
LIBRA	Venus	Air	male
SCORPIO	Mars	Water	female
SAGITTARIUS	Jupiter	Fire	male
CAPRICORN	Saturn	Earth	female
AQUARIUS	Saturn	Air	male
PISCES	Jupiter	Water	female

Here, briefly, are the influences exerted by the planets:

THE SUN:

this is the source of life, the male, active, creative factor, often connected with positions of authority, and with religious and political leaders.

THE MOON:

this is to do with the imagination, sympathies, preservation; it represents domestic life and relationships within the family. It stands for the mother, and in a man's chart, for women in general.

MERCURY:

this represents active intelligence, rationality, the need to know; often connected with education, travel, writing, communications generally.

VENUS:

the personification of love and beauty; personal magnetism and physical attractiveness. It is related to all artistic occupations, as well as to those close to nature.

MARS:

stands for personal drive; the urge to win and to succeed; courage and stamina. It relates to all war-like occupations, and those using tools; as well as research and surgery.

JUPITER:

is the giver of wisdom and understanding; the urge to explore physically and philosophically. It is connected with occupations like the law, religion, teaching, banking.

SATURN:

stands for structure and consolidation, and represents self-discipline and the limitation and redirection of energies. It is connected with the occupations in the building and architectural areas, finance, government work.

There are also, of course, the three relatively recently discovered planets of Uranus, Neptune and Pluto, but the energies in their vibrations tend to affect mankind in general and do not often show themselves in a personal sense in the lives of each individual. As a matter of interest, however, we are including them here:

URANUS:

represents intuitional originality, and includes everything really way-out and genuinely new and different in art and thought and living. Associated with new occupations such as rocket technology, satellite communications, computer science.

NEPTUNE:

the principle of universal love and perfection; it has to do with mysticism, artistic creativity, vision (natural and artificially induced by drugs, etc.). Connected with occupations dealing with film and dance, also with healing, and psychiatric work.

PLUTO:

represents regeneration; provides the necessary energy to break down psychological blocks which hold back development; it is the inner force, the seed, ready to break through and start growing. Is associated with all forms of underground work, mines, caves, etc., as well as undercover activities like spying, detection, and the work of psychic healers.

And here, very briefly indeed, are the principles associated with the elements and the sexes:

FIRE	dynamic creativity
EARTH	practicability, stability
AIR	communication, human interaction

WATER —emotional being, sensitivity

MALE —the outgoing, self-expressive principle

FEMALE —the inward-looking, self-repressive principle

And now, with these brief meanings to add to the interpretation of your particular character through your birth sign, we will give you a short general outline of the sort of characteristics to be expected in a person born under each of the twelve signs of the Zodiac. We do want to stress again that, without the specific information of your birth place, and time of birth, let alone the various positions of the planets, this will be a very general outline only. If you are becoming really interested in the whole subject we strongly recommend you to follow the suggested reading list at the end of the book:

ARIES—The Ram—Fire sign ruled by Mars—male

21 March-20 April

Each sign is connected with a part of the body and roughly represents that part. You may be able to see that the Aries symbol looks like the eyebrows and nose of the face. In fact, Aries is the head sign, and one of the first things about Arians is that they want to be at the head of everything they do, and they don't much like subordinate positions. They have tremendous energy, enthusiasm, idealism and are full of activity. In fact, they're so full of drive that they may overshoot themselves, have brilliant ideas they don't carry through, and are not in any case good at method and detail and can get very impatient with slower, more thorough people. They can also become dangerously self-absorbed and are nearly always egoists, though they are generally well-liked because they are stimulating and lively company.

TAURUS—The Bull—Earth sign ruled by Venus—male

21 April-21 May

This symbol is associated with the shoulders and neck—and one sure thing about Taurans is their ability and willingness to work hard (physically and mentally). They are very good partners in any enterprise. They are security conscious and comfort-loving, and put a lot of their energies into making financially and materially sure of life. With Venus as their ruling planet, it's not surprising that Taurans are ruled by their hearts rather than by their heads—they are steady and loyal friends and lovers, and if they are born when Venus itself is in Taurus they may be the kind of people who love once and for always. The dangers of a Tauran nature lie in their becoming too keen on possession—and too possessive in love—and too settled into a comfortable rut. They also tend to be reserved and find it hard to express their deep feelings.

♊ **GEMINI**—The Twins—Air sign ruled by Mercury—male 22 May–22 June

This symbol can be interpreted as the two lungs of the body—parts which are vital in all physical activities, including talking, which most Geminians are good at. They are full of ideas, outward-looking and sensation-seeking—flitting about the world of sights and sounds and ideas like restless bees. They can become Jacks of all trades if they are not careful, and will have to learn to concentrate all their mental and physical energies if they are to carry things through to a successful conclusion. They are highly intelligent, gifted and sensitive people, often good writers as well as speakers, hiding their essential nervousness and uncertainty about themselves under a bold and lively exterior. In love, as in everything else, Geminians have to guard against darting from one promising relationship to another.

♋ **CANCER**—The Crab—Water sign ruled by the Moon—female 23 June–23 July

This symbol is a stylized representation of the breasts—and it is the chest with which the sign is associated. Cancerians are frequently maternal (even the men) and very domesticated. Although they are sensitive and imaginative and very susceptible to both their own environments and to other people's pains and pleasures, they can be very practical when necessary. The chief danger with Cancerians is that, being easily hurt and affected by others, they may retreat into their shells and spend too much time day-dreaming. Also, being so highly imaginative, there's a tendency to build things up in the mind and to worry over things that are really small and unimportant. Cancerians are often strikingly intuitive, particularly about people with whom they are closely involved. If you are a friend or a lover of a Cancerian, you must be prepared for pretty rapid changes of mood. Cancerians are, after all, ruled by the Moon and their emotions ebb and flow under its influence much as the oceans do.

♌ **LEO**—The Lion—Fire sign ruled by the Sun—male
24 July-23 August
This symbol is a representation of the heart—which is the centre, the focal point of the human system. And Leo people are frequently the centre of their circle. They are born rulers, are personally attractive and usually have a cluster of loyal and admiring friends round them. They are proud, and like the good things of like—including intelligent and beautiful people—though Leo people can also be self-indulgent and self-centred and boastful if they are not careful. They are generous and brave and, provided you are willing to let them be boss, make good warm-hearted friends and lovers.

♍ **VIRGO**—The Virgin—Earth sign ruled by Mercury—female   24 August-23 September
This rather curious coil-like symbol can be seen as a representation of the inner coils of the body—which perform various complicated services in the human system. And service is the keyword of this sign. Virgoans are excellent at learning in detail and then applying that learning practically. They are frequently self-educated, and in any case will go on picking up subjects and learning about things all their lives. They are often drawn to occupations which need detailed study and application—such as chemical and psychological analysis—and their greatest danger is in being nit-picking, getting tangled up in tiny unimportant details and worrying too much if they can't sort everything out to their own satisfaction. They tend to be shy and retiring in personal relationships.

≏ **LIBRA**—The Scales—Air sign ruled by Venus—male
   24 September-23 October

As well as being the mid-point of the Zodiac, this symbol corresponds to the middle of the body—(the navel)—and as such, acts as a balance. Librans have a strong feeling for balance in all things—they are mentally sensitive, have a great feeling for beauty in form and colour and sound, and can be thrown off balance when their environment is inharmonious or uncongenial to them. If they are born when Venus is in their sign, they may well be artists in some medium or other. Librans can indeed be expected to be "feminine" (both men and women), being intuitive and charming, sociable and gentle-mannered. The main danger for Librans lies in their becoming effeminate and over-reliant on other people. Otherwise, they make good companions, and tend to marry young.

♏ **SCORPIO** —The Scorpion—Water sign ruled by Mars and Pluto—Female   24 October-22 November

This symbol is not unlike that for Virgo and indeed represents another complicated part of the body, the sexual organs—and the overall significance of this sign lies in sensation and regeneration. Scorpionians are dynamic, strong-willed, passionate and sensitive. They are good at stimulating growth—both materially and spiritually -for other people. They are never afraid to show their very strong feelings (including sexual ones) and this can sometimes be alarming to others. They have to be careful because they can become bullies and ruthless go-getters at other people's expense. Because Scorpionians are so positive and frank, they are either very much liked or disliked.

♐ **SAGITTARIUS** —The Centaur—Fire sign ruled by Jupiter —male   23 November-22 December

This symbol is related to the thighs and upper parts of the leg in the human body. Sagittarians have a markedly dual nature - they excel at physical activities, sports, and the outdoor life, but can also be deeply serious and even religious at heart. They are generous, self-reliant, knowledgeable and courageous. Because they are optimistic and cheerful people, everyone loves their encouraging company. Some people sometimes mistakenly feel Sagittarians are hypocritical because they seem to be at home in so many widely different groups. The danger for most Sagittarians lies in firing too many bright ideas and ideals into the air (like arrows) and not bothering to see where they land or what happens to them. They can also be self-opinionated and tactless in their strong feelings for the truth. In love and friendship with a Sagittarian you'll often have to learn to live with two people in one.

♑ CAPRICORN – The Goat – Earth sign ruled by Saturn – female   23 December-20 January
This symbol is connected with the knee and the shin in the human body, and Capricornians are a bit like sure-footed goats, climbing carefully and nimbly about in their lives. They are deep thinkers, but always with a strong practical strain. They are ambitious and will plod on, alone if necessary, to complete their undertakings. Because they don't open out much, Capricornians are apt to be suspicious of other people, to be afraid of material insecurity and to save too hard towards imagined disasters. They don't make friends or lovers easily, but are steady and faithful to the few they have.

♒ AQUARIUS   The Water Carrier   Air sign ruled by Saturn and Uranus   male   21 January-19 February
This symbol is connected with the ankles of the human body. Aquarius has also been called the sign of the inventor, and certainly Aquarians want to make everything new. At their worst, they can be eccentric and unpredictable, inconsiderate and selfish. They are in any case highly unconventional, work out their own codes of behaviour and want others to feel as free as they do. At their best they are humanitarians who want all the good things of life to be shared by everyone – the world is all one to them. Even in love and friendship, Aquarians don't exclude anyone from their affections.

♓ PISCES   The Fishes   Water sign ruled by Jupiter and Neptune – female   20 February-20 March
The symbol which is connected with the heels of the human

body. One of the outstanding characteristics of the Pisceans is their extreme sensitivity — they are so easily affected by the thoughts and emotions of others that from time to time they have to protect themselves by being alone. They are in any case naturally quiet people; trustful and loving, with high ideals and a lot of imagination. Their main danger is in being over-affected by outside atmospheres and other people's personalities, and getting lost themselves. They also identify themselves so closely with the sufferings of the world, that they tend to feel martyred themselves and to rebel against God for allowing so much pain. So long as they keep their balance, Pisceans are highly sympathetic and make loyal, loving friends and lovers.

✦✦✦✦✦✦✦✦✦✦✦✦✦

All we've been able to do in a chapter of this size and scope is to indicate some of the basic assumptions and approaches of astrology. At the risk of repeating ourselves, we must emphasize that the sweeping, over-simple predictions made in the star-gazing sections of the popular press have little or nothing to do with real serious astrology — and they may be, in fact, one of the reasons why the subject has up to now had such a bad name among scientists.

There are signs, however, that the attitude of many scientists is changing quite considerably. In many parts of the world (including Soviet Russia and other East European countries) there are scientists who now accept that there's a great deal more to astrology than they would have been prepared to admit a few years ago. One of the main reasons for their more respectful attitude has been the comparatively recent realization of the importance of the earth's electro-magnetic fields in affecting various life patterns, including human behaviour; and the growing understanding of the extent to which these electro-magnetic fields are in turn affected by phenomena outside our own world.

This is, of course, basically what the astrologers have claimed for many centuries, even though they may have used archaic and often semi-mystical ways of saying it. Take, for instance, the influences of the moon which, together with the sun, has always been considered astrologically as very important indeed in our lives. From the earliest times it has been thought that the full moon had a particularly unsettling effect on the mentally unbalanced (the word lunatic comes from the Latin word for moon, i.e. luna). It seems now that these old theories were perfectly justified. The periodic changes in the moon, it is now generally accepted, do modify the earth's magnetic field, and this in turn affects all living things. The pull of lunar gravity is naturally at its greatest when the moon is approaching fullness, and there is plenty of evidence to suggest that this affects our bodies and nervous systems in all sorts of ways and that it may very well raise tensions and aggravate whatever mental conflicts may already be there.

Another ancient folk belief was that the moon controls our blood flow in much the same way that it controls the tides. Some recent research now suggests that there may very well be something to it. There have also been scientific investigations which suggest the possibility of a direct relationship between the lunar cycle and both the menstrual cycle and ovulation in women. What is more some researchers have also investigated the idea of the moon as "the great midwife", which is held among a number of peasant and primitive communities in various parts of the world. These researchers have produced results which show that (on the basis of a very large sample) more births take place during the waning of the moon than during its waxing. Other investigations have not yet satisfactorily confirmed this possible relationship, so although it is not scientifically established so far, it will now at least be clear that scientists really are moving into an area which they previously left to the astrologers.

The sun too, has its cycles, and there is now direct evidence to support the astrologers' ancient belief that these have a powerful effect on life on earth. A Japanese scientist, Maki Takata, has demonstrated, for example, that there are certain changes in our blood serum which mainly take place when the big sun-spots are affecting the earth's magnetic field. Recent scientific investigations in the Soviet Union also suggest that the blood (and therefore various diseases and malfunctions connected with it) is directly affected by the sun's activity. Two French heart specialists have discovered a significantly high correlation between activities in the sun and heart failure caused by blood clots. Other researchers have shown that the changes in the earth's magnetic field caused by the sun affect our nervous systems (which, after all, depend very largely on electrical stimuli)— and therefore our behaviour too. Thus, a survey of pit accidents in the Ruhr and studies of traffic accidents in Germany and the Soviet Union, both point to a significant rise in numbers after bursts of activity on the sun. As one scientist has put it, ". . . man is, among other things, a remarkably sensitive living sundial".

And since the effects of the sun's and moon's activities on life on earth   and particularly on the sensitive and complex human being—have been scientifically demonstrated and accepted, it won't surprise you to learn that a large number of scientists now agree that the positions and movements of the planets (or perhaps the infinitely vaster cosmic pattern of energy to which they, like ourselves, belong) also affect us.

In other words, the scientists are now, generally speaking, in agreement with the astrologers' basic belief that life on earth is influenced by what is happening in the cosmos surrounding it.

But the common ground between astrologers and scientists is much wider than that, and is growing greater all the time. There is, first of all, the question of the exact time and date of your birth, which is so vital to astrologers. Eugen Jonas, a Czech scientist, seems to have proved pretty conclusively not only that the time of a woman's ovulation is connected with the moon's activity, but also that her ability to conceive is linked with the phase of the moon that prevailed when she herself was born. Jonas has provided many women, in Czechoslovakia and other East European countries, with charts based on each individual's connections with the moon, and it is claimed that these charts prove 98% effective in preventing conception—which is as good as the famous Pill, and has the advantage of no chemical side-effects! The charts can also indicate, apparently, which are the days on which individual women are most likely to conceive.

So there—assuming these findings and results are fully confirmed—is the direct link between birth and one of the celestial bodies which the astrologers have always claimed to exist. Most scientists in fact would now probably accept the idea that cosmic forces have an influence on the infant in the womb, although some of them disagree with the astrologers' emphasis on the importance of the moment of birth, maintaining that the cosmic influences must begin to operate much earlier than that—even indeed from the moment of conception when—as we already know—the individual combination of genes and chromosomes settles so much of what that individual will inherit from the parents.

And what of the astrologers' casting of natal horoscopes and their claims that these will reveal individual character and destiny? Well, there are scientists who are moving into this area too, and treating it with a good deal of care and respect. For over twenty-five years, for instance, Michel Gauquelin, of the Psycho-physiological Laboratory at Strasbourg, has been researching into the possible links between human life on the earth and the rhythms of the planets. He collected details from hundreds of birth registers, and set out to see if these details had any connection with the positions of the planets, as computed from the astronomical tables. He began by selecting two batches of top medical men (over 1,000 in all), and found that a very large number of them were born when the planets Mars and Saturn had either just risen or reached their highest point in the sky. This showed a definite statistical correlation between the rise of these planets at a child's moment of birth (they could, of course, have begun to exercise their influence earlier than that) and his future success in the field of medicine. It may seem that the samples were too small and culturally localized, but the odds against this correlation taking place by chance alone were 10 million to 1 against.

Gauquelin went on to study other professions, and again came up with impressive correlations between them and the positions of the various planets, though the relations weren't always as clear-cut as in the case of the doctors. Later he extended his researches to other parts of Europe, until eventually he had some 25,000 records. The results confirmed those he had made earlier. Here are some of them:

Scientists and doctors were positively linked at birth with Mars and Saturn (and avoided Jupiter).

Soldiers, politicians and team athletes were positively linked at birth with Jupiter.

Painters, musicians and some kinds of writers were not linked at birth to the presence of any of the planets, but definitely avoided both Mars and Saturn.

Solo performers, like writers and long-distance runners were much more closely linked at birth with the moon than with any of the planets.

The only real disagreement between scientists and astrologers may well be the way in which the astrologers interpret the horoscope. While scientists, by and large, have come to accept that changes in the cosmos may affect human life and behaviour, many of them think that the astrologers' claim to know exactly what these changes signify is far too sweeping, and that they rely far too much on the ancient and intricate traditional framework (which to many scientists seems an arbitrary one) to make their interpretations for them. Even astrologers themselves, in fact—or at any rate the best of them—admit that the laws and principles governing their study are often chaotic, illogical, and unco-ordinated, that their records are scattered and have many errors, and that the traditions behind them are wrapped in myth and ancient lore.

This doesn't mean that a horoscope is worthless—or even that the ancient traditions underlying it are worthless, just because they come from a pre-scientific age. The real test, after all, is what kind of results a good astrologer can obtain from the horoscopes he casts, in spite of their defects. As far back as 1959, Vernon Clark, an American psychologist, decided to test the astrologers' claim to be able to predict future talents and aptitudes from a birth chart. He collected ten horoscopes of five men and women, each working in a different and clearly defined profession, all of them born in America and all of them between the ages of forty-five and sixty. He then handed the completely unidentified horoscopes and a separate list of various professions to twenty different astrologers—and asked them to pair off the appropriate horoscopes and professions. The same information was also given to a group of twenty psychologists and social workers who knew nothing about astrology. This group's matching of horoscope with profession corresponded only to the laws of chance—but 17 of the astrologers achieved results 100 to 1 against chance.

This result, it is claimed, proved not only that people's characters are influenced by cosmic patterns, but also that a good astrologer can tell the nature of the influence by studying the horoscope.

This test was followed by other more complex ones, and at the end of them, Clark came to the cautious scientist's conclusion that "astrologers working with material which can be derived from birth data alone, can successfully distinguish between individuals".

Other scientifically conducted inquiries have pointed in the same direction, and although this doesn't mean that all the claims of astrology have been proved, there is no doubt that an increasing number of scientists in many parts of the world consider that the subject should be taken seriously and investigated further.

So if you've always had a hankering after astrology, you need no longer be afraid you might be a bit of a crank!

CHAPTER FOURTEEN

KNOWING YOURSELF—
IN THE FUTURE

CHAPTER FOURTEEN

KNOWING YOURSELF—
IN THE FUTURE

Asking and answering questions about yourself is perhaps one of the most important ways of getting to know yourself better. But as we live in an age of technology it's hardly surprising that a number of gadgets are being devised to help you do that job too—insofar as any mechanical means can provide true understanding of the self.

You can, for example, buy a simple battery-operated machine called a *Relaxometer* for monitoring your galvanic skin response. It consists of a panel to which are attached two electrodes, which you fasten to two of your fingers. The point is that changes in your nervous and emotional state (variations in the over-all level of neural activity, to put it in more scientific language) affect the amount of sweat on your finger-tips—and the sweat in turn affects your skin resistance. The more upset you are the more you sweat, and the greater the influence on your skin resistance. By measuring this skin resistance the Relaxometer tells you how upset you are at any rate at that particular moment. It does so either by giving you a sound signal, or by means of a needle on a dial. The more tensed up you are the higher the pitch of the signal, or the higher the reading on the meter. The very fact of having auditory or visible proof of your state of mind (or, rather, that aspect of it which causes you to sweat) may in itself make you more aware of it. By trying to reduce the sound signal or meter reading you may be getting practice in reducing tension as well—and it is claimed that regular use of the Relaxometer may help you to exercise some control over your own bodily and mental condition.

At about the same price and size as a pocket calculator you can also buy a *Bio-Calculator* which (in addition, in fact, to doing the jobs of a simple calculator) gives you information about the three basic biological rhythms—physical, emotional and intellectual—which are supposed to control your everyday functioning. The Biorhythm theory is that such rhythms begin to operate from the day you were born (and perhaps before it) and then occur cyclically within a set number of days. The gadget works out all the time periods, and then translates them into the three basic Biorhythm stages, shown by code numbers on the display panel. By reading off these numbers on a Biorhythm chart against the three basic wave forms, it's claimed that you can find out your condition on any given day. The theory is that this will help you to arrange your activities according to the rhythms of your own probable life cycle, so that you will know when you are likely to be at your best . . . or worst. It's suggested, for instance, that with the help of the gadget an athlete could plan his training programme in tune with his personal biological clock.

Another gadget is the *Alpha-Sensor*. It's based on the big EEG machines you find in most hospitals. EEG is short for Electroencephalograph—that is the drawing or graphing of the electrical wave patterns that come from the brain. The EEG machines have identified four separate brain wave patterns, together with their relationship to various mental states. The commonest of them is the beta wave (beta—or B —is the second letter also in the Greek alphabet), which seems to be associated with the kind of mental concentration needed for tackling day to day problems, including studying for exams. At a much lower frequency comes the theta waves (after another letter in the Greek alphabet, for which there isn't a single exact English equivalent) and these apparently go with creative hallucinations (and also sometimes with anxiety). The delta waves (delta is the Greek D), at a much lower frequency again, belong almost exclusively to sleep. And in between the beta and the theta waves are the alpha waves (alpha is the Greek A), and these seem to be associated with a slowing down of the brain activity—and hence with feelings of relaxation and passivity which can (though not always) be very pleasurable.

What the technologists have done with the Alpha-Sensor is to translate the occurrence of alpha waves, as measured by the EEG machines, into a sound signal. So when you switch on your Alpha-Sensor (after first, of course, attaching the electrodes to your scalp) it will make a humming noise when your alpha waves are working—and the noise will stop when they stop. In order to enjoy the dreamy, contemplative high of your alpha waves (if that's how they act on you) you have to keep the signal going as long as possible—and for some reason which isn't yet properly understood, you can easily increase the duration of this alpha wave signal with a bit of practice.

All sorts of claims have been made for alpha wave training—that it relieves anxiety, provides a safe substitute for drugs, helps yoga-like states of meditation, and so on. Many of the experts in this field though, recommend caution. There is evidence to suggest, for example, that there may be a connection between alpha waves and lack of positive achievement—and that frequent training with them may reduce the user's drives and desire to succeed in life. Some experts point out, too, that in some people (again for reasons not yet understood) alpha waves activate anxiety rather than relieving it; and others that some alpha wave patterns are pleasurable and others not—and that the more readily available gadgets aren't yet subtle enough to record the differences.

There are several other gadgets—one, for example, that aims at inducing muscular relaxation, and another that aims at control over changes in bodily temperature. As the technology becomes more sophisticated, in fact, we can be pretty sure that an increasing number of mechanical devices of this kind will arrive on the market.

The proper technical name for all of them is *Biofeedback machines*. Feedback is a term which was coined by the pioneers of radio around the beginning of this century. It has been defined as "a method of controlling a system by reinserting into it the results of its past performance". Obviously this is what a number of complex machines do among them of course the computer when it "remembers" or stores away data in the process of working out a problem.

But it can be said that human beings do it too. If you're playing tennis, for example, you learn (hopefully!) to improve your shots by taking note of, and acting upon, the shocking results of your previous attempts.

Biofeedback, then, is a special kind of feedback one that comes from various parts of your body (the Greek word *bios* means life)—from your brain, heart, circulatory system, the various groups of muscles, and so on. The specialists in biofeedback training believe that it's possible, with the help of their electronic devices, to tune into all these bodily functions, and eventually to control them. They argue that most of us (at any rate in the western world) are by now so out of touch with our inner selves that it's next to impossible for us to change the behaviour patterns that may be making us ill, or causing us distress, or blocking our self-fulfilment merely by outside instruction or advice, by hard thinking or an act of will, no matter how determined. By looking into our bodies and brains, and hearing or seeing what is happening to the various functions there, the theory is that we have the information needed to begin controlling them.

Biofeedback research has already helped to bring about a drastic revision of our ideas about the nervous system. At one time it was assumed that there were two quite distinct systems: the voluntary (or somatic) system, which was responsible (through the appropriate nerve cells, fibres and muscles) for all those movements of arm, leg, jaw etc. which we normally regard as deliberate: and the involuntary (or autonomic) system, which acts on the pupils of our eyes, our blood vessels, our glands, and all those functions which had been always considered entirely automatic, and entirely beyond our conscious manipulation. The biofeedback researchers, however, have shown that this so-called involuntary nervous system can be brought under voluntary control (in animals, incidentally, as well as in humans), so that it is possible, to some extent at any rate, to learn how to vary our heart-rate or blood pressure at will.

The potential implications of this as far as medicine is concerned are obvious. The biofeedback specialists believe that in the future they may be able to help us to play a far greater part in regulating our own health. The American psychologist, Gardner Murphy, for example, has declared: "a very significant control of cardiovascular (relating to the blood vessels of the heart) and gastrointestinal (relating to the intestines in the stomach) responses may be anticipated, not only with immediate clinical values in bringing in or shutting out various classes of information, but with the deeper scientific value of giving a much wider view of what the human potentialities for such inner experience and such inner control may be." As a matter of fact biofeedback techniques have already, it appears, achieved very promising results in the treatment of high blood pressure, as well as in that of migraine headaches and various speech defects by helping the sufferers to help themselves! There is evidence, too, that they can be helpful in treating various neurotic disorders, by familiarising the sufferer with the physical manifestations that often accompany anxiety or depression such as tensing of the muscles, palpitations of the heart etc.—and by teaching him to control them, perhaps also to control the mental patterns and blockages that brought them about in the first place. One specialist indeed has argued that if healthy mental states can be satisfactorily defined it should be possible to train people to go on reproducing them so that instead of swallowing a tranquillizer when you felt strung up you might instead conjure up at will the condition of tranquillity which you had learned from biofeedback training. Needless to say, although self-help and self-knowledge would be a central element in any such treatment, it would still in most cases need to be carried out under expert supervision.

Many biofeedback specialists are particularly anxious to contradict any suggestion that the application of technology to the study of the human mind and personality means reducing them to the status of machines. They argue that, on the contrary, they are pointing the way to a tremendous extension of our knowledge and understanding of human consciousness, and setting it free from many of the restraints that have hitherto held it back. Incidentally, you can get some idea of how seriously these new techniques are already being taken in some parts of the world from the fact that in Japan pilots aren't allowed to fly if their biofeedback devices register that they have a bad day.

There are many, of course, who disagree with their more extreme expectations. A psychoanalyst, for example, might argue that there can only be a limited value in merely recognising the purely physical symptoms of deep-rooted conflicts, and in attempting to control these conflicts without fully understanding their hidden causes and that there can be no substitute for a thorough psychic exploration which uncovers these causes and allows the personality to reconstitute itself from within. To this the biofeedback specialists would perhaps reply that their techniques might at least help to short-circuit the lengthy business of analysis by orthodox methods.

The oriental practitioners of the various forms of deep meditation, which have been in existence in the east for centuries, might very well point out that they can achieve far more spectacular results in the control of the body and the involuntary nervous system than anything the biofeedback experimenters can do. Many of their feats, indeed, have been scientifically tested and authenticated among them the slowing of the heart rate, raising or lowering the temperature in different parts of the body, and opening up the intestinal tract and cleaning it with a cloth passed down by the power of the abdominal muscles!

The advocates of biofeedback don't question any of these feats, but they do claim, as far as brain waves are concerned, that whereas a yogi may take years of rigorous meditative training to learn how to control them, almost anyone can be taught, with the help of biofeedback machines, to achieve it in a matter of hours, and that their techniques, moreover, provide in effect a short cut to genuine meditative conditions. Against this it could be argued that there can be no real comparison between the kinds of meditation brought about by technological brain wave training, and that achieved by

Zen, the various paths of yoga, transcendental meditation and various similar techniques which, their adherents believe, lead to states of being that just aren't susceptible to mere physical description. Christian and other mystics would probably say much the same thing and the authors of this book would on the whole agree with them.

At the same time, the practitioners of biofeedback, in spite of their reliance on technology, certainly aren't afraid of venturing far beyond the commonly accepted boundaries of conventional, established science. On the contrary, they have been among the boldest in research into para-psychology that is the exploration of behavioural or personal exchanges which are *extra-sensorimotor* – not dependent on the normal working of the body, muscles or nervous system.

In this they have been influenced by the researches carried out between 1927 and 1965 by Dr J. B. Rhine in the Parapsychology Laboratory at Duke University, USA, and later (together with his wife) at the Institute of Para-psychology at Durham, North Carolina (part of the Founda-tion for Research on the Nature of Man, of which Dr. Rhine is the head). These scientifically controlled researches pro-vided evidence, absolutely water-tight in the view of many, that some people do indeed possess extra-sensory perception (ESP for short), which has been defined as: "Experience of or response to a target object, state, event, or influence without sensory contact."

But they have been even more influenced by the work carried out in recent years behind the Iron Curtain. It may come as a surprise to some people to learn that it is in Com-munist countries that research into paranormal phenomena, with state backing, is taken most seriously. The main reason probably is that the Russians, and their fellow-researchers in the other Iron Curtain countries, do not make a distinc-tion between science on the one hand, and the study of psychic phenomena on the other—whereas we in the west have, in our anxiety (for religious reasons) to keep the soul separate from the body, tended to confuse all mental phenomena, including paranormal ones, with our concept of the soul, so that our scientists when faced with mysterious mental events, instead of extending science in order to investigate them, have traditionally preferred to dismiss them as non-existent or illusory. At the same time those in the west who still believed in paranormal happenings, came to accept that they must lie beyond the boundaries of science.

As a matter of fact the Russians don't like the term extra-sensory perception (ESP), because they think that the prefix extra carries the suggestion of something in addition to, or outside science. They prefer the term *supersensory perception* (SSP), seeing it as a way of communicating which is not yet understood, but which must be ultimately explicable in scientific terms—after all, they are dialectical materialists!

They have, in consequence, for some years now been systematically investigating all kinds of psychic phenomena, and especially the three basic ESP (or SSP) capacities— *telepathy* (perception of the mental activity or state of another person without any physical contact); *clairvoyance* (perception of objects or objective events without contact or previous information); and *precognition* (prediction of future events, the occurrence of which cannot be inferred from present knowledge). It is said that they have achieved some quite astonishing results, especially in the field of telepathy. As long ago as 1967, for instance, they claim to have success-fully transmitted (and unscrambled) a code message by means of telepathy, from the mind of one gifted subject in Moscow to another in Leningrad (a distance of some four hundred miles). If this claim is established (there are many who think there can be no possible doubt about it) the practical implications for communication, say, between space-ships and earth, or between a submarine deeply submerged (and therefore beyond the reach of radio signals) and its base are obvious—and there are some western observers who believe that successful experiments in both these contexts have already been carried out.

The Russians are also believed to have made considerable

progress in understanding another paranormal capacity—
psychokinesis (PK for short), the power, that is, apparently
possessed by some people of causing objects to move without
any physical contact with them. Some American observers,
in fact, are convinced that the august Soviet Academy of
Science is strongly backing full-scale research into the
physics of psychokinesis.

But the Russians have been working, too, on a wide range
of other alleged psychic phenomena and paranormal
powers—among them *water divining* by means of dowsing
sticks; *psychic auras* (one Soviet scientist claims to have
discovered a method of photographing them—in techni-
colour); *folk healing*; *prophecy*; *eyeless sight* (the power
apparently possessed by some people to pick up colours and
other visual data with the finger tips alone); and many
others, some of them very way-out indeed. By arrangement
with the Indian government, they have also received visits
from specially gifted yogi, fakirs and mystics, so that they
could be investigated in the Soviet parapsychological
laboratories. At the same time ancient sciences or forms of
thought, like *alchemy* and *astrology*, are being studied for the
light they may throw on baffling parapsychological problems.

Similar developments have been taking place in the other
countries of the East European bloc. In Bulgaria, for
example, a famous peasant prophetess has been installed
(on a state salary) in a department of the Institute of
Suggestology and Parapsychology in Sofia. In Czechoslovakia practically every aspect of parapsychology is
researched into at Prague University (and there is also,
incidentally, a Centre for Scientific Astrology).

Most of these researches behind the Iron Curtain have
centred round people apparently possessed of special psychic
gifts, but the purpose behind them, of course, is to try and
discover whether their powers (assuming that these really
do exist) can be scientifically studied and understood—and
so perhaps made more generally available.

Biofeedback research impinges on the field of parapsychology in a number of ways. For one thing, as we have seen, it claims to have shown that it really is possible to exercise control over the involuntary nervous system and to learn how to alter brain waves and body radiations. If it can be conclusively demonstrated that you can, for example, switch your alpha waves on and off at will—then it's not so very difficult to envisage the possibility of brain waves being so arranged as to form a message which can then be recorded by brain waves arranged in the same pattern in somebody else's head. What is more, in view of the fact that the biofeedback researchers have developed machines that can monitor mental energies and translate them into signals, it should also be possible to analyse, interpret and duplicate parapsychological experiences.

The biofeedback specialists have, moreover, shown that we all produce electro-magnetic body waves which can be organised in order to furnish a coded message—and that the waves can be transmitted. The American Dr. W. A. Schafer, for example, has built an electronic instrument which can pick up electro-magnetic waves produced by heart-beats at some distance from the body to which the heart belongs.

It has therefore been suggested that paranormal phenomena might be related in some way to body waves. The possible association of such phenomena with alpha waves, or their association with different body rhythms coming together into some sort of special pattern, are among the theories that have been put forward. Another theory is that the faster-than-light particle called the *tachyon*, which some scientists now believe to exist, is the physical basis of parapsychological phenomena.

On the practical side, the biofeedback researchers are confident that they have achieved a number of positive results. One of them is that biofeedback training can apparently improve the performances of those who possess the ability to read the ESP test cards at a distance—in other words that it can consistently raise their score even higher than usual above that which would have been achieved by mere chance.

Another claim is that biofeedback research in the general area of electro-magnetism indicates that we are far more susceptible to changes in our environment—which may comprise extra-terrestrial bodies as well as our own earth—than most traditional scientists are prepared to admit. Biofeedback investigators have shown, for example, that there is a marked connection between the ways our body waves behave, and variations in the earth's electro-magnetic field. To put it another way, it appears that the frequencies of the pulsations coming from the earth correspond with our alpha, beta, delta and theta brain waves. This might explain why many animals (and some human beings too) "know" in advance when an earthquake is on the way and get out of the way if they can—they've picked up the changes in the earth's magnetic and electrical fields which precede the actual arrival of the earthquake itself.

It is again the Russians, though, who have carried out most research into the effects of electro-magnetic fields. In this area they have achieved particular success with a technique which they call *electro-sleep*. Basically this consists of a pulsating, low frequency electrical current applied to the subject's head, in order to cause relaxation, sleep, or even (in suitable cases) complete anaesthesia, according to the amount of power used. To come back to our own western world, there is another American scientist who has constructed a biofeedback device which, it is claimed, proves that plants are sensitive to energy waves emanating from living organisms—including human beings. So perhaps those old tales of people who have green fingers or who talk to their plants have something to them after all!

It's true, of course, that most of the traditional scientists are still extremely wary of all the way-out claims of the biofeedback researchers—though it must be added that most of these are highly-trained scientists themselves. What seems certain is that the future will witness a considerable increase in the investigation of human personality and behaviour by means of biofeedback and perhaps other kinds of electronic devices—and that researches into the more mysterious and hitherto little explored areas of the human psyche will be greatly extended. In other words, the prospect is that you will not only have more mechanical aids in getting to know yourself—but that you may also find that there is far more of yourself to explore than you had ever suspected!

None of these possible developments, however, need go against any convictions you may hold as to the limitless and unfathomable depths of human personality, or against any religious faith you may have. It is difficult to see how any machine, no matter how complex, can explain the ultimate mysteries of human existence and destiny, or solve the perennial problems of good and evil. The question of who uses the machines, and how, will always remain. As for the possible release of psychic energies hitherto ignored or denied by science, it must be remembered that there is no guarantee that they will be beneficent. The quality of the people who possess them, investigate them, and apply them, and of their motives, would still be an absolutely vital consideration. It's worth recalling that the ancient seers and mystics believed that evil psychic forces might be released as well as good ones, and so spoke of both black and white magic— and that Adolf Hitler for one was a great believer in the occult.

Nevertheless, provided we keep these kind of considerations in mind and provided we don't jump to the conclusion that machines can solve everything (including the pain of living, which has been responsible for some of the greatest achievements of human history), or that all the mysteries of life are about to be revealed, we should welcome the prospect of a further opening-up of human self-knowledge and of human potentialities, and of a possible extension of man's awareness of his relationship to the universe as a whole.

BOOKS FOR REFERENCE

If you want to start on a deeper study of the subjects in this book which particularly interest you, here are some titles which will help you. The editions given are the most recent, the most readily available—and wherever possible —in paperback.

CHAPTER ONE
Body Consciousness by Seymour Fisher (Fontana 1976).
Body Image and Personality by Seymour Fisher and S. E. Cleveland (Dover Press (New York) 1968).
White Racism by J. Kovel (Pantheon Books, Allen Lane 1970).
The Self and Others by R. D. Laing (Tavistock Publications 1959).

CHAPTER TWO
Social Interaction by M. Argyle (Methuen 1969).
The Psychology of Interpersonal Behaviour by M. Argyle (Penguin 1967).
Social Encounters ed. M. Argyle (Penguin 1975).
The Expression of the Emotions in Man and Animals by Charles Darwin, with Preface by Konrad Lorenz (University of Chicago Press (Chicago & London) 1965).
The Naked Ape by Desmond Morris (Cape 1967).
The Human Zoo by Desmond Morris (Literary Guild 1969).
Intimate Behaviour by Desmond Morris (Cape 1971).
Human Behaviour by C. Russell and W. M. S. Russell (Deutsch 1961).
Human Expression by Anthony Storr (Penguin 1968).

CHAPTER THREE
Fashion and the Unconscious by Edmund Bergler (Brunner (New York 1953).
Dress, Drinks and Drums by Ernest Crawley, ed. T. Besterman (Methuen 1931).

The Psychology of Clothes by J. C. Flugel (Hogarth Press 1950).

The Presentation of Self in Everyday Life by E. Goffman (Penguin 1972).

Clothes by James Laver (Heinemann 1969).

Modesty in Dress by James Laver (Heinemann 1969).

CHAPTER FOUR
Psychopathology of Everyday Life by Sigmund Freud, trans. from the German by A. Brill (Benn 1960).

CHAPTER FIVE
Dreams: Their Mysteries Revealed by Geoffrey A. Dudley (Aquarian Press 1969).

Dream Power by Ann Faraday (Hodder 1972).

The Interpretation of Dreams by Sigmund Freud, trans. from the German by A. Strachey (Allen & Unwin 1955).

Memories, Dreams, Reflections by C. G. Jung (Fontana 1967).

Creative Dreaming by Patricia Garfield (Futura Publications 1974).

Dreams and Nightmares by J. A. Hadfield (Penguin 1971).

Dreams and Dreaming by Norman Mackenzie (Aldus Books 1965).

CHAPTER SIX
Your Character from Your Handwriting by C. Harry Brooks (Allen & Unwin 1930).

The Psychology of Handwriting by Robert Saudek (Allen & Unwin 1954).

CHAPTER SEVEN
Causes and Prevention of Road Accidents by John Cohen and Barbara Preston (Faber 1968).

Aggression on the Road by Meyer H. Parry (Tavistock Publications 1968).

Criminal on the Road by T. C. Willett (Tavistock Publications 1964).

CHAPTER EIGHT

Test Yourself by William Bernard & Jules Leopold (Corgi Books 1975).

Know Your Own IQ by H. J. Eysenck (Penguin 1962).

Check Your Own IQ by H. J. Eysenck (Penguin 1975).

CHAPTER NINE

Memory: Facts and Fallacies by Ian M. L. Hunter (Penguin 1970).

Memory and Intelligence by Jean Piaget & B. Inhelder (Routledge 1973).

Disorders of Memory and Learning by George A. Talland (Penguin 1958).

CHAPTER TEN

Know Your Own Personality by H. J. Eysenck & Glenn Wilson (Penguin 1976).

The Personality Test by Peter Lauster, trans. by Susanne Flatauer (Pan Books 1976).

The Lüscher Colour Test by Max Lüscher, trans. and ed. by Ian Scott (Pan Books 1976).

CHAPTER ELEVEN

Palmistry: Your Destiny in Your Hands by Mary Anderson (The Aquarian Press 1973).

Paths to Secret Power by Mary Anderson (Aquarian Press 1972).

The Complete Gypsy Fortune Teller by Kevin Martin (Mayflower 1975).

CHAPTER TWELVE

The Horoscope, the Road and Its Travellers by Alan Oken (Bantam Books 1974).

Astrology: Evolution and Revolution by Alan Oken (Bantam Books 1976).

Your Character from the Stars by T. Mawby Cole (The Aquarian Press 1976).

Raphael's Ephemeris published by W. Foulsham & Co. Ltd., Slough, Bucks. Annually since 1860.

CHAPTER THIRTEEN
The Tarot by Alfred Douglas (Penguin 1974).
The Key to Tarot by Arthur Edward Waite (Rider & Co. 1972).

CHAPTER FOURTEEN
Biofeedback by Marvin Karlins & Lewis M. Andrews (Sphere Bofiks 1975).
Psychic Discoveries Behind the Iron Curtain by Sheila Ostrander & Lynn Schroeder (Sphere Books 1976).

ACKNOWLEDGEMENTS

We would particularly like to thank the following authors and publishers for specific permission to reproduce their material:

1. "Your Character From Your Handwriting"
   Author: C. Harry Brooks
   Publisher: Geo Allen Unwin (Publishers) Ltd

2. "Test Yourself"
   Author: William Bernard and Jules Leopold
   Publisher: The Chilton Book Company

ILLUSTRATIONS

All the illustrations in this book have been produced by George Robinson.